On March 1, 1932, the 20-month-old son of aviator Charles A. Lindbergh was stolen from the Lindbergh home near Hopewell, New Jersey. Ten weeks later a badly decomposed body was found. The case was one of the most highly publicized of this century. And when Bruno Hauptmann was tried, convicted, and executed for the murder of the child, the nation and the Lindbergh family believed justice had been done.

Nearly 35 years later, Harold R. Olson, a Connecticut businessman, began the search for the identity of his real mother and father after the deaths of his adoptive parents. He followed a trail of evidence that led him to the Capone gang, to government coverups, and ultimately to the startling discovery that he might be the Lindbergh child!

Theon Wright covered the Hauptmann trial as a young reporter and felt that the true story of the Lindbergh kidnaping had never been told. Now, merging Harold Olson's efforts with new evidence Theon Wright himself uncovered, there may finally be an answer to the question. . .

WHAT *REALLY* HAPPENED TO
THE LINDBERGH BABY?

IN
SEARCH
OF THE
LINDBERGH
BABY

Theon Wright

TOWER BOOKS **T** NEW YORK CITY

A TOWER BOOK

Published by

Tower Publications, Inc.
Two Park Avenue
New York, N.Y. 10016

Introduction

History has a way of correcting itself. Sometimes it requires a few weeks; at other times it requires years—even centuries. History is not created by historians, or even newspaper reporters. It consists of events and facts, and sooner or later the truth emerges.

As a reporter and writer I have covered a number of cases where an error, misjudgment, or sometimes deliberate falsification has been rectified by a later disclosure of facts. Some of these facts were not known at the time of the event, or perhaps ignored for one reason or another. Two instances of this sort come to mind. In one, the Massie case in Hawaii, I covered the trial of four people accused of shooting to death one of five beach boys who had supposedly raped the wife of a Navy officer. Thirty-five years later I wrote *Rape in Paradise* which exonerated the beach boys and disclosed a monumental miscarriage of justice. In another book, *The Big Nail*, written some sixty years after the supposed discovery of the North Pole by Robert Peary in 1907, another miscarriage of justice was revealed. By no stretch of the imagination could Admiral Peary have reached the Pole. Dr. Frederick Cook, who said he reached the Pole a year before Peary, died a disillusioned and heart-broken old man, the whole world believing he was a cheat and fraud. Peary died a nation's hero.

I mention these personal references because in the present book I hope to rectify, to whatever extent is now

5

possible, another miscarriage of justice. One which resulted in the conviction and execution of Bruno Richard Hauptmann more than forty years ago for kidnaping and killing Charles Augustus Lindbergh, Jr., son of the most famous aviator of his day.

My interest in this case was at first rather indirect. I was at the Bronx Courthouse as a reporter for the United Press the night Bruno Hauptmann was taken from the Greenwich Police Station in Manhattan to the Bronx Courthouse to be grilled by detectives from New Jersey and New York. This was September 22, 1934, two days after he was arrested. Two years later I was at the home of Hauptmann's sister, Mrs. Emma Gloeckner, in West Hollywood the night Hauptmann died in the electric chair at Trenton. This was April 3, 1936.

Between those two dates I wrote a number of stories on the Lindbergh case. I also interviewed a number of people. I had assumed, as did most reporters of that day, that Hauptmann was guilty of the kidnaping, and possibly of murder. It was not until I dug into several aspects of the case and discovered queer little gaps in the story presented by the New Jersey prosecutor, State Attorney General David Wilentz, that my superficial conviction was shaken.

Among these gaps was the existence of a strange little group that gathered Sunday evenings at a spiritualist church, directly across the street in Harlem from a rooming house where several of the key witnesses in the trial of Bruno Hauptmann lived. The group that attended seances at the church also included two members of the Lindbergh household and a man named Isidor Fisch, who became a mystery figure in the Hauptmann trial.

Little attention was paid to these stories at the time I wrote them, chiefly because they did not fit into the prosecution's theory of the kidnaping and murder of Lindbergh's son. Since that time, however, many facts

—some known, but disregarded at the time—have emerged. Some have appeared in books reviewing the Lindbergh case, most agreeing with the prosecution's theory that a lone kidnaper accomplished the crime. Other facts, known at the time of the Hauptmann trial, were never made a part of the State case—such as the omission of evidence of an incorrect identification of the baby's body found on Mount Rose Heights near the Lindbergh estate at Hopewell, New Jersey.

Taken separately, these facts would neither prove nor disprove the position taken by the New Jersey prosecutor—that Hauptmann was the lone kidnaper. Put together, they form a skein of facts and speculation that makes the position taken by the prosecution not only improbable, but impossible.

A few years ago I found that a man named Harold Olson, living in Connecticut, had been engaged for about twelve years in a search to prove whether or not he was Charles Lindbergh's son. From his investigation and interviews, he had amassed a great store of records and reports of the Lindbergh Case, and had become virtually convinced that he was the lost Lindbergh child. He made the fruits of his research available to me, and my interest in the Lindbergh case was revived. Many of his facts conformed with my own suspicion that an error had been made—a miscarriage of justice in the conviction and electrocution of Bruno Hauptmann.

It has been said that old bones should not be dug up—that the dead past should bury its dead. But history abhors a vacuum. One man was sent to the electric chair, others went to prison on charges growing out of the Lindbergh Case. Governor Hoffman of New Jersey saw his political career disintegrate into ruins because he reprieved Hauptmann temporarily to sift out the facts, believing that there was more to the case than was presented at Flemington courthouse.

A review of the entire history of the cast at this point in time, when public opinion is not as inflamed as it was

7

during the kidnaping and trial, with some of the missing pieces presented as facts and others as speculation, seems not only advisable, but necessary.

Part One

THE
LINDBERGH
KIDNAPPING

1

A Matter of Identity

It was early afternoon in the small village of Wickford, Rhode Island, on the west side of Narraganset Bay—September 27, 1959. A young man about thirty, and a woman, slightly younger, walked down a street toward the Hains Boatyard. They had attended services at St. Paul's Episcopal Church in North Kingstown earlier and decided to look over the boats while waiting for the ferry to take them to Cape Cod.

The man was of medium height, rather thin, and on close inspection his face appeared to be marked with several scars. The woman was dark-haired and pretty. They had been married the day before in New York, and were on their honeymoon.

While they stood looking at the boats, an elderly woman who had been staring at the young man, suddenly approached the couple. A red-haired woman in her late twenties was with her; she was slightly crippled and walked with a limp. The older woman said, "This is your sister."

The young man seemed surprised and embarrassed. He evidently did not recognize the woman referred to as his sister.

"You were with us as a baby," the older woman explained. "I cared for you. This is my daughter."

The woman had been looking closely at the scars on his face. She said, "May I feel the dent in your

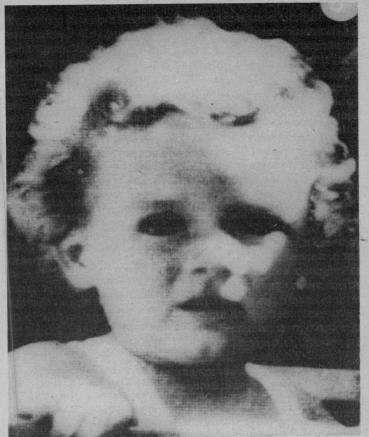

Charles A. Lindbergh, Jr., near his first birthday.

head?"

"I suppose so," he said, visibly embarrassed. He had been told the dent was from a slip of the forceps during delivery. But it was the first time a stranger had asked to feel it. The woman touched with practiced fingers, and nodded.

"You are the Lindbergh baby. I cared for you as a child."

By this time the young man was anxious to break loose from this unexpected attention. But the elderly woman seemed to persist in her inquiries. She mentioned the name "Lindbergh" several times.

The man was Harold Roy Olson, and his bride was the former Angela Hennessy. The Lindbergh name had no particular significance for him at the time. He had been a baby when the infant son of Charles A. Lindbergh was kidnaped and presumably killed by his abductor on March 1, 1932. It had even less significance for Angela. He decided, after breaking away from the elderly woman and her daughter, that it was a case of mistaken identity.

This was a long time ago. Today Olson only vaguely recalls what happened. However, Olson had the feeling that the woman, who seemed to know about the dent in his head, had been brought to the Hains Boatyard by someone, possibly to determine his identity. He recalled that earlier that year, when he was working as a boat painter at Nevins Boatyard on City Island, New York, a man had suggested to him that he resembled someone named Lindbergh. He paid little attention to this at the time, but later—after he had begun an intensive investigation into his own identity—he learned that the man who made the suggestion might have been Jon Lindbergh, son of the flier.

This was not the first time Harold Olson had been confronted by questions as to his identity. As a boy, growing up in Escanaba, Michigan, he had been told

12

that his father and mother, Roy and Sara Olson, were not his natural parents—that he belonged to a family of gangsters, who had placed him with the Olsons when he was too young to remember. He was told his real father may have been Al Capone, the Chicago bootleg mobster, who operated whiskey runs out of Escanaba.

In 1952, on his way to Japan with the U.S. Army, Olson stopped over in Evanston, Ill. to visit Fred and Hilmer Carlberg, his mother's cousins. As Olson was leaving from the train station at the end of his visit, they told him there was something he had to know about his parentage—especially as he was going into combat.

They said family rumors suggested that his father might be Al Capone. "But that may not be right," one of them added, "because your father may be Charles Lindbergh."

"The hair of the back of my neck stood up," Olson remembers. "Psychologically I ran from the idea." Olson totally rejected the idea of either Capone or Lindbergh being his father as emotionally unacceptable.

Upon discharge from the army in the fall of 1952 Olson returned to his job at McCann Erickson in New York and shortly thereafter got a telegram to come home—his mother was dying.

"I dreaded to see her die and prayed she would be dead before I got there. She was still alive and told me my father had asked the nurses to give her enough morphine so she would be dead on my arrival. But she resisted all needles and was alive and in great pain the next day when I got there. She said she had to stay alive so she could tell me something I needed to know. I said it didn't matter about all she was trying to tell me in great pain and she gave up and went into a coma and died during the night in early morning. I went for a crying walk by myself and in the dark vowed to God that I would do my best as I grew older to right wrong that had been done to people unfairly."

Olson had tried since he was a boy to reject the notion

that Roy and Sara Olson were not his real parents, just as he rejected Capone as his father. But he gradually became aware that he was somehow connected to a family of gangsters.

He found that his great-uncle, Werner Olson, had been known in Escanaba as a horse or local gang leader for Al Capone.

This did not seem to tie into the reference to the Lindbergh baby, however, and for several years after the Rhode Island incident Olson gave little attention to that phase of his past.

A few years before he married Angela Hennessey, he became friendly with a special agent of the Federal Bureau of Investigation, Henry Ruda. The FBI man showed an unusual interest in Olson, helping him obtain an apartment in Tudor City in New York, and also steering him toward the job as a boat painter on City Island, and attending Olson's wedding.

It was Ruda, however, who suggested Olson talk to William Dalton about his (Olson's) past. Dalton had been in charge of Capone's East Coast rum-running operation, and worked for Meyer Lansky, who more or less inherited Capone's bootleg business when he was sent to prison. Dalton suggested Olson see a woman named Gussie Johnson, who lived in Gladstone, Michigan, about six miles from Escanaba.

When Olson talked with Gussie Johnson she mentioned the Lindbergh baby, and said she had played with him as a child. She had also remarked that "it was easier to kidnap someone than to collect the ransom." One time she mentioned somewhat unaccountably, that her brother was a doctor in Escanaba and that she had assisted undertakers in embalming.

Olson had assumed from his mother's remark, and what he learned in Escanaba, that his actual parents were related to gangsters. In 1967 his father had visited Harold and Angela Olson at their home in Westport, Connecticut, and told his son he would explain later what his mother—or foster mother—Sara Olson had

The Lindbergh baby, left, and Harold Olson. Note the similar eye structure.

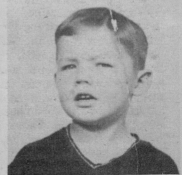

The Lindbergh baby.   Young Harold Olson.

been referring to. However, Roy Olson suffered a stroke in Escanaba and died without revealing any explanation of what Olson's mother said.

Just before he died he made a sign with his hand to Angela, who was with her husband. He tried to pull up the sleeve over her arm, then managed to point to the window shade, which was drawn. She realized that he was trying to draw attention to a birthmark under Olson's right arm that resembled a strawberry and a turtle. Olson recalled that his mother had also tried to have him look at a small photograph which she kept in a book, just before she died.

These miscellaneous and apparently unrelated events suddenly fixed in young Olson's mind a deep desire to investigate his past more intensively. He had resisted this during the years since Sara Olson died; he wanted to forget the uncertainty that had been nagging at him since he was a boy in Escanaba. He had not thought much about the incident in Rhode Island, when the woman said he was the Lindbergh baby; he was more concerned about the possibility that he was from a family of gangsters.

Several years later—in 1972—Olson met the red-haired daughter of the woman who had told him she was his sister. She said she was Mary Hertler and her mother was Mary Elizabeth Hertler; she was called Mazie and had died in 1964. She said her mother had worked as a nurse for Dr. Thomas N. Hepburn in Hartford, and they had lived at 109 Maltby Street in East New Haven in 1932.

This address was of significance to Olson. In his investigation, he was able to identify it as the house where the Lindbergh baby was reported to have been held in East New Haven in early March, 1932, while the FBI was investigating a tip that it was in New Haven!

The New Haven search for Lindbergh's son was never

disclosed to the press. It is not mentioned in any standard book or article on the Lindbergh case. Yet the fact that it occurred is confirmed by several reports of the FBI, obtained from the Department of Justice files under the Freedom of Information Act.

Reports on the New Haven angle are largely confined to various checks made on the people who gave the tip— David Kahn, head of a New York furniture firm; Grove Seely, a friend of Kahn; Major Thomas Lanphier, an aviator and personal friend of Lindbergh, who worked with the FBI in the New Haven investigation; and Edgar Cayce, the noted psychic from Virginia Beach, who furnished the tip. Several reports gave details of the New Haven search, and one—a general report on the FBI's role in the Lindbergh case investigation—included a single paragraph on the New Haven adventure. It is dated April 9, 1932; the paragraph says:

> The next direct contact was on March 10, 1932, when Lanphier came to the New York Office with the request that Connelly (Special Agent E. J. Connelly, in charge of the Lindbergh investigation for the FBI) investigate certain addresses in New Haven, Connecticut mentioned by an alleged soothsayer named Kahn of Virginia Beach, Virginia. According to Connelly this soothsayer had furnished information to the effect that the baby was held at a certain address in New Haven, Connecticut. Investigation proved the information to be of *no value*." (Italics mine)

The report was signed by Special Agent J. M. Keith, addressed to J. Edgar Hoover, the director of the FBI. Kahn was not from Virginia Beach and not a soothsayer; the information came from Edgar Cayce, who was a psychic and clairvoyant, not a soothsayer; and it resulted from a request by Kahn and Lanphier to Cayce to hold a clairvoyant reading at his Virginia Beach home, to try to locate the Lindbergh baby.

17

The New Haven search will be discussed in proper context later in this review; it is sufficient at this point to note that if the FBI had investigated the New Haven angle with anything approaching professional competence, the Lindbergh case might have been solved in less than two weeks after the baby was kidnaped!

What interested Olson at the time was the mention in the reports of a man he had come to believe was closely linked to his early life, who he once believed was his father, Al Capone, the Chicago bootlegger. A report dated March 21, 1932, signed by Connelly, said: "Kahn indicated that he had been connected with Albert Pick of Chicago which, eliminating any consideration of the fact that these parties were telling what appeared to be fortune telling (sic), which later we did not, of course, in any way believe, indicated that possibly he might be an emissary of the Chicago crowd, which has been previously mentioned, namely Alphonse Capone. . ."

Connelly's report suggested that since the situation seemed "to lead back to Chicago gangsters" it might be well to consider the possibility "that these people under the guise of telling fortunes would lead us eventually to the child and later indicate some way whereby Capone could get a certain amount of credit for same."

Aside from the wholly inaccurate reference to fortune telling and the fact that David Kahn was not a sooth-sayer but an intermediary, the report might have been pursued with useful results, but the final estimate that the New Haven effort was of no value precluded any follow up by the FBI.

It did not preclude Harry Olson from following this lead. Forty years later, in 1972, he heard about the Edgar Cayce activity from Tom Valentine, a Chicago newspaperman. He was given a rough account of Cayce's readings and he went to New Haven. Details of how he followed up will be covered in a discussion of the New Haven episode in Part V of this review.

Harold Olson as a Cub Scout, age 10.

Olson in his twenties.

Businessman Harold Olson today.

Aviator Charles A. Lindbergh's famous smile.

The mature Harold Olson.

I first became aware of Harold Olson's search for his identity in 1977—a decade after he had embarked on his intensive quest. My eldest daughter, Roxana Rogers, who lived in Weston, Connecticut near Olson's home, had become a newspaperwoman, covering the Weston news for a Westport newspaper. Through a colleague, Kenneth Dixon of the Bridgeport *Post*, she learned of Olson's effort to find out whether or not he was the son of Charles Lindbergh.

She met Olson and told him of my skepticism about the Lindbergh kidnaping. He gave her photocopies of much of the material he had assembled, and she sent them to me. The following year I visited my daughter in Weston, and met Olson. I told him of my own doubts, largely the result of the digging I had done as a newspaperman in the early 1930's. I had studied various reports and data he had gathered, including the FBI reports of the aborted New Haven investigation. It seemed to me much of what he had assembled fitted into my own theory of the kidnaping, which was quite briefly that two gangs had been involved, one as the kidnaper and another seeking to muscle into the extortion scheme.

My visit with Olson tended to confirm my conviction that there was more to the Lindbergh case than the public had ever dreamed of. The pieces began to fall into place; gaps in theories I had mulled over for nearly a half century began to close.

There were three aspects of Olson's search for his parents that were impressive: First, he was not certain he was Lindbergh's son; he described himself as being "about ninety-five percent sure." Second, he had resisted the idea that he was not a natural son of Sara and Roy Olson, and was psychologically hostile to the notion that he was the son of Charles A. Lindbergh. Third, he had waived all claims against the Lindbergh estate—something no other claimants have done. When he finally became convinced that there was a strong possibility he was Lindbergh's son, he began an

**Flanking young Olson are Hilmer (left) and Fred
Carlberg, Sara's cousins from Sweden, in January 1952.
Before his departure for Japan the two men told him that
his father was Al Capone — or maybe Charles Lindbergh.
It was the first mention of Lindbergh in Olson's life.**

intensive effort to prove the case, one way or the other —not because he wanted to be Lindbergh's offspring, but because he wanted to find his own roots.

It was this possibility that stirred memories of the past. More than forty years ago I had asked the question: What really happened to the Lindbergh baby? It might now be possible, by merging Harold Olson's efforts with what I had found during my years as a newspaperman, to find the answer.

2

An Unanswered Question

To ask, what really happened to the Lindbergh baby, would have been regarded as totally irrelevant, if not impertinent, by most people nearly a half century ago. The 20-month old son of Charles A. Lindbergh had been stolen from his crib in the Lindbergh home on Sourland Mountain in central New Jersey, near the town of Hopewell.

It happened on March 1, 1932. Seventy-two days later a truck driver, William Allen, stumbled on a body in a shallow grave on Mount Rose Heights, less than two miles from the Lindbergh estate. The police were called and, under the watchful eye of Inspector Harry Walsh of the New Jersey police, the body was carefully removed from the grave. The strips of cloth wrapped around the badly decomposed torso were removed, and the body was taken to the Swayze Funeral Parlor in Trenton.

Colonel Lindbergh, conducting his own search for his kidnaped son, was on a yacht, the *Cachalot,* off the New Jersey coast trying to contact another boat, the *Mary B. Moss,* when he heard the news. His son had been found—dead! He hurried home and, in Trenton the next day, he briefly examined the body. After looking at the teeth and at the overlapping toes, he identified it as his son. A few hours later the body was cremated.

How then could anyone ask what had happened to the Lindbergh baby?

During the ten-week period following the kidnaping it had been supposed the Lindbergh baby was being held by a kidnap gang for ransom. After the father identified the body found near Mount Rose as his son, it was accepted that he was dead.

While the body lay in the Swayze morgue, it was also examined by Dr. Phillip Van Ingen. The Lindbergh baby was allergic to milk and, as a result, had developed rickets. Dr. Van Ingen, a specialist in children's diseases, had been treating the baby. After the kidnaping Anne Morrow Lindbergh released the baby's diet to the press. It included bone meal; a substance often used in the treatment of rickets. (Harold Olson is also allergic to milk.) Dr. Van Ingen had examined the baby on February 18, 1932, ten days before the kidnaping. Walter Swayze, the undertaker, reported that he had asked Dr. Van Ingen if the body found in the shallow grave was actually the Lindbergh body.

"He gave me a peculiar look," Swayze said. "He said, 'If you were to lay ten million dollars on that table and tell me it was mine if I could say positively that this was the Colonel's son, I'd have to refuse the money. I couldn't honestly identify this skeleton.'"

There were many other unexplained events in the Lindbergh kidnaping case. There was the mysterious suicide of Violet Sharpe, who drank poison several days after the body of the dead child was found near Hopewell. There was the strange case of J. J. Faulkner who deposited $2,980 of the Lindbergh ransom money in a New York bank on May 1, 1934—before Hauptmann was arrested. There was the unexplained change from the original police theory that the Lindbergh baby was kidnaped by gangsters, to a theory of Hauptmann as the lone kidnaper—after a man had been sent to prison for supposedly dealing with the mob.

But the main question that persisted both before and after the trial concerned the identification of the body found on Mount Rose Heights as the body of Lindbergh's son. Some of this uncertainty emerged when the body was found and it continued throughout the case.

Dr. Van Ingen's indecision when he examined the body taken from the grave and was asked to say whether or not it was Lindbergh's son, was based on several descrepancies.

First, there was a difference in measurements. Dr. Van Ingen had measured the Lindbergh baby ten days before the kidnaping. At that time it was 29 inches in height. Dr. Charles H. Mitchell, Mercer County physician, measured the corpse taken from the grave near Hopewell and found it to be 33-1/3 inches long. Some of the difference could be attributed to the growth of bones after death, but not four-and-one-third inches!

There was also some evidence that the body found on Mount Rose Heights might have been embalmed. The body taken from the grave had been badly decomposed. But the liver—last of the viscera to disintegrate after an embalming—was almost intact.

In a letter to Mrs. Dwight Morrow, mother of Mrs. Lindbergh, Dr. Van Ingen said: "I especially noted (while examining the baby on February 18) that *both little* toes were slightly turned in and overlapped the next toe." (italics mine)

In his report after examining the dead baby, Dr. Mitchell said: "The first toe of the right foot partially overlapped the *large* toe and the second toe of the right foot completely overlaps the *large* toe." (italics mine)

There was a good deal written about the overlapping toes of Lindbergh's son during the search for the baby, many stories in error. But this specific difference shown in reports of Dr. Van Ingen, who examined the Lindbergh child, and Dr. Mitchell, who examined the body taken from the grave, could only be explained if the missing Lindbergh baby and the body found on Mount Rose Heights were not the same!

All questions relating to the identification of the body taken from the grave as Lindbergh's son became academic as far as the case against Bruno Richard Hauptmann was concerned because of an incident that must have been the most unusual development in the trial. Since this incident bears directly on the basic theme of this review it will be taken out of chronological sequence and reviewed at this point.

Edward J. Reilly was a flamboyant Brooklyn lawyer whose numerous unsuccessful defenses of accused killers won him the nickname, "Death House" Reilly. Mrs. Anna Hauptmann went to Brooklyn shortly after her husband was arrested in 1934 to talk to James Fawcett, a Brooklyn lawyer originally chosen as Hauptmann's chief counsel. She was accompanied by a friend, who met another friend as they entered the building where Fawcett's office was located. It turned out that this friend of her friend was a reporter for the New York *Journal,* a Hearst newspaper that had already begun a campaign of accusations against Hauptmann as the Lindbergh baby kidnaper.

He said to Mrs. Hauptmann, "Fawcett will take your husband to the electric chair." He recommended another attorney, Edward J. Reilly! Mrs. Hauptmann accepted Reilly, whose fee was picked up to the extent of several thousand dollars by the New York *Journal.*

"I never heard of Mr. Reilly before, but I relied on the advice this man gave me," Mrs. Hauptmann told Governor Hoffman of New Jersey when he was investigating the case after Hauptmann had been convicted and sentenced to die.

It would be pointless to question Mrs. Hauptmann's judgment at this time. She was worried and harried, a lone woman seeking help for her husband who was under arrest. She later told Governor Hoffman, "I was told that in a suit filed by Mr. Reilly for fees the other lawyers filed affidavits saying Mr. Reilly was intoxicated at the trial. Maybe I was too ignorant about the law, and was motivated by things I cannot explain."

C. Lloyd Fisher, an attorney in Hunterdon County where the trial was held, and assistant counsel for the defense, later told me what happened in the court at Flemington.

Mrs. Edith Dormer, custodian of St. Michael's Orphanage in Hopewell, which was across a hill from the shallow grave where the body was found, was on the stand. It had been reported that a child from the orphanage was missing the night the Lindbergh baby was abducted; the prosecution was seeking to prove by her attendance records at the orphanage, that all children were accounted for that night. Mrs. Dormer had brought a set of books to confirm this.

State Attorney General David Wilentz, who was also the prosecuting attorney, was about to offer the books in evidence when Judge Thomas W. Trenchard called the attorneys to the bench for consultation. Reilly, Frederick A. Pope, and Fisher all came to the bench. The court record tells what happened.

Mr. Wilentz: If there is any dispute about the attendance records, I will offer them. If there isn't, I won't.

Mr. Reilly: There is no dispute.

Mr. Wilentz: There is no claim that the child came from the orphanage?

Mr. Pope: No.

Mr. Wilentz: Am I to understand that there is no claim that this child (the body taken from the grave) came from the orphanage?

Mr. Fisher: I thought your proposition was that if we didn't dispute the attendance records you would not offer the books.

Mr. Wilentz: If there is any claim about it, I will offer them.

Mr. Reilly: I will say now that there has never been any claim but that this was Colonel Lindbergh's child that was found there. We stipulate that.

The lawyers walked back to their seats. According to

Fisher, Pope said in a low voice to Reilly:

"You have just stipulated the life of your client."

The events of the trial will be taken up in proper order. This particular incident is introduced at this point because Reilly's stipulation closed all doors to any further efforts by the defense to challenge the identification of the child. Dr. Van Ingen was not even called to testify. The investigation into the identification of the body taken from the grave was no longer relevant: the difference in measurements, the possibility of embalmment, discrepancies as to overlapping toes, above all the location of the grave a mile from Hopewell, where state troopers, students recruited from nearby Princeton University for the search, and curiosity seekers must have tramped over the area for days after the kidnaping—all this was wiped out by Reilly's single stipulation.

All that was legally left were Colonel Lindbergh's rather cursory, and nurse Betty Gow's even more ephemeral identifications.

Lindbergh had just returned from the *Cachalot*, where he had spent days trying to contact the *Mary B. Moss*. For six weeks since the kidnaping he had gone through agonizing torture: the constant expectation that he would see his son, the continual failures, renewed searches, and finally the end of the trail, the announcement over the radio that his son had been found, dead! He had gone to the Swayze Funeral Parlor in Trenton believing he would see the body of his son. It was natural that he should not have looked very closely.

He was taken by Colonel Norman Schwarzkopf, head of the New Jersey state police, into the room where the body lay. A sheet covered the corpse.

"Take that off," he said. The sheet was removed.

Lindbergh stared for a time at the baby. He bent over and examined the mouth, counting the teeth. He looked at the overlapping toes on the right foot. The left leg was missing from the corpse. Then he left the table.

Four generations. At right, Anne Morrow Lindbergh with her mother and grandmother — and Charles Augustus Lindbergh, Jr.

The county prosecutor approached him.

"Colonel Lindbergh, are you satisfied that it is the body of your child?"

"It could be," he said quietly.

That was all. On the basis of Colonel Lindbergh's identification, which was all that was left to be admitted in the trial court, the *corpus delicti*—the "body of the crime"—was established. Without absolute proof as to the identity of the corpse, the case against Hauptmann might have failed. Chief Counsel Reilly's stipulation had foreclosed any further legal challenge, any possible questions that might have been raised.

There were many other odd contradictions, which will be taken up in the course of this review. But the *sine qua non* of the prosecution, the identification of the corpse as actually that of Lindbergh's son, which should have been a basic element of Hauptmann's defense strategy, was no longer to be questioned.

Reilly's stipulation may have sent Hauptmann to the electric chair; but it did not prevent further speculation about the case or future claimants from declaring themselves to be Lindbergh's son. On the night of Hauptmann's execution, April 3, 1936, Mrs. Emma Gloeckner, his sister, told me a five-year-old boy had already put in his claim to being the son of the "Lone Eagle."

"Someone wrote a letter. I do not believe it, but it is possible."

It is this possibility that is the theme of this review. What really happened to the Lindbergh baby?

3

A Crime Is Committed

The story of the night of March 1, 1932 has been covered in detail by books, articles, and newspaper stories. Many of the accounts were written shortly after the kidnaping, in the midst of the confusion and uncertainty as to what had really happened to Lindbergh's son. They constitute a continuing narrative, corrected and recorrected as the record unfolded.

Five major books have been written devoted to the Lindbergh case—the kidnaping of the Lindbergh baby, the search for the child, the discovery of the body on Mount Rose Heights, the subsequent trial and execution of Bruno Hauptmann. The first four are *The Lindbergh Crime* and *The Trial of Bruno Richard Hauptmann,* both written by Sidney B. Whipple; *The Hand of Hauptmann,* by J. Vreeland Haring; and *Kidnap*, by George Waller. The fifth book, *Scapegoat*, by Anthony Scaduto, presents the case from Hauptmann's point of view, and will be discussed later.

Sid Whipple covered the trial for the United Press; he was a colleague of mine in that organization, and his first story is a heavily biased chronology ending with Hauptmann's conviction by the jury at Flemington courthouse. Whipple was a capable reporter, but a conventional man with fixed opinions. I had the feeling he believed Hauptmann was guilty before the trial began.

Haring was a handwriting expert anxious to prove he

was the authority in the case. He had been called in by the prosecution when it became evident certain testimony on fingerprints as well as handwriting did not fit the State's theories. Dr. Erasmus Mead Hudson's preliminary analysis of fingerprints had been rejected. Waller's book is a journalist's recapitulation of the entire case based on reports, statements and other sources close to the investigation. His review adds little to what was already known, and is not an analysis of the evidence.

There have been other specialized books such as *A Psychiatric Study of the Lindbergh Case,* written by Dr. Dudley D. Schoenfeld, which covers particular aspects of the case. And there are also self-serving books by Dr. Condon and Paul Wendel, written chiefly to exculpate the authors. But the five books mentioned constitute the main sources, and represent what the American public —particularly those under fifty, who were not exposed to the events themselves—now knows about the Lindbergh kidnaping and the Hauptmann trial.

None of these books analyzes the unexplained events in the case. There were many contradictions in the stories told by various people involved. And the strange shift of the New Jersey prosecution from the theory of mobsters snatching the child to the theory that Bruno Hauptmann acted alone as kidnaper and killer of the baby is still not explained. To the extent that it is now possible, this review will be an effort to bring together the confusing facets of this case about which *Editor & Publisher* wrote: "No trial in this country has so degraded the administration of justice."

On Tuesday night, March 1, 1932, a cold, blustery wind was blowing over the Sourland Mountains where the estate of Charles and Anne Lindbergh lay amid sparse trees on the snow-covered ground. The Lindberghs usually spent weekends at their home near Hopewell, and weekdays at the home of Anne Lindbergh's mother, Mrs. Dwight Morrow, in Englewood, New Jersey. The baby had been sick during the day, however, and it was decided to remain at Hopewell. Colonel Lindbergh arrived from New York at about 8:15 in the evening. He inquired about his son's cold, and was told the baby was asleep.

The nursery was in the southeast wing, built above the library. Betty Gow, the baby's nurse, had a room opposite the nursery. The Lindbergh's bedroom was above the main living room, facing west. A door led directly from her room into the nursery. After dinner, Lindbergh went into the library with his wife. It was about nine o'clock, and suddenly Lindbergh turned his head.

"What was that?" he asked his wife. He had heard a noise that sounded like the breaking of wood. Anne Lindbergh listened, but heard nothing further. They decided it was the noise of the wind.

At 10 o'clock Betty Gow went into the nursery to see the baby. The crib was empty. She went into the Lindbergh bedroom, where Anne Lindbergh was preparing to go to bed. Two other members of the household staff —Oliver Whateley, the butler, and Elsie Whateley, his wife—were in their room over the garage, which was on the northwest side of the house, opposite the nursery.

"Mrs. Lindbergh, do you have the baby?"

She said, "No."

"Where is the Colonel? He may have him. Where is he?"

Betty Gow ran downstairs and found Colonel Lindbergh at his desk.

"Colonel, do you have the baby?"

"No. Isn't he in his crib?"

Betty Gow shook her head, and Lindbergh ran past her and up the stairs. Anne Lindbergh had returned from the nursery to her bedroom. They went back into the nursery. The bedclothes in the crib did not appear to be disturbed. The child could not have crawled out of his bedclothes. He was pulled out.

Lindbergh went into his bedroom and took a Springfield rifle from the closet. He turned and faced his wife.

"They have stolen our baby!"

He saw something on the radiator grating beneath the window on the southeast corner of the nursery. It was an envelope. He did not touch it, and told his wife and Betty Gow not to touch it until the nursery had been examined for fingerprints.

The window shutters were partly open. On a suitcase directly below the window were marks of yellow clay footprints. Lindbergh noted at the time that the clay was the same as the soil outside the window.

He called for Oliver Whateley and told him to call the chief of police in Hopewell, Harry Wolfe. Then he went downstairs and called Colonel Henry C. Breckinridge, a close friend and an attorney; he explained what had happened, and asked him to come to Hopewell.

He took the rifle and started down the road on foot; Whateley drove a car behind him. They met a police car and Wolfe got out, with Charles Williamson, his chief constable. They went immediately to the area below the window in the nursery, and found two holes in the ground, and a shallow impression that might have been a footprint. About seventy-five feet away they saw a ladder. It was in three sections. The top section was ten feet away from the middle and bottom sections, which were held together by a wooden bolt. There were rails along the side of the ladder, and one of the rungs and a rail of the bottom section was split. A chisel was found on the ground beneath the window.

The condition and structure of the ladder became a matter of supreme importance in the investigation by New Jersey police, and later in the Hauptmann trial.

Meanwhile Colonel Norman Schwarzkopf and his deputy, Major Charles Schoeffel, arrived at the Lindbergh home, with two detectives, Lewis Bornmann and Nuncio de Gaetano, and Joseph Wolf, a state trooper.

A few minutes later Colonel Breckinridge arrived from New York. Shortly after midnight Frank A. Kelly, a fingerprint specialist, joined them and went over the note found in the envelope on the radiator grating. There were no fingerprints.

Schoeffel handed the note to Lindbergh. It read:

Dear Sir

   Have 50000$ ready 25000$ in 20$ bills 15000 in 10$ bills and 10000$ in 5$ bills After 2-4 days we will inform you were to deliver the money. We warn you for making anything public or for notifying Pol (word blurred) The child is in gut care Indications for all letters are singnature (sic) and three holes.

The description of the events at the time the baby's disappearance was first discovered follows the script generally conceded by police. However, there were certain unexplained circumstances. The kidnaper's first note was left near the windowsill; with the wind blowing across the Sourlands that night, and the window partly open, it seems strange that it had not blown across the room. The ladder was found seventy-five feet from the window. Why was it dragged that far, and left? The absence of fingerprints on the message left on the radiator grating might have indicated that the kidnaper wore gloves. Above all, the kidnaper—if he entered through the window—most have had some idea of the internal habits of the household, the location of the baby's crib, and the fact that the Lindberghs intended to stay at the Hopewell house that night instead of at Englewood, where they would normally have taken the baby.

These points did not become too evident in the early stages of the investigation. After the body was found on Mount Rose Heights, and particularly after Hauptmann's arrest, when the prosecution changed its theory from a gang to a lone kidnaper, they became extremely important.

Lindbergh had asked Schwarzkopf to avoid any publicity. But this was like asking Niagara Falls to reverse its current. By morning the alarm had been broadcast to every state bordering on New Jersey. Newspaper reporters were heading for Hopewell. In Cook County jail in Chicago, Al Capone, waiting to be transferred to prison to serve an 11-year sentence for income-tax evasion, offered a reward for return of the child and told Arthur Brisbane of the Hearst newspaper chain he would contact every known gangster in the country if they would let him out of jail for a few days.

Meanwhile, a man whose relationship to the Lindbergh case still remains a mystery, sent a letter to the Bronx *Home News,* a small suburban newspaper in New York, offering $1,000 reward and saying he would act as go-between to bring Colonel Lindbergh in contact with the kidnapers. He was Dr. J. F. Condon, known later as "Jafsie." It was the beginning of a ten-week period of trying to establish contact with the kidnapers—an effort that ended when the body was discovered on Mount Rose Heights.

Dr. Condon's letter appeared in the *Home News* on March 8, 1932. Two days earlier a woman came to the Princeton Junction Hotel, near Hopewell, giving her name as Mary Cerrita. She was with her common-law husband, Peter Birritella. She said she was a psychic and had information about the kidnaping which she had gotten from the spirits. Every possible source was being checked for information, and spiritualists were no exception. Schwarzkopf and Breckinridge interviewed her. She called Colonel Breckinridge Mr. Breckenbridge and told him he would get a note from the kidnapers. She also said she had received a spirit message in which the name "Jafsie" appeared. She said, "The baby's body will be found on the Heights above Hopewell."

Three years later, before the trial of Bruno Hauptmann, I interviwed Mary Cerrita, accompanied by Joe Dunninger, a noted de-bunker of spiritualist frauds, and she repeated what she had said to Schwarzkopf and Breckinridge. Three things she mentioned that passed almost unnoticed at the time she gave the information to Schwarzkopf and Breckinridge were either the result of remarkable prescience, or she had information about the kidnapers. This was on March 6, 1932. The letter from Dr. Condon, as noted, was put in the *Home News* two days later. A letter was received at Colonel Breckinridge's office at 25 Broadway, New York, addressed to Mr. Breckenbridge, with the identifying symbol two days later: and 72 days after the kidnaping, a body was found on Mount Rose Heights!

This coincidence will be dealt with in a later development. Nothing was reported about this until much later, but as Joe Dunninger said after we left Mary Cerrita's house in New York, "I am sure the spirits did not give her this knowledge."

The second message from the kidnaper, mailed in Brooklyn on March 4, warned Lindbergh that the matter had been "made public" and that "we will have to hold the baby until everything is quite (sic)." The ransom was raised to $70,000. A third message, received by Colonel Breckinridge at his office, also warned Lindbergh against using marked bills, and added: "We will inform you later how to deliver the money but not before the polise is out of this cace and the pappers are quite."

There were many other questions raised during the first weeks of the investigation and search for the missing child. Some of the questions were never answered; others developed later and were for the most part ignored.

The case of Violet Sharpe has been mentioned. It was never explained by the investigators, although they were questioning her when she committed suicide. The curious case of J. J. Faulkner who deposited almost three thousand dollars of the marked Lindbergh notes was not explained, or even hardly mentioned in the trial.

The crudely built ladder, found near the place where it had leaned against the wall to the nursery window, had a number of fingerprints on it, but none were Hauptmann's fingerprints! Experts differed on whether or not the handwriting on the notes was Hauptmann's or a crude attempt to duplicate his writing. The change in the focus of investigation. The first theory that a mob kidnaped the baby, was later changed to the theory that Hauptmann was the lone kidnaper. Above all, there was the strange case of "Jafsie" Condon. Why had he injected himself into the case? Why did he use the code name Jafsie, which he presumably invented six days after Mary Cerrita had told Schwarzkopf and Breckinridge of her psychic reading of the name? Was it a code word he invented or was it given to him to enable him to act as a go-between in the contact between Lindbergh and the kidnapers? If so, who gave it to him?

It will be necessary to follow each of these unexplained events, or unanswered questions, relying on the records in the case, the opinions of various experts, including their contradictory statements, and, to whatever extent is possible, my own and other newspaper accounts and documents which came into my possession during the course of the investigation.

4

Jafsie Condon

Dr. John F. Condon, a retired schoolteacher who taught parttime at Fordham University, spent the evening of March 7, 1932 at Bickford's Restaurant in the Bronx with a group that often gathered there. In his own story, *Jafsie Tells All*, a maudlin mixture of self-appreciation, rambling anecdotes, and obvious efforts to explain various contradictory statements he made before, during, and after the Hauptmann trial, he tells of his personal reactions when a newsboy brought in papers telling of the Lindbergh kidnaping.

He had just been on the verge of fisticuffs with a man at a neighboring table, who had—in the doctor's view—insulted the United States Department of Justice. On his way home he berated himself—"a professor at Fordham University"—for threatening to hit another man in a public restaurant.

He began to think about the kidnaping of Lindbergh's son, and it suddenly occurred to him that it was his duty to help.

"What was I myself doing to help put down crime in my own country? What was I, as a citizen, doing to help?"

According to his own story he had gone home with this thought on his mind. He decided to write a letter—not to *The New York Times,* but the Bronx *Home News,* an obscure suburban paper, offering his life savings—$1,000, if the kidnapers would return the Lindbergh baby. The letter appeared in the *Home News* the next day, March 8.

Two days later he received, to his professed surprise, a letter: "Dear Sir, if you are willing to act as a go-between in Lindbergh case, please follow strictly instruction."

He was told to take an enclosed letter to Colonel Lindbergh. The manner in which this was accomplished has been narrated in great detail, not only by Condon but by various writers on the subject. Condon called the Lindbergh house and spoke to Robert Thayer, a family friend. Thayer told him to open the letter to Lindbergh. It contained a strange symbol similar to the one found in the first kidnap letters; two intersecting circles, the outer parts tinted blue and the inside intersected part red, with three dots of holes in a horizontal diameter across both circles.

Thayer became quite excited, and offered to drive to the Bronx. Dr. Condon insisted that he come to the Lindbergh home in Hopewell.

Thus was Condon established as the go-between.

Several stories, some in direct conflict with each other, have been told in an effort to explain why this erratic Brooklyn schoolteacher was selected as go-between by Lindbergh as well as the kidnap gang. Condon testified at the trial of Hauptmann that he thought he talked with Lindbergh. Lindbergh was not sure; he did not think he talked with Condon. Thayer, a son of Congresswoman Ruth Pratt, made the following statement to the New Jersey state police:

At about 12 o'clock on the night of March 10 I was answering the telephone. A voice on the telephone stated that he was Dr. John Condon of the Bronx and that he had received a letter addressed to him, containing a letter addressed to Colonel Lindbergh. He said he did not know if there was anything to it, that it might be just a crank; but that he had put an advertisement in the Bronx *Home News* offering $1,000 reward to anyone who returned the baby safely, and possibly this was an answer to the advertisement.

We had just been discussing the question of the difficulty of the kidnapers communicating with Colonel Lindbergh and Colonel Breckinridge, due to the great publicity in the case and the activity of the press, and had been discussing the possibility of the kidnapers sending letters to Colonel Lindbergh through a third party. For that reason my curiosity was particularly aroused and I asked Doctor Condon how the letter was signed. He stated that it was signed with the *sign of the Mafia*. (italics mine) I then asked him to open and read the letter addressed to Colonel Lindbergh.

I took this letter down on pencil and paper as he read it to me, and it was apparent to me from the first that this letter was from the same people that had left the ransom note. This was confirmed when I asked him to give me a vague idea of the signature. . .

It will be noted that when Condon was asked to tell how the letter to him was signed, he said it was "signed with the sign of the Mafia." At that time he had not opened the letter to Lindbergh, and the letter addressed to Condon *was unsigned!* If he described the letter to Lindbergh as being signed by a symbol of the Mafia, Condon must have known in advance what the signature would be!

Thayer never was called as a witness in the Hauptmann trial. If he had, this persistent mystery might have been cleared up.

Prior to Condon's entry into the case, a man who called himself a former government agent, Morris Rosner, had been suggested to Lindbergh as the go-between. He established himself in the Lindbergh house to direct efforts to establish contact with the kidnapers. He selected two notorious mobsters, Salvatore Spitale and Irving Bitz—both of whom were then under indictment as violators of the prohibition laws—as his assistants. Rosner had called a press conference on March 11 to announce that he was "in contact with the kidnapers."

He continued his role as contact man, but Condon

was established as the real go-between—a move that was for the time kept from the press. Condon arrived early in the morning of March 11 at the Lindbergh home and was given a written authorization, signed by Colonel Lindbergh and his wife, to act as go-between representing the Lindberghs.

He returned to his Bronx home at 2974 Decatur Avenue the next morning after arrangements were completed with Lindbergh and Breckinridge, the latter driving him back. Condon had spent the rest of the night in the Lindbergh nursery, and in the morning was found looking over several toys. He asked Lindbergh for some of the boys, a camel and an elephant, and also two safety pins used to fasten the bedclothes in the crib. He explained that these would be used to assure himself that he was dealing with the actual kidnapers.

It was during his conference at the Lindbergh home that Condon hit on the name "Jafsie" which he said would be known to the kidnapers but not to anyone else. The note from the supposed kidnapers had instructed Condon to put an ad in the New York *American:* "Money is redy," if he was willing to act as go-between. Breckinridge prepared the wording of the ad: "I accept. Money is ready. Jafsie."

The name Jafsie might have been understood by Condon's Bronx friends; it was composed of the first initials of his name, John Francis Condon. How it would have been known to the kidnapers is a matter for conjecture—unless, of course, it had been worked out in advance.

The ad appeared in the classified section of the *American* in the evening edition of March 11, and true to the script, a telephone call was received at noon the next day by Mrs. Condon. The caller instructed her to tell Condon to be at home about seven o'clock that night. That evening, with Colonel Breckinridge and Condon's close friend, Al Reich, a former heavyweight boxer, standing by, he received the call.

At this point something happened which was to cause

Condon considerable worry at the Hauptmann trial. The caller had interrupted his conversation with Condon when someone said, *"Statti citto!"* This is the Italian equivalent of "Shut up!"

The words might have been spoken to anyone—a child, perhaps, but the words were *Italian!* At the time this meant to Condon that an Italian was mixed up in the case. He assumed he was dealing with a gang. Later, when the State of New Jersey changed its theory from a mob to a lone kidnaper, Condon had some trouble explaining his earlier statement, but failure of the Hauptmann defense to probe seriously into this aspect of the case allowed him to skim by safely.

The caller told Condon to stay at home between six and twelve until he received another note. The following day, March 13, a taxi driver, John Perrone, appeared shortly after six o'clock with the note which instructed Condon to drive to the last subway station on Jerome Avenue in the Bronx, walk a hundred feet beyond, and there would be another note telling him what to do. "Act accordingly. After 3/4 of an hour be on the place. bring money with you." It was signed with the Mafia symbol.

The prosecution, in an effort to show that only one man kidnaped the Lindbergh baby, sought to identify the man who presumably wrote the kidnap notes, as the only one who knew this signature. As a matter of record, the original kidnap note had been given to Morris Rosner to copy; it had been seen by members of the Lindbergh household, and probably by Spitale and Bitz, Rosner's two assistants. Condon also made a copy.

Breckinridge had not given Condon the $50,000 ransom money at the time, but Condon decided to meet the kidnapers anyway. Al Reich drove him to the end of Jerome Avenue. They found another note in an empty frankfurter stand, beyond which lay the Woodlawn Cemetery. It read: "Cross the street and follow the fence from the cemetery direct to 233rd street. I will

43

meet you there."

This was a mile further. Across from the cemetery was Van Courtland Park, a huge, sprawling area of open ground and park buildings. A nine-foot fence surrounded Woodlawn Cemetery.

They drove along the side of the cemetery. Fifty yards short of the cemetery gates, across from 233rd Street, Condon got out and walked to the gates. He waited for a time, until a handkerchief appeared, held in someone's hand, on the far side of the gates. The man who held it was inside the cemetery.

The man spoke to Condon in which he described as the same voice he heard on the telephone; a thick, deep voice, with a pronounced accent. He was holding the handkerchief over his face.

"Did you got it—the money?"

"No," Condon answered. "I couldn't bring the money without the package." He obviously meant the baby.

According to Condon the man inside the fence then said, "Did you send the cops?" He had heard the sudden crunch of footsteps.

"No!" Condon said. "I gave you my word."

The man suddenly said, "It's dangerous!" and turned and fled. He hauled himself over a nine-foot fence, and ran toward Van Courtland Park. Condon, in spite of his seventy-two years, ran after him, hollering, "Come back! Don't be cowardly!"

At this point some mention should be made of the general nature of this situation. The body found several weeks later on Mount Rose Heights had been left, according to the State's theory, in a hastily dug grave as the kidnaper fled from the Lindbergh estate. Condon did not know this at the time, but the kidnaper must have been aware of it. Knowing that the New Jersey state troopers had combed the area, and knowing he had hastily buried the body—as the prosecution said he did—would he have faced a representative of Lindbergh in the cemetery? This question became even more acute two weeks later, in another cemetery, when the supposed kidnaper faced the father of the child, Lindbergh himself!

Condon managed to overtake the other man. They sat on a park bench in Van Courtland Park, devoting an hour and a half to discussing various aspects of the situation.

Condon asked the man his name, and he replied, "John."

"Are you German?"

"No. Scandinavian."

In a report made by Special Agent J. E. Seykora of the FBI, Condon is also quoted as saying that "John" spoke with a "Scandinavian accent." In the Hauptmann trial at Flemington he said he recognized a *German accent*, as he talked to "John" in the cemetery.

Condon also said in his testimony, "I got out of the car with the letter. . .and went over to the space in front of the gates. I took the letter out. One man walked down in the direction of the automobile. Mr. Reich was in the automobile, and I saw the man coming down, but *I didn't pay any attention to him.*" (italics mine)

Why not? Was there another man besides "John?" The matter was not even raised in the trial!

In the New Jersey police records on the Lindbergh case, according to Governor Harold Hoffman, who made an intensive investigation of the entire case, there is a signed statement by Robert Riehl, a guard at the Woodlawn Cemetery, who was later identified as the man whose approaching footsteps frightened "John." It reads:

I observed a man sitting on the top of the stone column of the gate, talking to the other fellow who was outside the gate. The man sitting on the column seen me. I was then about seventy-five feet away. He hollered to the man outside the gate, "There's the cop coming." The fellow on top of the column then jumped down and I thought he had broken his leg. Then he got up and ran across 233rd Street into the Park and disappeared. I went near the gate and questioned the other man who was outside as to what the young fellow was doing on top of the column, and his reply was, "I don't know, I have no idea. If you wait a minute I'll go over and ask him.

Riehl's statement added: "When this man hollered *I did not notice a foreign accent in his speech.*" (italics mine)

Riehl was never called to testify at the Flemington trial. Condon testified that the man who frightened "John" was identified as a "cemetery guard named Riehl."

The period of more than an hour—Condon said it was "an hour and forty minutes" in an earlier statement, and about an hour in testimony at the Flemington trial—spent in the cemetery furnished some enlightenment to Condon, and resulted in statements he later retracted or modified. At the end of the session, "John" said, "I will send you the baby's sleeping suit."

Condon, in his earlier account on May 13, 1932, does not mention the safety pins he took from the Lindbergh nursery, with Colonel Lindbergh's permission, as a means of identifying the kidnaper. He does not mention the pins in a recorded statement to the Department of Justice, or in a statement given to Assistant District Attorney Breslin of the Bronx on May 14. On May 20, 1932, he appeared before the Bronx grand jury and said, under oath: "I spoke to Colonel Lindbergh and asked him if I might take the two safety pins for this reason: the crib was long and wide enough to pin the over-blanket of the child with large pins to the undersheets . . .I had an object in view. I determined to have at least something (to show the kidnapers). *I didn't show that to the kidnapers* as stated in newspapers." (italics mine)

Again under oath at Flemington he testifed as follows, quoting from the record:

Dr. Condon: In order to find out whether he ("John") was the proper party, I said, "How am I to know that I am talking to the right man? Tell me."

Mr. Reilly: What did he say?

Dr. Condon: I trust I may be excused. "The baby was held in the crib by safety pins."

Mr. Reilly: Who said that? "John?"

Dr. Condon: "John."

Mr. Reilly: Did you have the pins with you?

Dr. Condon: I had the pins with me because I took them out of the baby's crib the night I slept there.

The stories Condon told to the state police, the Department of Justice, and the Bronx grand jury contradict this testimony; yet it was allowed to pass unheeded by both prosecution and defense!

After Jafsie's first meeting with "John" in the Woodlawn Cemetery, Condon and Breckinridge agreed to place the next ad in the Bronx *Home News*. "Baby alive and well. Money is ready. Call and see us. Jafsie."

On March 16 a package was laid on top of Condon's mailbox. It contained a child's woolen sleeping suit and a letter. He called Breckinridge and that night Lindbergh appeared at Condon's home in the Bronx.

The letter raised the ransom from $50,000 to $70,000. It said: "Ouer man faill to collect the money. There are no more confidential conferences. This arrangements too hazardous for us."

During the meeting in Woodlawn Cemetery "John" had mentioned that the baby was "on a boad" six hours distant from New York, and two women were taking care of the child. "John" also said his share of the ransom was $20,000 and the other members of the gang would each get $10,000, leading him to believe a gang was involved.

Meanwhile they continued sending messages. One letter included on the reverse side a special note: "Mr. Lindbergh is only wasting his time with his search."

Condon had become aware that another search was going on. A newspaper story, datelined Norfolk, Virginia, had appeared March 12 stating that three important people were in communication with Colonel

Lindbergh: Dean Harold Dobson-Peacock of the Christ Episcopal Church in Norfolk, Admiral Guy H. Burrage, retired, and John Hughes Curtis, a prominent Norfolk boat builder. They were also in communication with the Lindbergh baby kidnapers.

This apparently explained the words on the reverse side of the last letter to Condon from the kidnapers. He must have wondered if he was not being passed over in the search for the Lindbergh baby!

On March 29, however, he received a letter with the familiar symbol; two intersecting circles with three holes marked along the diameters. It was in reply to the latest ad inserted in the Bronx *Home News* the previous Saturday, March 26. The letter warned that if the deal was not closed by April 8, the price would go up another $30,000—to $100,000. It also mentioned the false clues that Lindbergh seemed to be following.

Lindbergh had meanwhile called in the United States Treasury Department's chief enforcement officer, Elmer Irey, to advise him. Irey suggested he prepare an additional package of bills totalling $20,000, in which he would insert a sufficient quantity of gold certificates in sequences of serial numbers to enable the Treasury Department to trace the bills.

On April 2 the acceptance of the kidnapers' latest ultimatum appeared in the New York *American:* "Yes, everything O.K. Jafsie."

That night a cab driver delivered the letter of instruction. Condon was to go to a nursery on Tremont Avenue; a letter fastened underneath a table would tell him what to do.

This time Lindbergh accompanied him. They found the nursery, across from St. Raymond's Cemetery. Condon had heard that Italians frequently held business meetings in a graveyard; this seemed, in Cordon's opinion, to confirm that the gang was a mixture of Italians and the Scandinavian, "John." This was changed, of course, during the Flemington trial: it was a lone German carpenter who conceived and carried out the kidnaping!

Lindbergh had started to get out of the car when Condon stopped him. He said "John" expected only Jafsie. Lindbergh agreed. The reports of this meeting in the Bronx cemetery—St. Raymond's—later became so complex and full of contradictions that it became necessary to use several sources, rather than rely solely on Condon's rambling account.

The instructions said to "cross the street, walk to the next corner and follow Whittemore Ave to the soud." Condon apparently decided not to follow these instructions. He said later he wanted to see who was lurking behind tombstones, so he followed Tremont Avenue to the east. After walking about three hundred feet past the cemetery gates he heard a voice.

"Hey, Doctor!"

A man was behind a gravestone inside the cemetery.

"Hey, Doctor! Over here!"

Condon started toward the tombstone, but the man moved away, jumped over a five-foot wall, and waited beside a clump of bushes. At this point the question of inflections, intonations, foreign accent, and gutteral tones began to take shape. Condon at first said he would recognize "John" by his voice. Lindbergh, in a statement to the Bronx grand jury, wasn't quite sure. He first said the man said, "Ay, Doctor!" and later "Hey, Doc!" Asked if he had a foreign accent, he said, "Undoubtedly, it was a very distinct foreign accent." Later he told the grand jury, "I can't say positively. I remember the voice very clearly, but it would be difficult for me to sit here and say I could pick a man by that voice."

This was about three weeks after he heard the voice, on April 21, 1932. Two-and-a-half years later Lindbergh's recollection became more firm. And so did Condon's.

Lindbergh identified the voice at the Flemington trial as Hauptmann's and Condon's identification was so definite that it appeared to preclude any doubt.

Attorney General Wilentz asked Condon, "Who is 'John?'" The Bronx schoolteacher replied, "John is Bruno Richard Hauptmann!"

After Condon joined "John" in the cemetery, the man said, "Did you got it, the money?"

"No. It's up in the car."

"Who is there?"

"Colonel Lindbergh."

"Is he armed?"

"I don't know." Then after a minute, Condon said, "No, he is not."

"John" demanded the money, and Condon said, "Not until you give me a receipt showing where the baby is."

According to Condon's story, there followed a brief dickering over the amount of ransom—whether it should be $50,000 or $70,000. "Listen, John," Condon finally said, "Colonel Lindbergh is not so rich. These are times of depression—why don't you be decent?"

After a moment of apparent indecision, "John" capitulated—a startling development in itself. "All right," he said, according to Condon's story, "I suppose if we can't get seventy, we take fifty."

This, in Condon's mind, seemed to indicate that "John" was not merely the bagman, but the leader of the gang. Otherwise he would not have settled for $50,000 instead of $70,000.

Again it is necessary to interpolate certain relevant points. Gaston B. Means, whose part in the Lindbergh case will be reviewed later, wrote a memorandum to his lawyer from the District Jail in Washington, D.C. on May 27, 1933—more than a year before Hauptmann's arrest, and a year after the body had been found near Hopewell—in which he made a trenchant observation.

"Nobody with any commonsense would believe the body was where it was found while negotiations were going on with Dr. Condon and through him with Colonel Lindbergh and Colonel Breckinridge, which lasted a number of days. This could not be true because

50

at any moment the body might have been found. . . . Those who were conducting the negotiations had to know, while they were going on, that the body was well concealed and there was absolutely no chance of finding it by mere accident, and only by a tip-off."

When "John" left to get the receipt, Condon went back to the car where Lindbergh was sitting to get the ransom money. At this point a third man appeared for the second time, that is, one in addition to Condon and "John." Oddly enough, this third man was mentioned only by Lindbergh in his testimony before the Bronx grand jury; Condon did not refer to him in his account of the meeting at St. Raymond's cemetery in his trial testimony.

Lou Wedemar, a newspaperman and writer for the Universal Service, appears to be the only reporter who did mention him. He wrote in his series on *Fifty Unanswered Questions in the Hauptmann Case:*

> When Colonel Lindbergh went to St. Raymond's Cemetery on the night of April 2, 1932, to pay the ransom to John he saw, according to his testimony before the Bronx grand jury, a man with a handkerchief. This man walked with a stoop and wore a brown suit. He twice passed Colonel Lindbergh's car, looking in every direction carefully while Condon was in the cemetery waiting for John. This man, whom Colonel Lindbergh then believed to be a lookout, held a handkerchief in his hand, partly covering his face. After twice passing Colonel Lindbergh, he ran to a spot some distance away. There Colonel Lindbergh saw him drop the handkerchief, as if giving a signal. Then he disappeared.
>
> The handkerchief was recovered later by detectives, and efforts were made to trace its owner. But it was not introduced at the Hauptmann trial, and no mention of it, or the man, was made to the jury. The possibility had been considered that this man was Isidor Fisch.

This possibility will be discussed in a later context, in an examination of the story of Paul Wendel, who confessed to the kidnaping of Lindbergh's son, and later repudiated the confession. Wedemar adds this significant bit to his story:

> During the fifteen minutes Lindbergh and Dr. Condon waited outside the St. Raymond's Cemetery for John to reappear, Dr. Condon *also saw this man*. When the man passed Colonel Lindbergh for the second time, Dr. Condon was emerging from the cemetery, after vainly seeking John. He saw and followed the man around a curve until they were both out of sight of Colonel Lindbergh. Whether they spoke to each other is not known; Dr. Condon would not tell. But while the man with the handkerchief was still on Tremont Avenue, *John hailed Dr. Condon from within the cemetery wall.* (italics mine)

Wedemar asked one of his unanswered questions: "Why did Dr. Condon follow the man with the handkerchief?"

Lindbergh, in a statement made to police after Hauptmann was arrested, said he believed it possible that the man with the handkerchief was Hauptmann, or "John." Yet he saw the man running down Tremont Avenue and he saw "John" across the road in the cemetery. Was Lindbergh confused, or did he lie to support the State's theory that it was a one man job? If so, he was contributing to sending to the electric chair a man who may have been innocent of murder—the charge on which Hauptmann was convicted.

After Condon got the ransom money from Lindbergh, he met "John" in the graveyard and handed it to him. The box contained only the package of $50,000. "John" handed Condon a note, which read:

> the boy is on the boad (sic) Nelly. It is a small boad 28 feet long. Two persons are on the boad. they are innocent. You will find the boad between Horseneck Beach and Gay Head on Elizabeth Island.

They drove back to meet the others—Breckinridge, Irey, the Treasury Department investigator, and his assistants. Condon explained how he had saved Lindbergh $20,000. Irey blew up. He told Condon the second package contained more than a hundred gold certificates of $100 denomination that could readily be traced if they were turned in at any bank!

Condon shook his head. He had not been told.

The search for the "boad Nelly" began at two o'clock the following morning. Lindbergh took off from the airport at Bridgeport, where a Sikorsky amphibian was waiting. The area described was Vinyard Sound, north of Martha's Vinyard—a series of islands along the southern side of Buzzard's Bay. There was no sign of the boat. Coast Guard cutters from Cuttyhunk Island joined the search. The following day, April 5, the search continued. There was no further evidence that the boat was in the vicinity. Lindbergh went back to Hopewell to break the news to his wife. Condon put another ad in the New York *American:* "What is wrong? Have you crossed me? Better directions. Jafsie."

Then a new development cropped up. The serial numbers of the ransom money paid the kidnapers had been listed by the clerks at J.P. Morgan & Company, where the package was made up. A circular was distributed by the Treasury Department to all banks giving this listing. This aroused the curiosity of the Newark *News,* which published a story indicating this list was probably a record of the payment of $50,000 by Lindbergh to the kidnapers, and surmising that the ransom had been paid but the baby was not returned.

Lindbergh, fearing this story might cut off all further communication with the kidnapers, authorized a statement explaining that he had delivered the ransom money to the kidnapers and the baby was not found at the place designated.

His statement said: "It was not intended to use the numbers on the specie in which the ransom was paid, but inasmuch as the kidnapers have failed to keep their agreement and have not communicated since the ransom was paid, every possible means must be utilized to accomplish the return of the baby."

Condon was back in his Bronx home, where reporters —now aware of his part in the ransom payment—were besieging him with questions. He explained that the initial failure to recover the stolen baby was due to the fear of a trap by the gang.

"There were too many airplanes and Coast Guard cutters in the vicinity where the child was to be turned over."

However, there was no further word from "John" or anyone else. Condon made many trips to the Greenwich police headquarters in New York. He looked at rogues gallery pictures, gave his description of "John's" voice, led detectives to St. Raymond's Cemetery and to the Woodlawn Cemetery, and enacted his meetings with "John."

In spite of his continued efforts, Dr. John Francis Condon faded from the scene—for a period. It was not until two-and-a-half years later, when Bruno Hauptmann was arrested as the kidnaper of the Lindbergh baby, that Condon returned to the front pages. The scene had shifted to Norfolk, Virginia, and to the home of Mrs. Evalyn Walsh McLean, in the Georgetown section of Washington, D.C. The names in the news were John Hughes Curtis, of Norfolk, and Gaston B. Means, of almost anywhere.

Several pertinent questions that might have been asked at the time, were not asked; so they may as well be asked in this review. It will be recalled that Mary Cerrita and her husband, Peter Birritella, were interviewed by Schwarzkopf and Breckinridge on March 6, two days before Condon sent his first letter to the Bronx *Home News,* and received a letter from the supposed kidnapers in reply. Sid Whipple mentions this in *The Lindbergh Crime:* "Spiritualists and pseudo-spiritualists made the occasion a field day for their operations. . . .Two others, professing to be in communication with the spirits, told Colonel Breckinridge that he would do better to go back to his office in New York and 'await a message there.'" Later Whipple says: "The soothsayers

54

had been right." The third message from the kidnapers was received at Breckinridge's office in New York! The soothsayers were from the Bronx!

Why was this clue overlooked? The name Jafsie was mentioned by Mary Cerrita and this was later picked up in a story in the New York *Daily News*. This was known when Jafsie came into the case. Why did not investigators follow up on this extremely significant clue? If Jafsie's name was known to the psychic, Mary Cerrita, it probably was known to the kidnapers—four days before Condon supposedly adopted that name when he was seeking a code word to identify himself!

When Joe Dunninger and I talked with Mary Cerrita, on December 30, 1934, she used the name Mr. Breckenbridge for Colonel Breckinridge. The same name was used in the third kidnap note, sent to his office at 25 Broadway. An investigation might have disclosed the reason *why* Jafsie injected himself into the case. Was he acting purely out of the desire of a good citizen to help? Or had he been picked as go-between by the kidnapers well in advance? Was he aware of this role, or was he selected without knowing it?

In the third letter from the kidnapers, or kidnaper, the writer said: "We will not accept any go-between from your sent." It was assumed this meant either "side" or "sent by you." Jafsie Condon was accepted. Was this coincidental, or did it follow the script set forth in the kidnapers' note?

Some of these points will be clarified as this review progresses. Some will never be explained, because the doors are now closed.

5

Gaston B. Means

Jafsie was right. There were other sources of information, and Lindbergh was looking into them: John
Hughes Curtis, the Norfolk shipbuilder, and Gaston B.
Means, once a detective with William J. Burns, an ex-
salesman for Cannon Mills, a Department of Justice
undercover operative, as well as a free-lance con man
known to the police, once tried for murder and
acquitted!

Means came on the scene first. Mrs. Evalyn Walsh
McLean, estranged wife of the publisher of the Washington *Post*, daughter of Thomas Walsh, a Colorado
mining magnate, and owner of the ill-starred Hope
Diamond, wrote in an article she prepared several years
after the Lindbergh kidnaping:

> I kept wondering who was the cleverest crook, in my
> opinion, I had ever known. Gaston B. Means was the
> name that kept coming back to me. . . .Here was a man
> who had every underworld connection; he had worked
> for Burns in the Department of Justice, he had been
> tried for murder, and even with his past record had
> served only a couple of years in the penitentiary. That
> showed me the man was really clever.

It was on this basis that Mrs. McLean located Means,
on March 4, 1932, asked him to come to her house, and
proposed that he attempt to contact the kidnapers.
Means told her he had already contacted them.

Late in 1935, when Hauptmann was still awaiting execution in the electric chair at Trenton, I came into

possession of a letter written from a jail cell in Washington by Gaston Means to his attorney, B. Mercer Hartman. It was from this letter that the excerpt in the last chapter is quoted, noting that "no one with any common sense" would have confronted the father of the kidnaped baby in the Bronx cemetery, knowing that a body left in a hastily dug grave as the kidnaper ran from the Lindbergh house, might have been discovered by New Jersey state troopers, or anyone else, tramping over the ground near Hopewell.

Means' letter had been given me by Vincent Marco, a Los Angeles attorney whom I knew quite well. He had been retained by Mrs. Emma Gloeckner, Hauptmann's sister, to investigate several circumstances in connection with her brother's conviction.

The letter, written almost in the form of an affidavit, advised Attorney Hartman that on May 26, 1933, "all litigation was ended by the action taken in (Judge Daniel O'Donahue's) court" and in accordance with Hartman's advice, Means was setting down a statement of facts in the Lindbergh case. There followed a lengthy recital of Means' participation in behalf of Mrs. McLean, who had hired him.

The letter was not introduced in the Hauptmann trial at Flemington for obvious reasons; Means said he was dealing with mobsters. I have no knowledge that it was ever used in any of the investigations, or is even a true account of Means' part in the Lindbergh case. But many facts mentioned by Means are consistent with a number of other facts developed by the various investigations, and some cast new light on the unexplained parts of the Lindbergh case.

Means was a mysterious character, a plump, affable man who had handled payoff money for President Warren Harding's administration, and had even been hired by Mrs. Harding to check on the President's reported romance with Nan Britton!

Despite his record, and the two-year prison stretches he served for violating the Prohibition Laws and swindling, there is much in his affidavit that can be related to known facts in the Lindbergh case. In her article published in 1938, Mrs. McLean wrote: "Gaston Means as he lies today, a stricken man in a federal prison hospital, must be thinking of things, which if known, would go a long way toward clearing up the Lindbergh case."

Returning to Means' letter to his attorney, he wrote:

From Feb. 16, 1932 to Feb. 26, 1932 I was in New York City registered at the Imperial Hotel. I had gone to New York City from Washington, D. C. for the purpose of locating Wellington Henderson in connection with an investigation that had been assigned to me.

In my efforts to locate Wellington Henderson I contacted James Feldman, alias Irving Fenton, and learned from him about Wellington Henderson being in Jersey City. I requested Feldman alias Fenton to reach Henderson and ask him to come to New York City at the Imperial Hotel.

Feldman alias Fenton called my attention in my first interview with him that he knew of a kidnaping that was going to take place and tried to interest me in this matter.

Means told Feldman alias Fenton he was not interested, and says he formed the impression that the kidnaping had to do with "some bootlegger and thereby make some money out of the situation."

Shortly afterward he met Feldman alias Fenton with a well-known member of the bootlegging business, Max Greenberg. Feldman told Means, according to his story, that he wanted to discuss the matter of kidnaping in greater detail, and Means added, "It was not necessary for me to take any part in it but they had to have a contact man for the purpose of collecting money." Feldman also said there would be no publicity "as things were properly planned, but if every detail were not carried through successfully there would be the widest publicity ever known in such a case."

Means says he told Feldman and Greenberg he was

not interested in any kidnaping, as a contact man or in any other capacity, and that he "did not want him (Feldman) to discuss the subject with me or give any other information in regard to it."

Means' letter states he returned to Washington February 26 and remained at his home in Chevy Chase, Maryland. On March 2, 1932, he read in the newspapers that Colonel Lindbergh's child, Charles A. Lindbergh, Jr., had been kidnaped from their home in New Jersey. He wrote in his letter: "Feldman alias Fenton had said enough to me and his references to New Jersey on several occasions led me to form the opinion that the kidnaping he said was going to occur had occurred, and the kidnaping he referred to was the kidnaping of Charles Lindbergh, Jr." This seemed to arouse Means' patriotic instincts.

On Wednesday, March 2, Means telephoned Colonel Robert Guggenheim, of the wealthy Guggenheim family, and asked for a meeting. He said he believed he knew who the kidnapers of the Lindbergh baby were, and with his knowledge of underworld personalities he believed he could find the baby and restore it to the Lindberghs. Guggenheim was interested; he arranged for Means to meet him.

Meanwhile Mrs. Walsh reached Means by telephone, and asked him to come to Friendship House, her home in Georgetown. She had known Means through her husband's connection with the Department of Justice. She said she was also a friend of the Lindbergh's, and of Captain Emory Land, Mrs. Evangeline Lindbergh's cousin. Means asked that Captain Land be present at their meeting.

Means said in his letter: "I did not discuss the kidnaping with Mrs. McLean, except that both of us made reference to such a horrible thing having been perpetrated."

Mrs. McLean did not know when she telephoned Means that he believed he already had a contact with the kidnapers.

Before going to Mrs. McLean's home, Means called on Judge Marion De Vries in Washington and explained that he had information he believed might lead to the location and return of the Lindbergh baby, and asked his advice on how to proceed. Judge De Vries asked whether Means could contact the party or any other parties he thought might be involved. Means said he could, and the judge told him to contact the party and return to his office, and he would see about arranging a meeting between Means and Colonel Lindbergh.

Before going to the McLean home, Means says he sent a special delivery letter to James Feldman at the Elizabeth-Cartaret Hotel in Elizabeth, New Jersey, asking that he call him at his Chevy Chase home, or come to Washington.

"From the newspapers," Means wrote, "I formed the opinion that the plans for the kidnaping had gone wrong and therefore they would be anxious to get rid of the child at the earliest moment possible."

He then went to the McLean home and explained to her what he had done. He also mentioned that he had called Colonel Robert Guggenheim but had not followed up the call because he wanted to consult with Judge De Vries. She knew Colonel Guggenheim, and suggested that a friend, Robert Fleming, who was also well-acquainted with the Guggenheims, might arrange the meeting with Lindbergh.

Means' letter was a bit rambling at that point, but the substance of the arrangements he described was that Fleming would come to his home and arrange for a meeting with Colonel Guggenheim. Meanwhile, Means notes, Mrs. McLean, "although she did not drink herself, had an extremely good brand of whiskey from which I made a few highballs in order to take advantage of the good whiskey and extended my visit until about 11:30 P.M., when I left for home."

Fleming had already arrived and left, and Means remained at home most of the following day to receive the telephone call from Feldman. In the afternoon

Means was informed by Fleming that Colonel Guggenheim would meet him at Fleming's house. That afternoon, he went over and explained the situation to the Colonel. He returned about eight o'clock and received a local telephone call from Feldman, who had already arrived in Washington. He also had a call from Mrs. McLean asking him to come to Friendship House to meet Captain Land.

Before arriving at Mrs. McLean's home, Means met Feldman on the sidewalk near her house and, according to his letter, "he told me the situation in regard to the kidnaping" and said the prospective kidnaping he had told Means about in the Imperial Hotel in New York City concerned the Lindbergh baby. Feldman added, "All concerned in this were now in a most dangerous situation." Plans had not gone as they expected, and Feldman said he was "certainly glad to get the letter from me, and hoped that I had some way in which the child could be returned to the Lindberghs under immunity conditions and without requirement of any ransom."

Means told Feldman to meet him "in the basement of my home at 11:30 o'clock that night." He then went to Mrs. McLean's home where she and Captain Land were waiting, and said he had "contacted one of the parties" but did not go into any details.

This series of events, culled from the letter Means wrote to his attorney, is explained in full detail because it was quite evident that Means, always looking for a profitable enterprise, was arranging a scheme in which both sides could be played against each other. The letter says:

> Up to this time no question had arisen in any respect in regard to any money or any ransom or any expenses of any kind. All of my work had been absolutely sincere and solely for the purpose of bringing about the return of the Lindbergh child without expense to anyone. Mrs. McLean, in discussing the matter with Captain Land told him that he could say to Colonel Lindbergh that the

work in connection with the case would be entirely at her expense and that all financing that had to be done would be paid by her and that she would pay the ransom for the return of the child to her.

Captain Land said he would go to Hopewell to obtain his promise of immunity for the return of the child and the authority of an experienced investigator to work on the case for Mrs. McLean.

Whether or not Means was making a self-serving statement, engaged in blatant hypocrisy, or setting the stage for a financial coup of his own, can only be surmised from the events as they occurred; but Mrs. McLean's interest was undoubtedly sincere. There had been a tragedy in her own life. She had been fearful, as the owner of the Hope diamond, a symbol of bad luck, that her son might be kidnaped and had hired a guard to watch him. When he was eight years old he had run through an open gate and was killed by a passing car.

Her memory of this event had triggered her reaction. She later wrote: "Perhaps I am thought of as a meddlesome old woman; that can't be helped. But if I had this to do all over again, I would do it."

Means' last words to Captain Land when they concluded the meeting at Mrs. McLean's home were, "I know the head of the Lindbergh kidnap gang. With your help, I can have the baby back to his mother inside of two weeks."

Land asked if any payment would be demanded. Means suddenly said, "They want a hundred thousand dollars."

This was Sunday, March 5. On Tuesday, March 8, Jafsie Condon placed his first letter to the kidnapers in the Bronx *Home News* and on March 10 received a reply asking $50,000. It seemed at the time that Means and Condon were dealing with two different gangs, and it also seemed reasonable to suspect that one gang had the Lindbergh baby, and the other *knew of the kidnaping*, but did not have the baby.

Means returned to his home to meet Feldman alias

Fenton in the basement. He went over all the matters discussed with Mrs. McLean and Land, including his somewhat impromptu suggestion that the kidnapers wanted $100,000. According to Means, Feldman's first comment was, "I do not suppose there will be any trouble for Captain Land to get authority for you to work on the case, and a promise from Colonel Lindbergh of immunity for the return of the child." He added that he regretted Mrs. McLean's stipulation that the child be returned to her, and "on the strength of this stipulation and her willingness to pay the ransom, he did not see why they should not require payment."

This turn-about seemed reasonable to Means, according to his letter. That afternoon Mrs. McLean telephoned that Colonel Lindbergh had agreed to authorize Means to work on the case, and had also agreed to the promise of immunity if the child were returned safely. He repeated their request for a ransom. She told Means she would provide the $100,000. The following day she gave Means the $100,000, plus $4,000 expense money. Means said Feldman had advised him that a Catholic priest should be present when the baby was returned, and she asked Father J. Francis Hurney, pastor of the Church of Immaculate Conception, to act in that capacity.

The reason the preliminary arrangements with Gaston B. Means have been covered in considerable detail is that what he wrote in his letter to Mercer Hartman, his attorney, and accounts of what happened as reported in the newspapers, are almost identical. In Means' letter, however, certain additional details are included which were not disclosed in later published reports.

The entire McLean-Means arrangement had been completed in secrecy, with only the principals aware of what was going on—Gaston Means, Mrs. McLean, Captain Land, Lindbergh and Breckinridge, Father Hurney, and presumably Feldman alias Fenton. It is necessary at this point to rely on Means' affidavit-like letter and Mrs. McLean's story written several years later for *Liberty* magazine.

Means returned to his Chevy Chase home, took the $100,000 to the basement where Feldman and Wellington Henderson, whom he had picked up in Washington, were waiting, and they counted the money. They then announced they would pick up the baby (apparently then in Baltimore) and take it to Mrs. McLean's home, Farview, in Maryland. Three days later, Feldman told Means, "Something unusual has happened, a terrible tragedy." The baby had been hidden in a dugout where whiskey runners kept concealed quantities of liquor, and in being carried up a ladder had fallen and was killed. It was in a hideout used by Max Hassel, otherwise known as Mendel Gassel, a prominent man in the whiskey running business.

Gaston Means used every trick in his bag during the next month to evade being exposed as a possible faker. He still had the $100,000 from Mrs. McLean, and as far as she knew the baby was still alive. She had also told Means, according to her later story, "If you don't play straight with me, I'll lock you up."

On April 2, the day Condon and Lindbergh were to meet "John" in the Bronx cemetery and pay the ransom, Means telephoned to say he had the feeling they would be "out of the woods" within the next few hours. Mrs. McLean had read in the newspapers that three men in Norfolk, Virginia, were reported *dealing* with the kidnapers; and she had heard that a man in the Bronx was already in contact with them. Her suspicions became aroused.

Which gang was Gaston Means dealing with?

She telephoned Means and asked that he come to her home in Georgetown to explain a few things.

It was the same gang, he told her. They were dealing with Curtis, and also a schoolteacher in New York. They had originally asked for $50,000 ransom, but now the figure was $100,000, the amount Mrs. McLean said she would pay. This was before the Jafsie story was in the newspapers. What Means did *not* say, however, was that he already had information which led him to believe the baby was dead, and that he had known of this for two weeks! In his letter to Hartman, he said: "The body of the Lindbergh child was taken as near the house as could be dared, where it would be found and thereby leave the impression that it was not the work of kidnapers, but an 'inside job.'"

Means had a genius for mixing facts with his clever imagination. What he did not know at the time, of course, was that subsequent investigations, stimulated by Mrs. Evalyn McLean and Governor Hoffman of New Jersey, would virtually prove that the body found near Hopewell was a substitute corpse, placed in the shallow grave in the hope it would be found and end the search for Lindbergh's baby.

At the end of his eight-page letter to Attorney Hartman, Means wrote:

> The kidnaping was carried out by Max Hassel's connections who were selling beer to Colonel Lindbergh's servants, or a servant. Colonel Lindbergh had played an innocent practical joke on one occasion by hiding the child and pretending it had been kidnaped. The beer sellers, knowing of this joke, went to Colonel Lindbergh's home on the night of March 1, 1932, and to the child's room and picked him up and walked out of the house. They had three bottles of imported beer, and if they had been stopped they would have said they brought over the three bottles of beer as samples, but when they came in the house, seeing none of the servants, they picked up the baby and left some notes to make out that he had been kidnaped.

Means' story is undoubtedly his usual mixture of fact and fiction. The earlier joke played on the household by Colonel Lindbergh is in all probability imagination. Some of the rest of the story would go a long way to explaining many unexplained parts of the Lindbergh kidnaping case—including the suicide of Violet Sharpe. This will be dealt with later in this review.

Means was still fighting for time to work his way out

of the situation. He told Mrs. McLean he had *seen* the child at Aiken, North Carolina, where Mrs. McLean had a summer home. The kidnapers felt this was a safer place to return the baby than Fairview, in Maryland. If Mrs. McLean would go to Aiken they would arrange to deliver the baby.

She drove to Aiken with Means and a man with a mustache and horn-rimmed glasses, whom Means called "The Fox." When they reached her home in Aiken "The Fox" moved around the place, apparently looking for bugging devices. He then said he would have to report to the other members of the gang. The next day he returned and said the others were not satisfied; they decided to turn the baby over to her at El Paso, Texas, across the Mexican border from Juarez! He also said she should bring a nurse to take care of the baby, who suffered from a minor cold.

That night—April 3—Mrs. McLean wrote to Father Hurney that she was going to El Paso, and might not come back. She said, "You and Capt. Land know what has happened but in case I do not come back I want you and the world to know what things have happened." She told of the man with the mustache and horn-rimmed glasses, known as "The Fox," who said he had the baby and it was well and strong. Later, she said, she "received a long distance call from Orange, New Jersey and then from Elizabeth, New Jersey" from this man, saying that things had gone wrong and Means should come at once. When Means returned, he told Mrs. McLean that "hi-jackers had almost gotten the baby and Curtis and that crowd were dealing with the hi-jackers."

The existence of two rival gangs seemed at variance with what Means had told Mrs. McLean in Washington; that they were all dealing with the same gang.

She told Father Hurney "The Fox," whom Means brought to her home in Aiken, had told her they must switch to El Paso to deliver the baby; it was too risky to try to return the child in Washington or Aiken. Mrs.

McLean and the nurse, Elizabeth Nelson, took the train for El Paso with Means, and found out that the supposed gang had raised the ransom to $135,000. This appeared to be the last straw. Mrs. McLean returned to Washington, discussed the matter with her attorney, and then phoned Means that she did not believe he could return the Lindbergh baby. She asked him to return her $100,000.

Early in May, 1932, agents of the Department of Justice arrested Gaston Means on a warrant charging larceny after trust—a form of embezzlement—and he was sentenced to serve fifteen years in a Federal penitentiary. His explanation of what happened to the $100,000 was ingenious. He said he was on his way to Washington to return the money to Mrs. McLean when a car drew alongside his car on the Potomac River Bridge and a man leaned out and gave the number "11." This was the code word for Mrs. McLean, so he assumed it was on her instructions and turned over the money. Later he said it was "Feldman alias Fenton" in the car.

"I was certain of it, so I gave him the hundred thousand."

Later his principal kidnaper—"The Fox"—was arrested as Norman T. Whitaker, alias Neil Williams. He appeared in court a year later with Means, who had been brought from his prison cell, on charges of attempting to defraud Mrs. McLean of the extra $35,000. Whitaker was rather bedraggled, wearing shabby clothes, and did not look as if he had participated in the hundred thousand dollars donated by Mrs. McLean.

Means died several years later in the Federal prison at Fort Leavenworth, but to the very end Mrs. McLean believed he had been in contact with the Lindbergh kidnapers.

"How did he know that the ransom had been increased (to $100,000) before that information was made public? How did he know about the entrance of Jafsie into the case before the police gave out that information? How did he know what would happen to Jafsie's negotiations—before it happened? And how did it happen that Means told me about the gang at Norfolk at the same time that John Hughes Curtis was telling the police the same story?"

In the closing page of Means' letter to Hartman, he mentions "certain mystic or symbolic" identification used by rum runners to spot their customers, apparently referring to the bizarre "signature." He added: "Investigate Max Hassel and Max Greenberg's records. The records will prove they were the kidnapers, and engineered more than one kidnaping for ransom."

Max Hassel and Max Greenberg were shot to death in the Elizabeth-Cartaret Hotel in Elizabeth, New Jersey, on April 12, 1933, in a gang-war shooting.

Means also said in his letter to Hartmann: "The ladder was used to look into the window to make sure the child was in the room, and not to bring the child out of the room." This might explain why the ladder was found seventy-five feet from the window.

Whether or not Gaston Means' story was fiction, and he believed he was dealing with a gullible woman, or he had established relations with the kidnap gang can only be surmised. Glib explanations offered by accounts of his participation—particularly that of Sidney B. Whipple in *The Lindbergh Crime*—do not answer every question, although they conform to the New Jersey police theory.

Some of this information came to light in the investigation of the Lindbergh case by Robert Hicks, the Washington criminologist who was retained by Governor Hoffman of New Jersey as well as by Mrs. McLean. This will be discussed in a later context.

6

The Norfolk Connection

John Hughes Curtis was a builder from Norfolk, Virginia, who came into the Lindbergh kidnaping case as an "outsider." A man whom he knew as Sam stopped him one night and said he had been selected as a contact man by the kidnapers of the Lindbergh baby.

Of all the go-betweens in the Lindbergh case, Curtis was least likely to be considered a swindler and crook. He was a solid citizen of Norfolk, with an impeccable record for honesty and integrity. Jafsie Condon had proved himself to be a posturing eccentric, shifting his stories with every change of wind; Gaston Means was a self-confessed confidence man and in the estimation of Evalyn Walsh McLean, who hired him, "the world's greatest crook."

Yet Condon continued to enjoy Colonel Lindbergh's confidence, a man he believed had contacted the kidnapers and paid $50,000 ransom. Means was later convicted of swindling Mrs. McLean out of $100,000. Curtis, on the other hand, had never asked to be involved in the Lindbergh case. In the end, shocked by the discovery of what was believed to be the baby's body on Mount Rose Heights, he signed an affidavit which the newspapers interpreted as a confession stating that at no time had he contacted the kidnapers.

There are several factors which might lead one to believe that Curtis, more than Condon, was in actual contact with the kidnap gang. It is also possible that he might have recovered the child if greater attention had been given his story. Mrs. McLean was among those who believed, in spite of Curtis' confession, that he was in touch with the kidnapers.

More of this will be developed later; but one is inclined to wonder whether Curtis' confession would have been made on May 17, 1932, a few days after the body was found on Mount Rose Heights, had he known at the time that there was legitimate doubt that it was the body of the Lindbergh baby!

Curtis did not come actively into the search for Lindbergh's son until March 19, 1932, but on March 10 he had been told by a man named "Sam," whom he later identified as Morrie Truesdale, that he had been chosen to be the go-between by the supposed kidnapers. Sam, a rum-runner of sorts who was known to Curtis, had jumped on the running board of Curtis' car as he drove out of the Norfolk Country Club grounds late in the evening of March 10.

"What are you doing here?" Curtis asked.

"Please don't get sore, Mr. Curtis!"

Sam slipped into the front seat of the car.

He appeared quite nervous. He asked Curtis to promise that he would not tell anyone what he was about to reveal. Curtis said he would tell no one. Sam then explained that he had been picked by the gang who stole the Lindbergh baby to contact Curtis and ask him to serve as a go-between to arrange for the return of the baby and payment of a ransom.

"Why me?" Curtis asked. "Why not someone in New Jersey?"

Sam explained that the kidnapers feared a hi-jack by another New York mob and Curtis was known as a reliable man. The Norfolk shipbuilder shook his head.

"I couldn't reach Colonel Lindbergh. He's too busy."

"Please think it over," Sam said, and left the car.

The next day—March 11—Curtis talked the matter over with the Right Reverend Harold Dobson-Peacock, dean of the Christ Episcopal Church in Norfolk, who agreed to try to reach Colonel Lindbergh.

Oddly enough, three days later Jafsie Condon told Assistant District Attorney Breslin of the Bronx, after his first meeting with "John" in Woodlawn Cemetery on March 12, that "John" had said, "The baby is *not in Norfolk.*" (italics mine) He also said Colonel Lindbergh "should not pay attention to the other gang (meaning Curtis) as they were not the right parties."

The conversation between Condon and Breslin was on March 14. While Curtis had been approached by the man he knew as Sam on March 10, it was not until March 19 that Lindbergh accepted Curtis. The Norfolk newspapers had hinted earlier, apparently on a leak from Dean Dobson-Peacock, that "three prominent citizens" of Norfolk were dealing with the Lindbergh case, but this was a week before Curtis actually entered the case.

How did Condon's mysterious "John" know, a week in advance, that Curtis would enter the case? How did Condon know this *five days* in advance, when he talked with Breslin about his meeting with "John?"

Dean Dobson-Peacock had tried since the morning of March 11 to reach Lindbergh. They called in Admiral Guy H. Burrage, who had escorted Lindbergh back from Paris after his flight in 1927. He wrote Lindbergh and finally got an answer to his letter on March 19. Lindbergh agreed to meet Curtis and his two friends on March 22. When Curtis, Dobson-Peacock, and Burrage arrived in Hopewell on March 22, Lindbergh said he thought Curtis was being deceived (apparently because he believed Condon was dealing with the gang that stole his son) but did not want to overlook any chance of making a further contact with the kidnapers. Curtis suggested that Lindbergh put $25,0000 in a bank as "earnest money." Lindbergh demurred at this; instead he suggested they ask the kidnap gang to give Curtis a photograph of the baby taken since the night of his abduction and a few words signed with a "certain

71

symbol.''

Curtis said he had already told Sam that *no ransom would be paid* until the baby had been actually returned to Lindbergh. Sam reported to Curtis that the gang had agreed to this proviso.

At one point Curtis brought an alleged member of the kidnap gang, along with a list of the baby's physical characteristics to the Lindbergh house. Lindbergh's attention at this point was wholly engaged with Condon's activities in the Bronx and he showed little interest in Curtis and his supposed connection with the kidnapers. Neither Lindbergh or his representatives met with Curtis, who left without having the description read; the alleged kidnaper having gotten frightened and left while they were waiting.

The story that three prominent citizens of Norfolk were involved in the search for the Lindbergh baby was, in the words of Sidney Whipple, "leaked" to the newspapers. He added in *The Lindbergh Crime,* with what amounted to an unmistakeable bias and prejudgment, "Curtis and his two credulous assistants. . .unable to keep such a glorious secret," had "talked" and on the following day a Norfolk newspaper "announced to the wide world that a baby was being held on a boat in Chesapeake Bay and three distinguished citizens were negotiating for its return."

Aside from rather sloppy newspaper reporting, Whipple's story of the leak indicated a general sentiment against Curtis that began in the days that followed the discovery of the body on Mount Rose Heights. It is also to be noted that in spite of the intensive coverage of the events following the finding of the body, not a single story at the time carried the information, readily available from Dr. Mitchell's examination of the corpse and from Dr. Van Ingen, that the body taken from the grave was four-and-a-third inches longer than the Lindbergh baby, and had possibly been embalmed. Hicks revealed this four years later.

Had this been disclosed at the time, Curtis' story might have been more carefully investigated.

On April 7, Lindbergh released to newspapers and radio networks the fact that he had paid $50,000 ransom to the kidnapers, and the baby was not returned. Lindbergh then turned toward the Norfolk group in virtual desperation. Apparently they had something to report.

On April 18, Curtis called the Lindbergh house at Hopewell and said he would arrive later that day. He had established himself in the Prince George Hotel, on 28th Street in New York. He had also obtained the aid of Edward Bruce, a friend and business acquaintance from Elmira, New York, who drove him to Hopewell.

He announced to Lindbergh that he had contacted several members of the kidnap gang. He met Sam in Newark, and a man called "Dynamite," whose real name was Olaf Larsen. A third man called John was with them. John spread some bills on the table and Curtis thought they had serial numbers which corresponded to the list of bank notes given by Condon to "John" in St. Raymond's Cemetery, which had been given to banks.

They had set a rendezvous at Cape May, on the southern tip of New Jersey; Curtis suggested Lindbergh take a room in Cape May and call him at the Prince George Hotel. The next day Lindbergh, Bruce, and a Navy pilot, Lieutenant George L. Richard, drove to Cape May and called Curtis at the Prince George Hotel. Curtis said he had heard from the kidnap gang and would go to Cape May, where a Gloucester fishing boat, the *Mary B. Moss,* was anchored.

The following day Curtis reported back to the group at the rooming house; he had been on the *Mary B. Moss* and had seen the gang, augmented by a blonde named Hilda, the wife of Dynamite, and another woman, Inez. They had told him how the kidnaping took place. A servant in the Lindbergh home met John in Newark and they had planned the abduction. John and Hilda, with two other members of the gang, Nils and Eric, had driven to the Lindbegh estate in a green Hudson sedan on March 1. In another car Sam and Nils were posted as lookouts. The servant in the house signaled "all clear" and John and Eric, after parking the green Hudson sedan, had placed the ladder against the wall, leading to the southeast window of the nursery. They climbed the ladder, used chloroform to keep the baby quiet, and walked down the steps and out the front door.

Certain parts of this story, it will be noted, are similar to the tale Gaston Means had told Mrs. McLean: the connivance of a servant in the house; the departure with the baby unnoticed by anyone in the household except the servant. There were certain variances. The ladder was used in Means' story only for the purpose of looking into the room to see that the baby was there; in Curtis' account it was used to enter the nursery. The ransom note left in the nursery supposedly was written by Hilda. The ladder had broken when they were looking into the nursery, or entering it.

Curtis had been told by Dynamite that they would rendezvous near Block Island, east of Long Island Sound, in the *Mary B. Moss;* he suggested they rent a small craft and head for Block Island.

At daybreak on the 21st they reached the area, but there was no sign of the *Mary B. Moss*. They returned and decided to go to Norfolk and board the *Marcon*, a fast yacht put at Curtis' dispoasl by a fellow yachtsman, Colonel Consolvo.

The rest of the Norfolk story was well-known at the time, and to those who have followed the Lindbergh case: a series of failures to contact the Gloucester fishing boat that lasted from April 23 until May 12, 1932. Curtis once reported that he was in contact with the kidnapers through Hilda. On the first day on the *Marcon,* he went ashore in Norfolk after they returned and phoned Hilda. She was at Freeport on Long Island and had a message: "Has the yacht a double exhaust? Heard your exhaust. Had company. Be patient. Will break through."

The weather was a constant factor; it had been stormy from the beginning of the search. Curtis had another yachtsman-friend in Atlantic City who offered them the use of his yacht, the *Cachalot*. On May 6 the group—Curtis, Lindbergh, Bruce, and Richard, the Navy flier—shifted to the second yacht. Curtis had obtained a new rendezvous point off Five Fathom Banks.

Inez told Curtis in Cape May, on May 10, the crew was becoming surly, and they had suggested handing over the baby without waiting for the ransom money. He reported this to the others, and the following morning—May 11—the *Cachalot* headed for Five Fathom Banks, flashing recognition signals. They found no trace of the Gloucester fishing boat, and returned to Cape May. Bruce and Richard went into New York, and here they heard the news over the radio: the Lindbergh baby had been found in the grave near Hopewell. They returned and met Lindbergh; he reported another day of failure. It was evident he had not heard the news. Bruce finally summoned enough nerve to say, "Colonel, your son has been found."

"Found?" Lindbergh stared at the two.

"Dead," Bruce said.

Lindbergh left immediately for Hopewell. Colonel Breckinridge arrived the next morning, with Dr. Phillip Van Ingen. Schwarzkopf had asked Curtis and Condon to come to Hopewell. He had one thing on his mind: find out what happened and above all clear the New Jersey state police of any accusation of bungling, in the newspapers or elsewhere!

Schwarzkopf's questions betrayed this primary interest. He talked first to Condon; he mentioned that Morris Rosner, the selected go-between man, had told Lindbergh on March 12 that he had definite knowledge the baby was alive and well. A similar report had been given by Curtis more than a week later. Was this a hoax? Had Condon been deceived by "John?" Why had he chosen the Bronx *Home News* to publish his first letter to the kidnapers? And why had they responded immediately?

The question Schwarzkopf did *not* ask was why "John" should have met Condon in the cemetery the first time, and also the second time, with the father a few yards away, if *he already knew* the baby was dead?

Gaston Means had pointed to that factor a year later; why was it overlooked by the State Police unless it was to cover up any question that related to the identity of the body found on Mount Rose Heights?

Captain John Lamb, of the state police, and Frank Wilson, special agent of the Internal Revenue Service, questioned Curtis. The next day they asked him to accompany them to Cape May and show them the place where he had talked with Inez on May 10. The visit to Cape May turned up no new evidence and they returned to Hopewell. Curtis had not even located the cottage where he met Inez; they were all alike!

Two developments seemed to have transpired: First, the police had a theory which in many ways was about as tenuous as the one the prosecution later adopted for the Hauptmann trial, except that it was a kidnap gang, not a lone kidnaper, who accomplished the abduction. The baby had been chloroformed, as Curtis' report from the gang said; he was carried alive from the house. He may have been dropped or hit his head on the wall, but more than likely was still alive when they left the house. As the kidnapers reached their car and started along the road, passing the place where William Allen would find the body more than two months later, they saw the lights suddenly go on in the darkened Lindbergh house. This must mean that the kidnaping of the baby had been discovered; every road in the area would be closed. So the kidnapers did what comes naturally to people in that business: they killed the baby!

What the theory did not explain was the realization that only someone lacking in "common sense" as Gaston Means said, would have carried on negotiations for ransom knowing that the dead body was left in a hastily dug grave, trampled over by the police and others, a telephone wire strung within seventy-five feet of the place, and that the body must have been discovered by this time—unless the body was not in the grave!

The second development for Curtis was more personal than the first. Condon was being treated with deference and respect, even though he had parted with the $50,000 ransom money, while Curtis was being treated like a dog. Lindbergh even wrote a letter to Condon, at Colonel Breckinridge's suggestion:

> My dear Dr. Condon:
>   Mrs. Lindbergh and I want to thank you for the great assistance you have been to us. We fully realize that you have devoted the major portion of your time and energy to bring about the return of our son. We wish to express to you our sincere appreciation for your courage and cooperation.
>
> Sincerely,
> Charles A. Lindbergh.

There was no such encomium for John Hughes Curtis; and at this point one wonders why. Condon led Lindbergh on a wild goose-chase in the Bronx. He had made statements, retracted them, changed them. On one occasion, in a conference between Schwarzkopf, Inspector Harry Walsh of the New Jersey State Police, a Mr. Nathan of the Department of Justice, and others, Nathan said to Walsh, "Are you convinced that Condon is on the level?"

"No," Walsh replied.

This was on May 18, 1932, less than a week after the body was found on Mount Rose Heights. Walsh later said, according to the records of that conference, that "discrepancies" in statements by Condon were being investigated. One of the statements made by Schwarzkopf at that conference referred to Condon's report of the meeting with "John" in St. Raymond Cemetery, where he handed over the $50,000 ransom money. "John" said to Condor, according to the latter's version: "Your work has been perfect in this arrangement." He also said, Condon reported, "I will have to talk to my partners." Condon said "John" went off to *two men standing in the background* some distance off. Schwarzkopf heard this. Why did he not report it?

The record of this meeting was not made a part of the case against Hauptmann at Flemington for the reason that it was then the State's theory that Hauptmann acted alone. But Schwarzkopf was present at this meeting. Why didn't he mention it? It was not disclosed until after Hauptmann's conviction, when Governor Hoffman included it in his report.

Meanwhile, Curtis was being given the silent treatment at Hopewell. The only tangible criticism of the Norfolk shipbuilder at that time was that he might have failed in the effort to contact the kidnap gang. Yet he wandered around the Lindbergh house alone; no one seemed interested in him. About midnight, Inspector Walsh came into the room assigned to Curtis, and they talked. Walsh finally suggested they take a walk. He finally said, "If you haven't told the truth, it would be a good time to do it now."

Curtis stared at him.

"But I have told the truth!" Walsh did not reply.

Finally Curtis said, "The only thing I said that wasn't true was about seeing the ransom money."

"Why did you make up that part?"

"I wanted to convince Colonel Lindbergh that I had talked with the kidnapers."

"That's what convinced him," Walsh said. "Why don't you go in and tell the Colonel? It will get it off your mind."

Curtis finally agreed; he returned to the house and in a few minutes Lindbergh joined them. Curtis explained that he had lied about seeing the ransom money and checked the serial numbers. He said he wanted to convince the Colonel of the need for immediate action. The Colonel listened to the man from Norfolk; then, without a word, he got up and left the room.

Walsh sent for another State Police officer,

Lieutenant Arthur Keaton, and asked Curtis to repeat what he had said. Curtis said it was true he had not seen the ransom bills; otherwise, he said, his story was the truth.

They talked for about two hours. Walsh finally arose and yawned. "I'm going to bed," he said. As he started to leave, Curtis suddenly said, "Get me a typewriter. I'll make a statement and sign it."

It should be recalled that Curtis had not wanted to get involved in the Lindbergh case. On March 15, when Lindbergh did not reply to Dean Dobson-Peacock's urgings, he was ready to drop the whole matter. He did not expect to receive anything for his efforts, although newspapers later noted that his business, the Gas Engine and Boat Company, had declared bankruptcy, with liabilities of over $35,000. He had suffered a nervous breakdown.

The question must arise: Was his statement a complete confession, as the news stories said; or was he on the brink of another nervous breakdown and made his statement because he was now sure he had been the victim of a hoax? Did he want to confess or simply get away from the blunder he seemed to have made?

He sat down and began to type:

Statement of John Hughes Curtis, 702 Redgate Avenue, Norfolk, Va. Made by my own hand and free will. Referring to the two statements made previously by me in regards to the Lindbergh (sic) Case. At the present time I am sane, but I honestly believe that for the last seven or eight months I have not been myself, due to financial troubles.

I was apparently brought back to my senses by my telephone conversation with my wife this afternoon when she told me of the troubles she was having and how the children missed me, also by my conversation with Inspector Harry W. Walsh.

I desire to state that my remarks about the newspapers are true and can be verified, this in reference to my story about Mr. Haskell and Mr. Wilcox of the *Herald-Tribune,* Mr. Lee of the *News* and Mr. Turin and Fox offering me money of my knowledge of the Lindbergh case or pictures of the baby.

The matter was brought to my attention during a conversation and due to what I now believe was a distorted mind by brooding over it, I became insane on the subject for the time being, which caused me to create the story in its entirety which was untrue in every respect.

I never knew such people that I named to Colonel Lindbergh and they were creatures of a distorted mind, with the exception of Morrie Truesdale, who had no connection with the crime. I exceedingly regret that I caused Colonel Lindbergh and others any inconvenience and wish it were in my power to correct my wrong. In justice to my wife and two children I trust that it is in the power of Colonel Linbergh to forgive the inconvenience and worry I did him in his time of grief.

This statement has been brought about by the realization of the wrong I have done.

He signed his full name. The two officers signed their names, and Walsh wrote down the time: 4:35 a.m., May 17, 1932.

The newspapers accepted the confession eagerly, their accounts dripping with both scorn and sympathy for the shell-shocked Norfolk shipbuilder. The only question they didn't ask was, Why did he do it? Why did he borrow boats from two friends, and spend days zigzagging over the ocean from Block Island to Five Fathom Banks, and nights contacting the kidnapers—just for a hoax, with no prospect of gain?

Richard Lee of the New York *News* and Grafton Wilcox of the *Herald-Tribune* partially confirmed the deal Curtis said he had made with them; but their understanding was that Curtis *would not be paid until the baby was returned* to the Lindberghs, which in itself removed any suspicion that he hoped to make money out of a hoax.

The charge finally brought against Curtis was "for the purpose of hindering the apprehension of the person or persons guilty of the said crimes (kidnaping the Lindbergh baby) did knowingly and willfully give false and untrue reports of the person or persons guilty of the commission of the crimes aforesaid." This raised some legal tangles; Curtis would have had to know who the kidnapers were in order to obstruct justice. On June 27, 1932, Curtis was brought to trial in the Flemington courthouse where Hauptmann was later tried and convicted. He was found guilty—which, in a sense, proved he had contacted the kidnapers—and fined $1,000 and a year in jail, but Judge Adam Q. Robbins, in order to extricate the state from its legal problems, agreed to suspend the jail sentence.

Mrs. Evalyn Walsh McLean may have given the most definitive answer to the various questions involving Curtis. In her story, "I Am Still Investigating," which she wrote with Alan Hynd in 1938, she refers to a "remarkable affidavit" made by Curtis in 1935.

"As I have said," she wrote, "there are many who believe the whole John Hughes Curtis story was a hoax. I am one of those who believe John Hughes Curtis was actually in contact with the kidnapers."

Before meeting Curtis at her home, she called Admiral Burrage, Lindbergh's friend. He said, "Mrs. McLean, I have absolute faith and confidence in John Hughes Curtis. I was with him when he first went to Hopewell, and I have been back of him all along the line, whenever I could help."

Curtis had visited Mrs. McLean at Friendship House when he first heard of Gaston Means' involvement in the case. "I was impressed by the story he told me," she wrote. "The story John Hughes Curtis told me is one that, if he ever cares to publish it, will startle the world. . ."

In his affidavit, which concerned certain evidence he was prepared to give at the trial of Bruno Hauptmann, he described his meetings with members of the kidnap gang. In the last paragraph he says: "I have, from pictures in the press and newsreels, satisfied myself that Bruno Richard Hauptmann and the man whom I knew as John. . .*are the same person.*" (italics mine)

This, of course, raises some interesting points. It is

quite evident that Curtis' *second affidavit* is completely contrary to the statement he made at Hopewell, in which he said his story of meetings with the kidnapers was "in its entirety. . .untrue in every respect." His affidavit in 1935 disavows this, and details his actual meetings with members of the kidnap gang, including John.

Whether the "John" of Condon's story of meetings in the Bronx cemeteries is the same as the John that Curtis says he met as a member of the gang, is not at all clear, and possibly could never become clear as long as Curtis' story that he lied about the meetings was accepted as fact.

Curtis was never called to testify at the Flemington trial of Hauptmann, because—as Mrs. McLean points out—his testimony would not have "fitted" with what became the New Jersey prosecution's theory of the case of the lone kidnaper.

Mrs. McLean made another clarifying remark: "According to the Norfolk man (Curtis) and other pretty sound testimony, Hauptmann was involved in the crime. Other things pointed to the possibility that he was innocent. But the further I got into this hideous mess, the clearer it became to me *that Hauptmann had not acted alone.*"

What might have been of overriding importance, particularly for John Hughes Curtis, is that if the body found on Mount Rose Heights was *not* the Lindbergh baby, there is a completely new dimension to the case—and one that might have been discerned in Curtis' story if it had been investigated properly at the time.

There is a definite possibility that if the Lindbergh baby was not the body found on Mount Rose Heights, he may be alive today. Bruno Hauptmann, who died in the electric chair, may have been one member of a gang that bungled the kidnaping, however no evidence was ever produced beyond that presented in the Flemington trial, that Hauptmann had any connection with the kidnaping or extortion plot.

The Curious Case of Violet Sharpe

One of the most baffling mysteries in the Lindbergh case—a mystery that was finally dropped from the police agenda in its investigations, since it fitted no theory and appeared to have no solution—was the strange suicide of Violet Sharpe.

Violet Sharpe was a maid at the Morrow home in Englewood. She was born in England, twenty-eight years old, and had been in the Morrow household for two years, having come down from Toronto, Canada. She was pretty, although a bit plump, vivacious, and at times sharp-tongued. Her sister, Emily, also worked in the Morrow family as a maid in the children's home in Englewood operated by Anne Lindbergh's sister, Elizabeth Morrow.

The New Jersey State Police, questioning all members of the Morrow household, turned their investigative eyes on Miss Sharpe on March 10, 1932. She was taken from Englewood to the Lindbergh home in the Sourlands. While she was questioned, a crew of detectives was prying into her room at the Morrow home in the hope of turning up some bits of evidence: her friends, habits, interests. It was known that she was interested in Septimus Banks, the middle-aged butler at the Morrow home, who had been with the Morrows for many years and in Sid Whipple's words, a "gentleman's gentleman."

It developed from questioning Violet that shortly

before eleven o'clock in the morning of March 1, 1932, she knew the Lindberghs planned to stay in Hopewell a few days, because of the baby's illness, instead of coming to Englewood as they usually did during the week. This was important information to the police. It indicated that information about the changed plans might have been passed on by Violet. Anne Lindbergh had telephoned for Betty Gow, and Violet took the call.

At this point Violet's answers became vague, and even confusing. She said she had a date that night, but not with Septimus Banks. A friend asked her to go to the movies, calling on the telephone just before eight o'clock. He arrived shortly after eight, with a young couple in his car—a green sedan! She didn't remember their names. In fact, she didn't even recall the name of her date. Later she said it was Ernie. She had met him two days before when she was walking home with her sister, Emily. He had waved from his car; she thought it was someone she knew and waved back. The young man drove up beside them and insisted he drive the two sisters to the Morrow home.

During the questioning, which was conducted by Inspector Harry Walsh, she was asked if Ernie or his two friends said anything about the Lindberghs.

She said, "Yes. They asked, 'How is Lindy's baby?'"

"What did you say?"

"I said he was cute."

Walsh seemed to be on the track of something, but apparently was not certain what it was. He decided on a new tack. Why did Emily, Violet's sister, apply for a passport to return to England on the day of the kidnaping? As it later developed, she sailed for England on April 6, shortly after Condon had paid the $50,000 ransom money to the supposed kidnap gang. Walsh's question was more or less rhetorical; she did not know.

Walsh continued questioning Violet Sharpe during the months of April and May. She appeared evasive about certain questions; some she told Walsh tartly were "too personal." At other times she was cooperative. But in two months he made very little headway. Then, on May 11, she went into Englewood Hospital to have her tonsils and adenoids removed. She was in the hospital when the body was found on Mount Rose Heights. It was evident to the Morrow household, when she returned to the Morrow home, that her usually good spirits had changed to a moody, almost withdrawn attitude.

Inspector Walsh sent word that she must be ready for further questioning on May 23. Schwarzkopf and Lindbergh were both at the Morrow house and sat in on the questioning. Walsh asked her to repeat the story of her meeting with Ernie and his two friends on the night of March 1. She had first said they went to the movies at an Englewood theater; later she admitted they had gone to a roadhouse, the Peanut Grill, in Orangeburg, across the New Jersey line in New York State.

Walsh asked why she had changed her story. She said she was nervous the first time; later she remembered more clearly. Walsh then asked her what time Ernie called that night. By this time Violet's nervousness was apparent.

"How often do I have to answer that?" she asked, sharply. "It was a quarter to eight!"

Walsh then asked if it was not true that Ernie had called her at eleven o'clock in the morning, just after she had heard from Mrs. Lindbergh that the baby had a cold and the Lindberghs would be in Hopewell for a few more days?

This was a question she need not have answered. How did Inspector Walsh know who called her? But she folded her hands in her lap, hesitated a bit, then nodded.

The New Jersey police who had checked on Violet's room when she was first being questioned by Walsh had found, among other things, several cards of a cab service, the Post Road Taxi Company, in White Plains, New York. Armed with this information, Walsh returned to the Morrow home for further questioning of Violet Sharpe. He had asked Laura Hughes, Mrs. Morrow's secretary, to take notes. Then he produced a picture, obviously from a rogue's gallery.

"Is that Ernie?"

She stared at the picture, and finally said, "Yes. That's Ernie."

Walsh knew that it was a picture of Ernest Brinkert. Detectives had checked on the Post Road Taxi Company, now out of business, and found that Brinkert had managed the company. He also had been picked up for petty thievery and assault. Why hadn't Violet mentioned his full name? At this point Violet broke into sobs, and soon became hysterical. Laura Hughes called the Morrow family doctor; he felt her pulse and told Walsh she should not be questioned further that day.

This was June 9, 1932. The following day Walsh planned to return to the Morrow home accompanied by several detectives. Walsh had called the house in advance, and Violet was told of this. She turned to Septimus Banks.

"He wants to question me again! I won't! I won't do it!"

Various accounts differ on exactly what happened. Whipple's story and George Waller's *Kidnap* agree in general. The newspapers of the time contained wildly differing accounts. A concensus seems to be that when Arthur Springer, former aide to the late Senator Dwight Morrow and now working for Mrs. Morrow, told Violet that Inspector Walsh was returning to question her again, she went past Septimus Banks into the pantry, took a bottle labelled "Poison" containing crystals of cyanide, and went to her room. She took a measuring glass from her bathroom, poured the crystals into it and then added some water. She drank the mixture and started downstairs, staggering first, then falling.

Septimus Banks reached her side, carried her to her room, and when the doctor arrived, she was dead.

There were many theories advanced as to why Violet Sharpe killed herself. Walsh and his superior, Colonel Schwarzkopf, took what might be described as a policeman's view. Schwarzkopf said in a statement to the press: "The suicide of Violet Sharpe strongly tends to confirm the suspicion of investigating authorities concerning her guilty knowledge of the crime against Charles Lindbergh, Jr."

These were words Schwarzkopf might have to swallow. Under the state's later theory, Hauptmann, and Hauptmann alone, committed the kidnaping and murder. However, at the time the head of the New Jersey state police was busy trying to prove that Inspector Walsh had not hounded Violet Sharpe until she killed herself.

The New Jersey police sent out an All Points Bulletin for Ernie Brinkert. They even called in Dr. Condon to look at the picture and tell them if it was "John."

"It looks something like the man who got the money, but the picture is too light. I can't be sure."

Detective Roy Turner, of White Plains, called on Thomas Fay who ran an answering service, with Brinkert as a client. While he was talking to Fay, the phone rang and it was Brinkert. He said he had telephoned because he heard the police wanted to talk to him, and he would come to Fay's home. The police found him there, sitting in his green sedan—in this case, a Nash. He told police he knew nothing about the Lindbergh kidnaping except what he read in the papers. He had been at the home of a friend with his wife on March 1; he had never met Violet Sharpe. Condon was brought in from the Bronx, and after examining Brinkert closely, shook his head. He wasn't "John."

It seemed to Schwarzkopf that with Ernie Brinkert safely in hand, the case could be wrapped up. But he was wrong. Ernie Brinkert waived extradition; he would go to New Jersey and answer any questions the police asked. Schwarzkopf and Walsh continued to pump questions at Brinkert, and he continued to answer them. About six o'clock Saturday night, as they were about to call it a day, the police brought in a man named Ernest Miller. He lived in Closter, New Jersey, a few miles north of Englewood; it was he who met Violet Sharpe on March 1. He described picking up Violet and Emily, telephoning for a date, and had two friends—Elmer Johnson and Katherine Minners—to prove it. They were the other couple described by Violet. Police found Miss Minners and she confirmed what Ernest Miller said.

When Walsh tried to explain matters to the newspaper reporters, they accused him of furnishing a fresh example of the inefficiency of the New Jersey state police. When he demanded, somewhat rhetorically, to know why Violet had identified the picture of Ernie Brinkert as the man who picked her up and dated her, one of the reporters suggested that if Walsh didn't know, nobody did. Presumably they had badgered Miss Sharpe until she was ready to say anything!

News stories from England, where Violet's sister, Emily, now lived, were even more violent and caustic in their reports. The New Jersey police had added the suicide of a helpless English girl to their record of failure to find out who killed Lindbergh's baby son! The London *Daily Telegraph* invoked the honor of the American people. The Manchester *Guardian* said the New Jersey authorities should "stand condemned in the eyes of all decent persons in the United States."

Schwarzkopf and Walsh may have reached a solution to Violet Sharpe's date on the night of March 1, 1932; but they were unable to explain her suicide when she learned that the Lindbergh baby was supposedly dead. It did not seem, as Walsh had at first theorized, that she was afraid Septimus Banks would hear of her pecadillo that night. This could hardly have provoked her to kill herself.

About two years later, when I was doing a series of stories with Joe Dunninger, on the peripheral aspects of the Lindbergh case, following the trial of Bruno Hauptmann, I ran across a strange series of coincidences that might have shed some light on the case of Violet Sharpe.

We had called on Mary Cerrita and her husband, Peter Birritella, to confirm her story told on March 6, 1932, to Schwarzkopf and Breckinridge. Birritella had banged his fist on a table and said, "It will come out! We will be on top. In two years it will all come out! There are more than Hauptmann in this case."

"How many?"

Birritella held up four fingers. "Not more than this— and one of them is dead."

"Was it Isidor Fisch?" He had died in Germany.

"No, no, no," Mary Ceritta suddenly said. "Fisch had nothing to do with it. She was a woman."

Dunninger suddenly asked:

"Was it Violet Sharpe?"

Mary Cerrita shrugged her shoulders. "If a person is not guilty they will not commit suicide."

Dunning asked Mary if she was subject to hypnosis. It was Birritella who replied.

"I can put her out—like that!" He snapped his fingers.

"How do you know these things you tell about, Mary?" Dunninger asked.

She struck her forehead. "I do not know. I go into a trance, and I say things. Later Peter tells me what I have said."

Later Dunninger told me Mary Cerrita could be made to repeat ideas while in a state of trance, under hypnosis.

"The woman is absolutely sincere! She believes herself to be possessed with psychic powers. The question is, where does she get these ideas? She did not know who I was, and her psychic powers did not tell her you were a newspaperman. Her powers reacted to one line of thought—the Lindbergh case. I have investigated thousands of cases of mediums, and have not found a single one capable of knowing things beyond what can be told them, or they can find out. I do not know who gave her the information, but I am certain it was not spirits.''

This interview with Mary Cerrita and Peter Birritella occurred on December 30, 1934. Less than two weeks later, Joe Dunninger telephoned me that he had learned of some strange coincidences in the case. Peter Birritella was a practicing spiritualist, pastor of a church on East 127th Street, directly across from a rooming house where several friends of Hauptmann had lived—among them, Isidor Fisch, the supposed holder of the Lindbergh ransom money later found in Hauptmann's garage.

Dunninger and I went to see a Professor Victor who seemed to be *au courant* with spiritualistic goings-on in Harlem. We asked him if he knew the Reverend Peter J. Birritella, pastor of a spiritualist church on East 127th Street. He said he did. Did he happen to know any outsiders who frequently attended the church services? He did. Among them he mentioned a maid and a butler from New Jersey. On further inquiry we learned that the maid was Violet Sharpe and a butler from the Morrow home. Both were occasional members of Peter Birritella's little flock.

At the time, Dunninger and I assumed the butler was Septimus Banks, but later I learned that Violet Sharpe's companion on these visits to Birritella's church was the staid old man of the Morrow household, Oliver Whateley—who was living at the Lindbergh's Hopewell estate the night of the kidnaping.

By one of those strange coincidences, or freaks of chance, that seemed to be characteristic of the Lindbergh case, I learned many years later of an incident partly confirming this connection between Violet Sharpe and Whateley. Anthony Scaduto described an incident—which he frankly admitted he could not verify —in *Scapegoat,* a defense of Bruno Richard Hauptmann. Among some documentation he received on the Lindbergh case was a statement sworn to by Gustave Mancke and his wife, Sophie, who operated a lunch room in New Rochelle, a suburb of New York. Scaduto wrote: "During an eight-week period in January and February, 1932, and up to the Sunday before the kidnaping, Isidor Fisch ate at their lunchroom on several occasions. Each time, Fisch was accompanied by Violet Sharpe, and by Oliver Whateley, Lindbergh's butler."

Gustave Mancke said more specifically in his statement:

> During these eight weeks and I believe on Sundays, at about 9 p.m. or later, a man and woman whom I identify positively from photographs as Ollie Whateley and Violet Sharpe came to my place four or five times to eat. On three of four occasions they were accompanied by a short, thin, dark man who looked like Eddie Cantor. He coughed badly and I slapped him on the back saying, "You resemble Eddie Cantor." His friend said, "No, his name is Isidor Fisch." This man who coughed always spoke to me in German. I positively identify this man as Isidor Fisch. The man whom I identify as Whateley. . .limped slightly and had blond hair thinning at the temples. . .
>
> The man Fisch never came to my place alone. He was there with Violet Sharpe and Whateley three or four times. None of these people above ever came back to my ice-cream parlor after March 1, 1932.

Scaduto adds, "I cannot characterize the Mancke's statement as absolute proof that Fisch was in contact with the two servants, for I have no corroboration." By an odd chance, Dunninger and I seem to have provided the corroboration.

Across from Peter Birritella's church, in a rooming house operated by a Mr. and Mrs. Wahl, there lived Karl and Gerta Henkel, Hans Kloeppenburg and Henry Uhlig, a roommate of Isidor Fisch—all of whom were witnesses in the Hauptmann trial! Kloeppenburg had moved to an apartment in the Bronx, where I found him with Karl Henkel. I asked them if any of Hauptmann's friends, living across the street from Peter Birritella's church, were members of the spiritualist cult. Henkel replied, "Isidor Fisch was."

Was Violet Sharpe, the maid from the Morrow home, and the butler, Oliver Whateley, ever at the church? He thought they were members; they often came to the church.

By another curious coincidence, a gold certificate listed among the Lindbergh ransom bills, had been turned in at a service station at the corner of Lexington Avenue and 127th Street, a half block from the rooming house where Isidor Fisch lived, and where Hauptmann frequently called. Since this led to Bruno Hauptmann's arrest this incident will be dealt with in greater detail later in this review.

Two others who assumed considerable prominence in the investigation of the Lindbergh case were also linked as possible members or frequent visitors to the Birritella church: J. J. Falkner, who had signed a deposit slip for $2,980 in bills listed as part of the Lindbergh ransom money; and Dr. John F. Condon. Dunninger and I questioned one of Condon's friends in a separate phase of our investigation, and he said the Bronx school-teacher was "quite interested in spiritualism" and had attended seances at Birritella's church.

Thus there were at least four people identified in other phases of the Lindbergh investigation—Isidor Fisch, Jafsie Condon, J. J. Faulkner—also known as Falconi—and Violet Sharpe, who at various times had visited the little spiritualist church where Mary Cerrita acted as a medium. She had been interviewed by Schwarzkopf and Breckinridge less than a week after the kidnaping and had predicted three things that could have been known only to the kidnapers, or planned by them.

All of these coincidences can be called purely circumstantial. None of the strange happenings prove the existence of a conspiracy to kidnap the Lindbergh baby. But for that matter, the entire case against Bruno Hauptmann—as will become quite evident in this review—was circumstantial. In an article written for the *Forum,* a legal journal, a distinguished New York lawyer, Richard A. Knight, said:

> Hauptmann was tried and found guilty, allegedly on circumstantial evidence, not of kidnaping or extortion, but of murder. . . .In the record compiled at the trial there is no more evidence that the man was guilty of murder than there is that you are I am. . . .No reasonable man can believe that an adult and a baby can fall off a ladder into the mud without making an impression in the mud. No reasonable man can believe that the baby, in falling, can have its skull crushed in three places by the wall of a house or the rungs of a ladder without its brains or blood staining either the wall or ladder, or the sleeping suit in which it is clad. In the alternative, no reasonable person can believe that a baby can be done to death in its cradle with a chisel without either the bedclothes or chisel retaining any evidence of the deed. . . . A child's murder can set no legal precedent; but a judicial lynching can.

This quotation introduces the second phase of this review: the character of the investigation and the statements of various people that for two and a half years occupied New Jersey authorities until Bruno Hauptmann was suddenly thrust on the scene and the case took the form of a one-man kidnaping and murder.

Before closing the review of events surrounding the kidnaping, it might be well to add a few comments made to Joe Dunninger and me by Karl Henkel. This, of course, was after the trial of Hauptmann had ended and he had been sentenced to die in the electric chair.

First, there was Henkel's remarks about several of Hauptmann's friends, including Isidor Fisch and Carl Arnold, a mysterious cobbler who did not live in the rooming house with the others but was a frequent visitor.

Henkel said Arnold wrote later from Germany: "I would not believe we had been in such company, and still cannot believe it."

About Isidor Fisch, who had, according to Hauptmann, given him the marked bills to hold, "Fisch was a strange sort of fellow. He lived in the house where I lived. He attended the church (Birritella's spiritualist church across the street) and said it was interesting."

Asked if Hauptmann was a member of Birritella's church, he said, "No, he was not. He was not interested in such things." Henkel then added something the cobbler, Arnold, had written from Germany: "Richard (Hauptmann) had something on his conscience that, if it is ever revealed, it will just be too bad for him."

Henkel said he had taken a motor trip with Hauptmann through Yellowstone Park and later told police that Hauptmann had told him something "so sensational that thereafter I shunned his company." He did not say what this was, nor do the New York police records of the case reveal what Henkel said.

As a final fillip, Dunninger and I asked the Rev. Mr. Birritella if he knew Fisch. He said he did.

"Did Fisch have anything to do with the kidnaping?"

"No, he was not in the case—I am sure of that."

"How do you know?" Dunninger asked.

"The spirits tell me."

One point became apparent to Joe Dunninger and myself, if not to the police or the New Jersey prosecution, led by David Wilentz. The kidnaping of Charles August Lindbergh, Jr., whether or not he was killed, did not necessarily rule out extortion as a separate matter. The coterie of amateur spiritualists using information possibly passed on by Violet Sharpe might have been involved in an extortion scheme without necessarily being the kidnapers.

This theory, to be discussed in the closing chapter of this review, might explain why Violet Sharpe, battered into a state of nervous hysteria by Inspector Walsh's questioning, might have been aware of what she told others and taken her life rather than face further questioning.

The theory that the extortion of ransom money from Lindbergh may have been the work of a separate gang was only casually mentioned during the investigation, and was dropped as soon as David Wilentz introduced his lone kidnaper theory.

Part Two

THE INVESTIGATION

8

The Hard Evidence

To gain perspective on the Lindbergh case, it is necessary to return to Hopewell on that fateful morning of March 2, 1932, when the world first heard that Lindbergh's son had been kidnaped.

Harry Morton Robinson, in his book, *Science Versus Crime,* gives us a panoramic view of that day:

> To summon up a ghastly remembrance of police tipstavery, bend your glance backward to the opening chapter of the Lindbergh case. Do you remember— could any one ever forget—the foaming and senseless cataract of gorgeously uniformed state troopers that descended on the Lindbergh home in motorcycles, roared up and down the road, trampling every available clue into the March mud, systematically covering with impenetrable layers of stupidity every fingerprint, footprint, dust traces on the estate? Hauptmann has been convicted and doubtless deserves the punishment that will be meted out to him, yet there are many impartial and legally trained minds which dispute the value of the evidence that placed him in the Lindbergh nursery on the night of the kidnaping.
>
> What wouldn't Prosecutor Wilentz have given for a lone conclusive fingerprint on the crib, windowsill or ladder? How effectively he could have introduced a moulage reproduction of that footprint underneath the nursery window? . . .

Governor Hoffman used this quote to explain his statement to Colonel Schwarzkopf that the Lindbergh investigation represented "the most bungled case in police history."

One wonders why some of the "impartial and legally trained minds" at the time of the Lindbergh investigation did not raise their voices against the execution of a man whom the State of New Jersey could not place in the Lindbergh nursery when the crime was committed!

A recapitulation of all the various elements of the hard evidence is not necessary for this review. But a brief account of the more salient facts is needed. The ladder found seventy-five feet from the nursery and efforts to tie that ladder to Bruno Hauptmann, the total absence of Hauptmann's fingerprints—or any known prints—in the nursery or on the ladder, the conflicting opinions of handwriting experts as to whether the writing was or was not Hauptmann's. These facts need to be reviewed carefully.

The ladder was the first of the hard evidence of the crime. It was a crudely built ladder made in three sections, first observed the night of the kidnaping by Chief of Police Harry Wolfe of Hopewell, and his assistant, Constable Charles E. Williamson. They had found two holes in the red-clay mud below the nursery window where Lindbergh had found the note; and several feet away they found two parts of the ladder, held together by a wooden dowel pin. Accounts differ as to how many feet away they lay, since both sections had been picked up and moved, but most agree that it was either sixty or seventy-five feet. Ten feet beyond lay the third section.

George Waller, in *Kidnap*, described the construction as "crude but ingenious." Whipple says it was "built with the skill of a craftsman." However, he caps this description with the statement that it was not strong enough to bear a man's own weight "combined with the weight of a sleeping child."

Corporal Joe Wolf of the New Jersey state police, who was the first of that arm of law enforcement to

Betty Gow, the nurse in the Hopewell house the night of the kidnaping, who helped identify the child's remains.

Isidor Fisch, "friend and business partner" of Bruno Hauptmann. Hauptmann claimed Fisch gave him the bundles of bills extorted from Lindbergh.

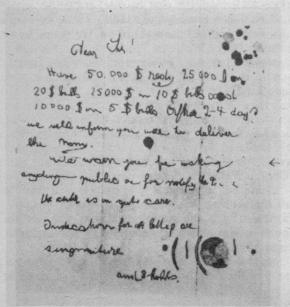

The Lindbergh ransom note. Note the peculiar symbol or signature in the lower right corner.

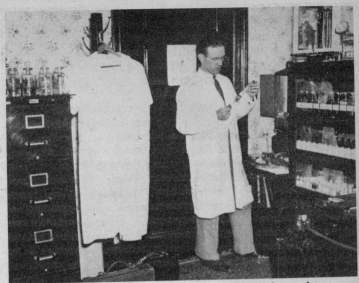

New Jersey state investigator Robert W. Hicks in his laboratory.

The remains from which identification was made.

arrive, wrote the original police report, in which he says: "Apparently *two members* (italics mine) of the party (of kidnapers) proceeded to the east side of the Lindbergh residence and assembled a three-piece homemade extension ladder." He determined this from seeing "two sets of fresh footprints leading off in a southeast direction."

The east side included the library on the ground floor, where Lindbergh was sitting and reading, the nursery above it, and Nurse Betty Gow's room on the northeast corner of the same floor. The house was well lighted. This was an anomaly in itself for the kidnapers to embark on an abduction party as carefully planned as the prosecution insisted in the Hauptmann trial with Lindbergh himself having the window against which the ladder was being raised well within his range of vision!

Wolf's report continues: "Three sections of the ladder were lying about seventy-five feet from the house, parallel with the footprints." He adds: "Obviously the crime had been carefully planned and the layout of the Lindbergh home carefully studied. . . . The kidnapers arrived in a car which was left parked some distance from the house, either in Lindbergh's private lane or a rough road known as Featherbed Lane. . . ."

This is almost exactly the report Curtis gave of the story of the kidnaping told him by the gang he supposedly contacted.

Later in the report Wolf says: "I detailed several troopers so that the footprints would not be destroyed."

The report of Corporal Wolfe, the first state trooper to reach the scene, was not made public until Governor Hoffman demanded and got it *after* the Hauptmann trial. In his testimony at the trial he was asked, "How many footprints did you see?" He replied, "I saw one." This was a large footprint near the place where the ladder had been placed against the wall, and indicated that a stocking apparently had been pulled over the shoe. He later mentioned another smaller print, identified as Mrs. Lindbergh's, made that afternoon when she stepped off the walk to wave to her baby who was held against the nursery room window by Betty Gow.

According to the official state police theory, the kidnaper had set the ladder against the wall, climbed up in full view of Colonel Lindbergh, stepped through the window, taken the baby from the crib (either alive, as at first insisted, or dead—having been strangled or beaten to death with a chisel in his crib, as Prosecutor David Wilentz described it in his closing address to the jury) and descended the ladder, which broke under the impact of the extra weight, without making a sound that could be heard on the floor below except for a noise Lindbergh thought was due to the wind.

The combination of many reports from officers who began investigating the crime that night was confusing. Wolf said "a strong wind was blowing." Major Schoeffel, asked by newsmen why the envelope with the ransom note did not blow across the room, said, "It was not very windy at the time." Constable Williamson, in his report, said "two sections (of the ladder) were lying together and one section eight or ten feet away." Detective De Gaetano said the ladder was in three sections, "all three separate and lying parallel."

Detective Bornmann picked up the ladder, dowel pin, and chisel and carried them into the house, so nobody knew where or how they lay!

Why or how the kidnaper, working alone, could have carried the baby, alive or dead, down the ladder holding the chisel, picked up all three sections of the "crude but ingenious" ladder, carried them seventy-five feet from the house and left them, together or apart, alongside the mysteriously vanishing footprints, is something the police never attempted to explain, and something that was left entirely out of the story told the jury in the trial at Flemington.

It is interesting to note Hauptmann's opinion of the ladder, since he was accused of making it.

"Would I, a carpenter, make for a crime like that a ladder that would not bear my own weight without breaking?"

During the trial he had replied to Chief Defense Counsel Reilly's question, "Did you build the ladder?" with a simple statement, "I am a carpenter."

After Hauptmann was arrested, and became by a sudden change of theory a lone kidnaper, the ladder assumed considerable importance, particularly in connection with "Rail 16," a portion of the ladder investigators said had been pried from the floor of the attic above the Hauptmann apartment in the Bronx, and used to bolster the homemade ladder. The wood had been identified by Arthur Koehler, a wood expert, as part of a piece of lumber, the other end of which was in the attic floor.

For two years prior to the arrest of Hauptmann, New York and New Jersey police had been working on the theory that the ladder itself was a key element in the case. Schwarzkopf had been prevailed upon by Major Robert Y. Stewart, head of the Department of Agriculture's forest service, to bring Koehler to Trenton and turn him loose on the ladder.

Koehler was given the ladder—which by this time had gone through the hands of the New York and New Jersey police—to begin his study, which Wilenz later declared he would use to "hang the ladder around Hauptmann's neck." After first viewing the ladder, Koehler said the man who made it "did not take pride in his work." In spite of the ingenuity which George Waller attributes to the carpenter in *Kidnap,* he also describes it as a slapdash job, a curious form of logic.

Koehler first dissected the ladder, taking it apart and assigning numbers to each piece. The bottom rung was "No. 1," the top "No. 11," and the rails in sequence, "Rail 16" being the top left-hand rail. It is hardly necessary to follow the involved process; the point that struck Koehler was that "Rail 16," the left-hand rail on the top section, had four nail holes in one end, which were "clean," that is, unmarked by rust, indicating the wood had been indoors rather than exposed to the elements in a lumber yard. The nail holes were also square. Distances between the holes were irregular; two holes were driven at an angle, and one was slanted sharply.

The marks on the wood also testified to the slapdash method of building. A handsaw had been used to cut the wood and had been carelessly used. Waller writes: "Looming up under a magnifying glass, they fell into patterns as unmistakable as a man's signature." This rather extravagant prose introduces a natural question: Whose signature?

This also brings up another question, which was never asked: If the examination of the various components was designed to identify the maker of the ladder, it was obviously intended to fix a pattern which might or might not apply to the man later arrested as the kidnaper of the baby. Was it the plan of New Jersey police to establish that pattern, and then fit the accused into it? Or were they simply depending on the lucky chance that the man who built the ladder—if he was the actual kidnaper—would fit into the pattern established by other evidence as well as Koehler's work with "Rail 16?"

A year had passed since Condon handed the $50,000 extortion money to "John" of the cemeteries, and the police were no nearer to finding "John." Possibly they were grasping at straws in a desperate effort to find someone who would fit the ladder pattern, as well as many other phases—such as the handwriting on various notes, fingerprints, and the gold certificates in the ransom money.

The attempt to build a case against a man who had not yet been apprehended was fraught with obvious difficulties—until the arrest of Bruno Hauptmann on September 18, 1934. Throughout the autumn and winter of 1933, Arthur Koehler had traced the wood for "Rail 16" through the Dorn lumber mill at McCormack, South Carolina, to Manville, New Jersey, and also to a Trenton box factory. The trail also led to Stamford, Connecticut and Springfield, Massachusetts, where the Dorn mills had shipped Southern Pine in carload lots. It finally led to New York and the National Lumber and Millwork Company in the Bronx.

What Koehler and detectives of the New Jersey police were seeking was a *pattern* of a man—a sloppy carpenter, with no feeling about wood. When they found "John" he would have to fit that pattern.

One begins to wonder at this point where the line of demarcation lies between honest zeal on the part of a prosecutor to convict a man accused of a crime, and the habit which seems to exist in many prosecutor's minds of seeking a conviction at all costs. If it becomes necessary to fabricate evidence, distort facts, omit pertinent testimony which might help the defendant—where does honesty lie?

Arthur Koehler's testimony, based on a carefully orchestrated effort to match grain against grain, wood against wood, could have been proved or knocked out by a simple statement from New Jersey Detective Lewis J. Bornmann, who was assigned to work with Koehler and had rented the apartment which the Hauptmanns formerly occupied. Did he or did he not take the "Rail 16" wood from the attic of Hauptmann's apartment? An affirmative answer would have negated all of Koehler's work; yet the question was never asked, either by Wilentz or the defense.

Bornmann had testified that he had searched Hauptmann's attic for days, and on the eighth day he found a pine board on the attic floor shorter than the rest. During the period after Hauptmann's arrest the place had been literally torn apart in the search for gold notes.

106

New Jersey and New York detectives had combed the apartment, attic and garage, and found nothing, except a few tools. Then came Bornmann. In his report, kept from prying eyes until Governor Hoffman asked for it, he says: "This date (September 26, 1934) detailed by Captain Lamb (John Lamb, who coordinated the detective work on the Hauptmann investigation) to continue search of the above-captioned home. . .we made a thorough search of the attic. Nothing of value was found." In a later report *the same day* he noted that a piece of wood flooring in the attic had been sawed off; this was the piece Koehler used so effectively in "hanging the ladder around Hauptmann's neck," as Wilentz described it.

The only possible explanation of the days of searching, the failure to find anything in the attic or anywhere else—and then Bornmann's sudden discovery of the missing floorboard and the fact that the attic wood matched "Rail 16" on the ladder—is that Bornmann or someone else pried that wood from the attic floor to make "Rail 16." Yet this obviously contrived evidence helped send Hauptmann to the electric chair!

Meanwhile other efforts were more or less in progress to find additional bits of hard evidence. One concerned the footprints found in the mud below the nursery window.

Corporal Joseph Wolf, it will be recalled, said the kidnap party consisted of "two or more persons." He had not only observed the marks of muddy feet on the suitcase beneath the nursery window, but tracked two sets of footprints along the path where the ladders lay. Detective Nuncio De Gaetano, in an official report, also dug up by Governor Hoffman, said: "We traced rubber boots or overshoes from the ladder down an old road to the chicken coop. The footprints went across the road and appeared to stop alongside the impression from an auto."

These are not random statements. They are official reports. It would have been possible for state police to make moulages of these footprints; and perhaps they did. But no mention of this was made at the trial. Wolf, asked how many footprints he had seen, said, "Only one!"

Fingerprints were found on the ladder before and after Hauptmann was arrested; but none of them matched Hauptmann's. The first kidnap note, left on the radiator, had been examined by Corporal Frank Kelly who also examined the shutters, crib, and other surfaces, and there were no fingerprints. Kelly made a similar examination of the chisel found in the mud outside the house; there were no fingerprints. Why were there no fingerprints *inside* the nursery? Were they rubbed off; and if so, by whom? The lone kidnaper, busy gathering up the child and chisel and escaping by way of a broken ladder, certainly had little time to clean up the woodwork. Did someone—possibly Betty Gow or Ollie Whateley—perform these chores for him?

As a matter of fact, there were latent fingerprints on the baby's toys and the crib. Governor Hoffman's investigator, Lieutenant Robert Hicks, is reported to have seen the baby's fingerprints during his researches just before Hauptmann was electrocuted. Years later Harold Olson, trying to prove whether or not he was Lindbergh's son, asked the FBI for the baby's fingerprints under the Freedom of Information Act, and found they were not available, but might be in the New Jersey police records.

These fingerprints could have conclusively proved, one way or the other, whether Olson and the Lindbergh baby were the same person. Olson went to Trenton, New Jersey, asked for the fingerprints and was told they were missing.

This was in 1977. Two years before, in 1975, Anthony Scaduto, author of *Scapegoat*, went to the New Jersey police headquarters in Trenton and asked for certain records of the Lindbergh case. He was taken to an old building and, as he later said in a letter to Hicks, dated August 14, 1978: "The most vital evidence I was able to find under restrictions placed on me was the child's fingerprints." These were in a shoebox, pushed back against the wall on one of the file cases, marked "Lindbergh fingerprints."

He found photographs of fingerprints, some of which he said were from a child's wooden block. Others seemed to have been taken from the crib, which Corporal Kelly had examined the morning after the kidnaping and reported "no fingerprints."

Dr. Erastus Mead Hudson, a fingerprint expert, offered in the early days of the investigation to consult with police on the fingerprint situation. He had developed a new method of raising fingerprints by using silver nitrate. He employed this process on the crib and high-chair of the baby and was able to raise several fingerprints of the child.

The search for Hauptmann's fingerprints was stimulated largely by Captain John Lamb, the coordinator of the New Jersey detectives. Hauptmann later told Governor Hoffman, who visited him in his cell at Hauptmann's request, that the police had taken prints from various parts of his hands many times—the sides, the palms, even the backs. Later they asked Dr. Hudson if it would be possible to counterfeit fingerprints. When he said he could easily tell the difference between real and counterfeit fingerprints, they stopped consulting him.

Dr. Hudson had examined the ladder and chisel found outside the house, and disagreed with Corporal Frank Kelly's report that he had dusted both and found no fingerprints. Dr. Hudson suggested he use his new method of applying silver nitrate to the surface; he was able to raise fingerprints on both the ladder and the chisel. Several were identified as those of the New Jersey policemen; others were not identifiable. After Hauptmann was arrested, his fingerprints were matched against those on the ladder and chisel. They did not correspond.

After Dr. Hudson's examination, Kelly and Sergeant Louis Kubler of the New Jersey Bureau of Identification sprayed both the ladder and the chisel with silver nitrate. They turned up 125 prints, and Dr. Hudson said his process would raise them for about six months, after which they would disappear. The police apparently took pictures of the raised prints, but when they failed to match Hauptmann's they presumably dropped that phase of the investigation.

George Waller, in *Kidnap*, cites this as a case of police bungling, but perhaps a stronger word could be used. Waller, unfortunately, was following police reports and the conventional view of the case. His account was taken largely from news stories and records and could hardly be called investigative reporting.

9

The Trail of Ransom Bills

For more than two years—from mid-April, 1932 to September, 1934—New York and New Jersey police traced one clue after another in pursuit of the elusive "John" of the cemeteries. The trail was marked by gold certificates listed as part of the Lindbergh ransom bills.

A little more than a week after Condon paid the $50,000 ransom to "John" the first of the bills appeared in Greenwich, Connecticut. The banks had furnished clients with a list of the bills. Mrs. Ella Decornille operated a pastry shop in that city, and on April 11, 1932, as she was closing her shop for the night, a car with a liveried chauffeur drove up. A well-dressed woman in a gray felt hat and tweed coat stepped out and entered the pastry shop. She asked for a loaf of bread and some strawberry pie. To pay for these, she presented a twenty-dollar gold certificate.

Mrs. Decornille glanced at the bill, and then at the list of Lindbergh bills as she sorted out the change. She stopped suddenly.

"Isn't this one of the Lindbergh ransom bills?"

The woman in gray grabbed the bill, left her purchases on the counter, and walked quickly out of the shop. The car drove away before Mrs. Decornille could get the license number. She called the police but there was little for them to act on.

During the last week in April, 1933, in the final rush to get rid of all gold certificates in accordance with

111

President Franklin D. Roosevelt's directive that all gold certificates of $100 denomination or more be turned in, there was a considerable movement at the banks. Fifty ten-dollar certificates had been deposited at the Chemical Bank in New York, all from the Lindbergh list. A few days later fifty more were turned in at Manufacturers Trust. The teller had not checked them against the Lindbergh list when they were deposited.

On May 1, 1933, the last day for exchanging gold certificates at banks, a deposit slip was made out at the Federal Reserve Bank in New York, which was signed with the name, "J. J. Faulkner." The teller did not notice that the bills were part of the Lindbergh ransom list, and did not look at the man who made the deposit. The deposit—$2,980—was later reviewed and all bills were checked. They were Lindbergh ransom bills; the police were called in.

The address on the deposit slip was 537 West 149th Street, New York.

Lieutenant James Finn, who had organized the New York police in the Lindbergh investigation, sent detectives to that address. There were no Faulkners living there, but several years before a Jane Faulkner had lived at the address. She was found to be living in Larchmont, a suburb of New York City, married to a Carl O. Geissler.

At this point, Messrs. Waller and Whipple, who wrote an account of this matter, should have been reading between the lines. As a matter of fact, they did not seem to be reading anything except police reports. Anthony Scaduto *did* ready between the lines, in researching *Scapegoat*, and came up with some interesting information.

Lieutenant Finn had issued a report on this phase of the investigation. Geissler, who had married Jane Faulkner in 1921, was found to have a sister who also lived in Larchmont with her husband, Albert Weigner; they had a daughter named Phylis.

Phylis had married a man named Henry Liepold, and Lieutenant Finn began to sense a clue. Liepold was found to have sent a cablegram to Willie Krippendorf in Munich, Germany. Finn found that Krippendorf had left for Germany shortly after the ransom money was paid by Condon on April 2, 1932. He was now returning to the United States, and the cablegram urged him to "take the cheapest steamer rate possible, even third class," apparently to avoid attention.

Finn had meanwhile asked Arthur Osborne, the handwriting expert hired by the New Jersey police, to compare writing found in Geissler's marriage certificate with J. J. Faulkner's signature on the deposit slip. The handwriting, according to Osborne, was similar. Finn's sense of smell became keener; things were getting hotter in search for "John" of the cemeteries.

When Krippendorf arrived in New York, Finn had detectives assigned to trail him. Immigration Bureau officials at Ellis Island produced records on Willie; he was thirty-five years old, weighed a hundred and fifty-five pounds, with gray eyes and blond hair. This almost fitted Jafsie Condon's description of "John."

The New York police began to trace Krippendorf's movements, suspecting he wsa probably connected with J. J. Faulkner. They found he had moved into the apartment of Leo Roden; both were associated with Ralph Hacker of Palisades Park, New Jersey—who was a son-in-law of Dr. John Francis Condon!

Oddly enough, this mish-mash of details seemed to mean nothing to the police, and even less to George Waller and Sid Whipple, who put together the police chronology of the Lindbergh case. Waller dismissed the line of contacts from Geissler to Liepold to Krippendorf to Hacker by noting that Geissler was merely identified as "a man who lived in Larchmont." Whipple was even more casual; he says, "Attempts to find J. J. Faulkner failed. . . .Investigation of this clue came to a dead end once the Geissler family proved they had no association

113

with the money." He described the use of the name and address of J. J. Faulkner as "pure coincidence."

Was it a coincidence that the address, which Waller said was "picked out of the air" and Whipple called "pure coincidence" led finally to Ralph Hacker, a son-in-law of Condon? Scaduto did a little more research; he learned that Hacker was involved in the ransom payment. He drew up plans for the wooden box which Condon used to pass the ransom money to "John," and when Condon decided to make a cast of "John's" footprint, it was Hacker who made it.

Police had begun to look into Krippendorf's and Geissler's activities, and this phase of the investigation was still on the agenda when Hauptmann was arrested September 18, 1934. After that it was dropped, presumably because the existence of additional members of the kidnap gang would not be consistent with the New Jersey prosecution's new theory, seeking to show that it was a one-man job.

Shortly after the conclusion of the Flemington trial I ran into something, in the course of Dunninger's and my unofficial investigation.

I had asked a member of the Federal Narcotics Squad, whom I knew, if he or any of his colleagues knew of J. J. Faulkner who had deposited several Lindbergh ransom notes in a New York bank. He suggested I go to an office in the Chrysler Building and meet a man who might give me some answers. I talked to the man, who said narcotics agents had traced a man named Falconi from New Orleans to New York. He said Falconi was the real name of J. J. Faulkner.

Falconi seemed to be engaged in a drug smuggling ring and worked out of Harlem, where there was a fairly sizeable community of Sicilians. He also said the drug smugglers in Harlem were interested in putting pressure on Colonel Lindbergh to stop reporting drug running operations along the New Jersey and New York coasts, which he apparently spotted during many flights he made in that area. I had the impression he was alluding to the kidnaping of the Lindbergh baby, although he told me he knew nothing about this.

There had been a report that a man named J. J. Faulkner had leaped to his death from a New York skyscraper, and I tried to tie the suicide to Falconi. The police had lost interest in J. J. Faulkner, however, and I got nowhere in my effort to pursue this lead.

The report of the suicide may have been incorrect, or —as the police reasoned—another J. J. Faulkner may have been involved. When Hauptmann was in the jail cell in Trenton awaiting execution, Governor Hoffman received a letter, signed J. J. Faulkner, advising him to take Condon's story "with a grain of salt." The handwriting was compared with the deposit slip and pronounced identical. Osborne had already compared the Faulkner signature with the writing of Carl Geissler and found them to be identical. Later, other experts said the writing in the Faulkner letter and deposit slips was not identical, adding very little to what was known about J. J. Faulkner.

This might have been a good time to ask Condon what he knew about Faulkner, or Falconi, but Condon had left with his daughter, Myra, on a vacation to Panama City. Thus the opportunity to trace the activities of Faulkner, Geissler, Liepold, and Willie Krippendorf to Ralph Hacker, Condon's son-in-law, and the possibility of tracking down the mysterious lookout in St. Raymond Cemetery—the man who wore a brown suit and walked with a stoop, who some thought was Isidor Fisch—was lost at a time when it might have done Hauptmann some good.

These questions unfortunately were not asked of Condon earlier and when Hauptmann was thrust into the picture as the lone kidnaper they were not relevant as far as the State of New Jersey was concerned. J. J. Faulkner and Carl Geissler, who had been foremost on Lieutenant Finn's mind for a period of almost a year, suddenly became myths.

During the year prior to Hauptmann's arrest, which occured on September 19, 1934, Colonel Schwarzkopf decided to organize a three-man team, consisting of Lieutenant Finn of New York, Captain Lamb of the New Jersey state police, and Justice Department Agent William Seery of Washington. Finn had drawn into this circle for a time a young New York psychiatrist, Dr. Dudley Schoenfeld. Schoenfeld's name is mentioned not because of any startling psychological developments he uncovered, but because the psychological profile he drew of the kidnaper—presumably "John" of the cemeteries—became a fixed picture, almost an obsession in the mind of Finn, and to some extent in the thoughts of Lamb and Seery, and the New Jersey police.

Schoenfeld's psychological portrait presented the kidnaper as a man influenced by strange psychic drives; he felt he was as good as Lindbergh and therefore wanted to surpass him—which took the form of kidnaping the son of the "Lone Eagle." The kidnaper believed he was omnipotent and Lindbergh stood in the way of that belief. Thus he was pictured as a hard, cold man who sought to demonstrate his superiority by showing that Lindbergh was not as strong as people supposed him to be. In his book, *A Psychiatric Study of the Lindbergh Case,* he wrote: "If the crime were governed by unconscious drives, these forces would be gratified only by the death of the child."

Schoenfeld's psychological portrait, as weird as it seems, became a fixed picture of the kidnaper. Apparently each time a suspect was investigated, he was accepted or dropped on the basis of this portrait—a thin-faced man, with high cheek bones and a pointed chin, who never seemed to wear an overcoat even in the most inclement weather, and who stared with scorn at each person to whom he passed a Lindbergh ransom note.

This conjured picture did not fit the well-dressed lady

in gray who tried to pass a twenty-dollar bill at Mrs. Decornille's pastry shop in Greenwich, Connecticut, so she was scratched from the list of suspects. Nor did it fit Oscar Geissler, a plump, dumpy little man who wrote like the mysterious J. J. Faulkner, so he was ultimately dropped from the list of suspects.

Finn thought so much of Schoenfeld's theory that he devised a map, stuck with green, red, and blue pins representing places where Lindbergh ransom bills had been passed. Oddly enough, they all seemed to revolve around the Bronx. Each time a ransom bill appeared, it was investigated to see if those who took the bills would recognize the man who passed them. Few remembered him, but those who did would be actively included in police files if they described a thin-faced man with a pointed chin, who spoke with a German accent, wore no overcoat, and looked with contempt on shopkeepers and others with whom he dealt.

However, during the latter part of 1933, the police had not given up on J. J. Faulkner and his write-alike, Oscar Geissler. They had tracked Willie Klippendorf to his association with Leo Roden and ultimately Condon's son-in-law. The fact that Klippendorf looked something like "John" of the cemeteries—about thirty-five, weighing a hundred and fifty pounds—intrigued their imagination. Unfortunately he did not have a pointed chin, and interest dwindled until suddenly an event occurred quite similar to the Violet Sharpe incident.

In October, 1933, Henry Liepold, the husband of Phylis Liepold—who had fled to Canada when she heard the police were after her—committed suicide. This drew an immediate comment from the police. Like Violet Sharpe, his death was an admission of guilt! It was not clear what they thought he was guilty of, but at this point nothing was clear to the police.

The trail of ransom bills at first seemed to be concentrated in the Bronx. On Saturday night, November 26,

1933, it switched to Greenwich Village. Mrs. Cecile M. Barr, the cashier at Loew's Sheridan Theater in the Village, was counting the money taken in that night when a bill, tightly folded, was tossed in front of her. She opened it; it was a five-dollar gold certificate. She glanced at the man; he wore a black hat pulled over his face, blue eyes stared at her from a thin face, somewhat triangular in form with high cheek bones, and he had a pointed chin. Mrs. Barr asked him what sort of seat he wanted; he looked at the price sign and said, "One forty." She gave him the change.

The next morning the theater's receipts for the night were deposited in the Corn Exchange Bank two blocks away. William Cody, the teller, glanced at the bill and checked the Lindbergh list; it was a ransom bill. That afternoon Lieutenant Finn came to her window and asked a few questions.

She described the man. He seemed to have a contemptuous look, and wore no overcoat. She noted that the bill had been carefully folded into eight parts—a point that was emphasized since other bills found to be on the Lindbergh ransom list, were also folded in that way, so they could fit into a pocket. She added one thing which Finn noted in his report, but did not mention at the trial: he was "apparently an American."

The manner of folding the bills—first lengthwise, then crosswise through the center, and finally lengthwise, making a compact bill—was noted on many of the bills. This way of folding bills was added to Schoenfeld's psychological portrait. He told Finn that when "John" was finally arrested, he would have a bit of ransom money tightly folded.

This evoked the curiosity of Scaduto, who had been researching the Lindbergh case some forty years after the Lindbergh baby was kidnaped. Was it Hauptmann's habit to fold bills tightly? He checked the records of Hauptmann's arrest and found that the bills he had with him were taken from his wallet, flat and uncreased. This, of course, did not prove he had not creased them before trying to pass them; yet it was an odd maneuver for a man trying to escape police attention.

One case of Lindbergh bill-passing presented even more peculiar circumstances. An East Side storekeeper was handed a ten-dollar gold certificate in March, 1933. This offered an interesting possibility to police, since it occurred *before December 6, 1933,* when Isidor Fisch, the man Hauptmann said left some of the Lindbergh money with him, left for Germany. The storekeeper said he would remember the man if he saw him. George Waller mentioned in his book that the East Side storekeeper would undoubtedly be called as a witness at the Flemington trial to identify Hauptmann. But the storekeeper was never called.

Scaduto draws a conclusion from this. If the man had seen Hauptmann and could identify him, why was he not called? Possibly because he had seen Hauptmann, and *did not* identify him as the man who passed the bill. Not only would this have been poor testimony for the prosecution; it would have defeated the claim that Hauptmann acted alone in the kidnaping!

Early in 1934—on February 14—a cashier at the Cross, Austir and Ireland Lumber yard, reported an incident which police seized upon avidly. The cashier, Alice Murphy, said two men had come into the yard carrying a large plywood panel which they selected from the company's lumber pile. One of the men—described as wiry, with flat cheeks and a pointed chin—wanted the plywood cut to a specific size, and asked the cost. She said it would be forty cents. Miss Murphy was handed a ten-dollar gold certificate, and since she had been warned about ten-dollar gold certificates, she called to the yard foreman, William Reilly; he came across the yard and the man who had given her the bill grabbed it back and gave her forty cents. The man said they would come back later to pick up the plywood, and the two left the yard. They did not return.

This tale was used at the Flemington trial to indicate that Hauptmann was one of the two men, trying to pass some of the ransom money, further proof of his guilt.

At this point one needs to pause and make a few observations. First, this was a period when many people who had hoarded gold certificates, refusing to turn them over to the government, were beginning to get rid of them. Since the certificates were illegal, having been called in by the President, it might seem natural to want to pass them off as regular currency.

Second, Hauptmann's behavior was as consistent with this theory as it was as a suspected kidnaper. It was even more consistent, because when he finally turned in a bill at a gas station, ultimately resulting in his arrest, in response to the service station manager's remark that "you don't see many of these any more," Hauptmann said, "No. I've only about a hundred left."

Was this the comment of a man who had extorted the money? Was Hauptmann likely to call attention to the gold certificates he still possessed—if he had kidnaped the Lindbergh child and then demanded extortion money?

Or were the police, and particularly Finn, so obsessed with the psychological profile of "John" of the cemeteries that they could not fairly analyze the situation? Were they upholders of the law, or policemen working off their frustrations of two years of fruitless investigation?

10

Problems of Jafsie Condon

For a period of about twenty-eight months—from May 12, 1932, when a body supposedly that of Charles A. Lindbergh, Jr. was found in a shallow grave on Mount Rose Heights, until the arrest of Bruno Hauptmann on September 19, 1934—Dr. John F. Condon lived a life alternating between a dubious belief in his sincerity and raw suspicion of his motives.

For a good part of that period he was the primary suspect on the police list. Although Colonel Lindbergh and his wife wrote a brief letter of thanks to the Bronx schoolteacher shortly after the discovery of the body, Lindbergh admitted he had many doubts about Condon.

Hugh Larimer, of the Department of Justice, in a report more than a year after the Lindbergh kidnaping, said, "Colonel Lindbergh made a remark that were Doctor Condon a younger man, he would be immediately suspicious of him, but in spite of his age there were several little things that raised doubt as to Condon's sincerity."

Larimer's report adds: "The Colonel was suspicious of Al Reich, who claimed he had observed John jump a fence and run" and Condon's own statement that he—a 72-year-old man—overtook "John" in the Woodlawn Cemetery. "Lindbergh was not impressed with the arrangement whereby Condon and Al Reich were to make contact and deliver the money," the result being that Lindbergh did not turn the money over to Condon until he could be present at the second meeting in St. Raymond's Cemetery.

Inspector Harry Walsh of the New Jersey police noted that "neither Violet Sharpe nor Condon, nor anyone else—except Curtis and Henry Johnson—were arrested and held pending an investigation."

Following the discovery of the dead body of a baby and the assumption that it was the Lindbergh child, Condon was asked to repeat his earlier descriptions of "John." These statements were made on May 14 and later on May 20, 1932. He said "John" was about thirty years of age, weighed a hundred and fifty pounds and had "almond shaped eyes, such as Japanese or Chinese have." Later he told Inspector Walsh of the man's "hacking cough" which gave him the "impression that pulmonary disease had started its inroads into this body." He also said "John" did not speak with a German accent; it was a Scandinavian accent.

Two years later, after Hauptmann was arrested, Condon was taken to a police lineup at the Greenwich Street Police Station in New York, with Hauptmann in the lineup. Condon completely failed to identify him.

In a report of that lineup, Inspector John Lyons asked Condon, "Would you say he (Hauptmann) is the man?" Condon replied, "I would not say he is the man." Lyons asked Condon if he were "positive" and he said, "No, I am not positive."

Agent Leon Turrou of the FBI later wrote a book, quoted by Anthony Scaduto, that he picked up Condon on his way to the Greenwich Street Station, and told him they had a suspect they wanted him to identify.

"Don't worry," Condon said, "if he's the fellow I met I'll know him. If I live a million years, I'll know him!" Then, Turrou says, Condon "tilted his head toward me and whispered, 'Now here, describe this suspect you've got.'"

Turrou said this surprised him. He said, "I'm sorry,

Doctor. The whole point of this is that you pick him out yourself.''

"Why? Just tell me why. That's a fool notion.''

On the way home, Turrou asked Condon why he had not identified Hauptmann. Condon said he was furious at the way the lineup was handled, "one German among a lot of bull-necked cops.''

"But have you seen him before, Doctor?''

"No. He is not the man. He looks like his brother.''

So much for Condon's earlier statements of identification. At the trial of Hauptmann he had no such reservations. When Attorney General Wilentz asked, "Who is John?'' Condon pointed unhesitatingly to the defendant, and said, "John is Bruno Richard Hauptmann.''

The reason for this diametrical change in Condon's story may never be revealed. Condon is dead and it was not revealed in his writings; if it had been, it would have taken the form of a confession. But perhaps the closest anyone can come is a statement Condon made to Bronx District Attorney Samuel Foley. Condon had been openly accused of being part of the extortion conspiracy. On several occasions he reported rough treatment by the New Jersey police. He had told of his fears of being indicted by a grand jury in New Jersey. In a statement, rather widely quoted by those who have written on the Lindbergh case, Condon said, "I would not like to be indicted in New Jersey by the grand jury. They would choke you for a cherry in New Jersey.''

Is it possible that his fear of Jersey justice may have been a contributing factor in his bewildering assortment of changed viewpoints and outright lies?

Later Turrou wrote in a report: "Dr. Condon impressed the agent that he had no desire, for some reason, to identify Hauptmann.''

Governor Hoffman wrote that several New Jersey troopers had told him Condon had been threatened with an indictment for obstructing justice if he did not identify Hauptmann as "John" of the cemeteries.

It is also possible that Condon was not only influenced by police threats, but with the possibility of what he knew being used against him. The fear of being exposed as an accomplice in the extortion plot.

With respect to the latter, there are several points that can be listed as bearing on Condon's role in the Lindbergh case:

First, Mary Cerrita's reference to Jafsie two days before Condon entered the Lindbergh case as a go-between. This was published in the New York *Daily News,* in a story written in 1933.

Second, the manner in which Condon inserted himself into the Lindbergh case, and the false or confused statement he made about his telephone call to the Lindbergh home the night he received a reply to his first letter in the Bronx *Home News*. He said he talked with Lindbergh, but it was actually Thayer he spoke to.

Third, his use of the *Home News,* a suburban newspaper with little circulation outside the Bronx, to send a letter the kidnapers. Why did he receive an immediate reply?

Fourth, his statement that the Mafia symbol was used to sign the kidnapers' first letter, when there was no signature on the letter to Condon. He was told to open an enclosed letter to Lindbergh *after* he mentioned the Mafia symbol.

Fifth, information from those who lived across the street from Peter Birritella's spirit church, indicating Condon often attended Sunday night seances and may have known Violet Sharpe, Ollie Whateley, as well as Isidor Fisch, and possibly J. J. Faulkner.

Sixth, Gaston Means reference to a Bronx schoolteacher as a possible contact man with the kidnapers *before* Condon's part in the Lindbergh case was disclosed by the press.

And possibly most significant, his remark—later reported by State Troopers to Governor

Hoffman—when he walked down the corridor after visiting Hauptmann in the Hunterdon County jail, "I will not testify against that man!"

Much of the above is circumstantial, based on reports that can no longer be verified; but much of it is fact, including queer changes in Condon's story, his failure to identify Hauptmann in the police lineup, and his emphatic identification later in the Flemington trial. His vacillations appear to be more than those of an erratic mind.

There seems little doubt that Condon was not blessed with what many describe as a steel-trap mind. Governor Hoffman notes in his articles in *Liberty* magazine, "What was Wrong with the Lindbergh Case," that Condon frequently contradicted himself. He told Assistant District Attorney Edward G. Breslin, of the Bronx, on March 14, 1932 that his reason for becoming involved in the Lindbergh case was "the derogatory talk" he heard about American law enforcement from people "with foreign accents"; later he said it was his "sympathy for the Lindberghs"; still later that he sent his letter to the kidnapers to the Bronx *Home News* because other papers "all pointed at one miserable fellow that I thought was innocent—Arthur Johnson." He had not met Red Johnson, whose real name was Henry, at that time; Johnson's name had not been mentioned in connection with the case—except the fact that he had a date with Betty Gow the night of the kidnaping.

He told Inspector Walsh he did not think about using the larger dailies because he was familiar with the *Home News;* in the articles he wrote in *Liberty* he said the Bronx was "an easy exit to Hopewell."

He was asked at the Flemington trial—where he admitted he did not even know Red Johnson—whether he knew that Johnson, a sea-going boyfriend of Nurse Gow, had phoned her at about eight-thirty the night of the kidnaping.

"I knew that on the night of the kidnaping!"

Later, in his customary lecturing tone, he said he had misinterpreted the question because of Defense Attorney Reilly's English. Did he? The question was in plain English, "Did you know that he (Red Johnson) had phoned Betty Gow at half past eight the night of the kidnaping?" He might have answered, in plain English, "Yes" or "No." Instead, he tried to explain his blunder. The question immediately arises: What was the reason for the blunder? Was it a simple mistake, or did he know about Red Johnson's call the night of the kidnaping?

This may not be an important point, but it raises the question of Condon's competence. Was he a blundering old fool, a psychopathic liar, or was he involved in the kidnaping in a way that was never disclosed? Or all three.

If either of the first two speculations is correct, Attorney General Wilentz, who was aware of most of Condon's eccentricities, should not have put him on the stand at Flemington. Instead, he made him the State's star witness. If the third point is true, and there is considerable reason to believe it is, what was Condon's part in the kidnaping or extortion plot, and can it ever be verified?

Probably not. But Governor Hoffman, whose investigation was made before Hauptmann was electrocuted, was able to produce several facts, based on reports that were not made public prior to the trial, that bear directly on Condon's complicity in either the kidnaping or the extortion plot.

Hoffman mentions Breslin's interview with Condon on May 14, 1932, in which Condon told him "John" had said the "people down south"—obviously referring to Curtis and his dealings with the other gang—had nothing to do with the actual kidnaping. This was five days before Curtis was brought into the kidnap case.

Anthony Scaduto, in *Scapegoat*, refers to Curtis as

126

"a swindler." There is no excuse for this term. Curtis did not confess to being a swindler, and there is nothing in the record that indicates he was a swindler. He stood to gain nothing if the Lindbergh child was not returned. If we were returned, Curtis would only receive payment for articles he had agreed to write for the New York *Herald-Tribune* and the New York *News*.

Had Scaduto paid more attention to Curtis, he might have evolved a theory of the Lindbergh case as well as proving that Hauptmann was not guilty of the kidnap-murder, with which he was charged. Curtis later repudiated his confession, which he made in a moment of frustration; and on evidence already established, there is reason to believe he was actually in touch with one of the extortionist groups.

It may be recalled that Curtis was convicted in a New Jersey court of having obstructed justice by interfering with efforts to contact the kidnapers. In order to obstruct justice, there must be someone to be obstructed. Curtis had to be in contact with a gang. He said in his second affidavit, offering to testify at the Hauptmann trial, that he identified a man named "John," one of the gang, as Bruno Richard Hauptmann. This, as Mrs. McLean said, would have been "excellent testimony" for the prosecution, but it would not have fitted into the theory that Hauptmann was the lone kidnaper, and for this reason it was rejected by the State.

Mrs. McLean talked with Curtis at Friendship House after he learned of her interest in the Lindbergh case. She was impressed by the story Curtis told her, and remarked that it would have been "a much more natural thing for the kidnapers to have picked out a man like him to act as intermediary than for them to have accepted an eccentric old character like Jafsie Condon."

Granting that Scaduto only built his story from newspaper clippings and his own research—some years after the Lindbergh case had ended to all intents and purposes with the execution of Hauptmann—Mrs. McLean's analysis of Curtis' character would seem more likely to be true than Scaduto's dismissal of Curtis as a swindler. This point is more than mere criticism of one researcher. It concerns a question central to the whole mystery of the Lindbergh case, and ultimately the possible answers to the question first posed: What really happened to the Lindbergh baby?

It will be recalled that on the back of one note to Condon from "John" after their meeting on March 2, 1932, in Woodlawn Cemetery, there was written: "Mr. Lindbergh is only wasting his time with his search." On March 14, 1932, Condon told Breslin, the Bronx assistant district attorney, that "John" also said, "The baby is not at Norfolk." This was *five days before* Curtis had contacted Lindbergh and more than a week before he entered the case. However, the remark of "John" in Woodlawn Cemetery was made *two days after* Sam had jumped on the running board of Curtis' car in Norfolk and told him he was selected by the kidnap gang to act as a go-between.

Was this an effort of one kidnap gang to select as many intermediaries as possible, in which case would this also have included Gaston Means? Or were *two gangs* involved, as first suggested by Gaston Means? Did Condon inject himself into the Lindbergh case as a conspirator, or simply to gain publicity for himself?

Condon's testimony at the trial, however, *did* fit the pattern of the prosecution, as long as he did not emphasize several comments that appeared in his previous statements describing his dealings with "John" of the cemeteries. He was quite careful in this respect, as can be judged from one specific series of incidents.

Condon and his ex-boxing friend, Al Reich, had observed a man coming down the street but he did not "pay attention or any account to him." This man had been described to police by Condon as a possible lookout when the gang theory was entertained by the New Jersey police. At the trial, when the one-man job theory was employed, Condon merely remarked that a man had passed the car and he paid no attention to him.

In the second meeting in St. Raymond's Cemetery, a man appeared again and was observed by Lindbergh, who testified at the Bronx grand jury to that effect. He was the "man with the handkerchief" who was also described by Lindbergh as a possible lookout; he dropped the handkerchief as Condon emerged from the cemetery, and Condon followed him! Lindbergh later told FBI Agent John Seykora the man "walked with a stoop."

Condon did not mention the man with the handkerchief at the Flemington trial—probably because it did not fit the State's theory of the lone kidnaper.

Lindbergh had listened to Condon's testimony at the trial, and he did not try to correct it—although he had told the Bronx grand jury about the man with the handkerchief. Was Lindbergh, as well as Condon, under instructions from the prosecution to say nothing that would not support the State's one-man theory? If so, his testimony is as suspect as Condon's.

Possibly the most penetrating comment, made on Condon's various statements, changes of viewpoint, and his final testimony at the trial, in which he levelled a finger at Hauptmann and said, "John is Bruno Richard Hauptmann!" was by Hauptmann himself. Sitting in his jail cell at Trenton, awaiting execution, he said, "Dr. Condon holds the key to my cell."

11

The Arrest of Hauptmann

During the early part of September, 1934, the search for
"John" seemed to heat up. There was a sudden rush of
reports from banks, indicating that whoever had the
Lindbergh gold certificates was beginning to pass them
more freely. The National Bank of Yorkville reported a
deposit from a Third Avenue grocery store that included
a Lindbergh bill. The storekeeper, Salvatore Levitano,
remembered he had argued with the customer who
wanted change for a ten-dollar bill for only a few cents
purchase. His description seemed to fit Dr. Schoenfeld's
"John" as well as Condon's. During that week a man
also fitting the description of "John" passed a dozen
gold certificates, all on the Lindbergh list.

On September 18, 1934, Finn hit paydirt. A teller at
the Corn Exchange Bank at 125th Street and Lexington
Avenue reported one of the Lindbergh bills had been
turned in by a service station manager.

Finn went to the bank and examined the bill, taking a
treasury agent and Corporal Horn of the New Jersey
police with him. He turned the bill over and there was a
notation, pencilled in the margin: "4U-13-41, N.Y."

It was the license number of a car; later it was found
to be issued to Bruno Richard Hauptmann, 1279 East
222nd Street, the Bronx.

Finn and his two men went to a gas station at 127th
Street and Lexington Avenue with the note. It may be
recalled that this station was located about a half-block
from the Reverend Peter Birritella's church and also

from the Wahl rooming house where Carl and Gerta Henkel, Hans Kloeppenberg, Henry Uhlig, and Isidor Fisch had lived. All but the latter were witnesses at the Flemington trial. Fisch died in Germany on March 29, 1934.

Finn spoke to the manager, Walter Lyle, and he remembered the customer who gave him the bill. He said he had made it a practice to jot down the license number of customers who gave him gold bills, due to police bulletins about the Lindbergh ransom list. Lyle said he had at first objected to the ten-dollar note, which by that time was illegal currency, and the man said, "They're all right. Anyone will take them."

Lyle remarked, "You don't see many of them anymore," and the man had said, as previously noted, "No—I have only about a hundred left."

This reported dialogue was carried by every newspaper in New York. It was known to the police. It should have aroused in Finn's mind the thought that people who are trying to pass off extortion money do not usually proclaim this by announcing that they have "only about a hundred left"—unless they are exceedingly stupid, and Attorney General Wilentz always referred to Hauptmann as "a clever man."

Perhaps Finn secretly wondered at this remark; perhaps he did not, obsessed as he seemed to be that he was on the trail of "John." George Waller might have picked up this strange statement; yet his only reference to it was the answer Hauptmann gave to Special Agent Seery's question: Why had Hauptmann told the gas station owner just a few days ago that he had "about a hundred (gold certificates) left." Was that true? Or was his denial to the police the truth?

"Well, no, it was not true," Waller quotes Hauptmann as admitting. "He did have about a hundred left."

This obviously was the point where Lieutenant Finn and Special Agent Seery should have pulled up short. Why would a man passing the well-advertised

Lindbergh ransom money have confessed to having a few hundred bills left, if he knew they were Lindbergh bills?

Whether Finn wondered at this, or thought that Hauptmann's later explanation was true: that he was afraid of being arrested for passing illegal currency, remains locked in Finn's mind. He appeared to have a fixed belief that he had at last caught up with the elusive "John" and may have simply assumed this was "John" of the cemeteries.

Waller, confining himself to police reports and trial records, merely reports that after Hauptmann admitted he had lied about the hundred bills when first questioned, he was taken home to produce them. He said, "They are up at my house. . .in a tin can."

Why is so much emphasis placed on Hauptmann's lying? A man picked up by a small army of policemen, bombarded with questions he may not have understood, probably fearing—as he said later—that his possession of illegal currency was the reason for police stopping him, might readily lie under the circumstances. It was at this point that the detectives who arrested him might have questioned their own initial judgment; but they did not.

Several questions were propounded to Hauptmann by detectives who swarmed around his home at 1279 East 222nd Street, in the Bronx. He had been arrested shortly after leaving his house in the morning of September 19. Three police cars converged on him. Special Agent Seery was in one, Special Agent Thomas Sisk in another, and Finn in the third. Hauptmann stood beside his car, handcuffed.

"Where did you get the gold certificates?" a detective asked. "Are there any more?" He waved a bill in front of the prisoner.

This was a question that should have confirmed in Hauptmann's mind that he was being arrested for possessing illegal currency. When Finn asked, "Why did you tell the attendant at the gas station you had only

The Lindberghs two years after the baby's kidnaping, greeting West Coast reporters.

Renowned psychic Edgar Cayce who was called in to help trace the missing baby.

Bruno Richard Hauptmann.

about a hundred left?'' this would have been even more proof of what the police were talking about: illegal currency.

Anthony Scaduto notes in *Scapegoat* that the first question made no mention of the Lindbergh case or the ransom money. He says, ''It became rather obvious that he believed the police and federal agents had arrested him as a gold hoarder.''

It should have been obvious to the police; but they had no interest in capturing a gold hoarder. They were interested in catching a wanted man, ''John'' of the cemeteries, the man who had taken $50,000 extortion money and did not deliver the baby because it was dead.

Perhaps it should have occurred to Waller as he checked over the police records; but judging from his book, it did not. He was sticking strictly to the reports and the New Jersey prosecution's theory that Hauptmann, and Hauptmann alone, kidnaped the baby. It did occur to Anthony Scaduto, of course; but he was interested in presenting Hauptmann's side of the case.

Again, the reader of today is faced with two conflicting stories, of which he knows little: the story largely accepted by the public, and certainly accepted by Sid Whipple and, in retrospect, by George Waller—that Hauptmann was the lone kidnaper; and the less widely known work of Scaduto, an investigative reporter whose principal aim was to prove that Hauptmann's trial and execution were a miscarriage of justice.

As the police drove Hauptmann back to his home, one of the detectives asked, ''Isn't it true that you extorted money from Charles Lindbergh? That you kidnaped the baby?''

This was the first word Hauptmann heard about the Lindbergh kidnaping. He seemed baffled.

''What are you saying? I know nothing about a baby.''

Sid Whipple's account, usually accepted as a description of all that happened in *The Lindbergh Crime*, included the dialogue at the gas station in which Hauptmann said he had "only a few left—about a hundred." As a writer, he might have speculated on the possible implications of that statement. As noted, an extortionist does not usually advertise the amount of extortion money he has left. But Whipple, like Waller, appeared interested only in the capture of the supposed kidnaper —not in anything that might tend to prove whether he was guilty or innocent. Whipple, of course, wrote his book from what happened when he was actively following the Lindbergh case; Waller's account was put together from existing records many years later. Both seemed to have assumed Hauptmann's guilt from the start. However, the two works represent what the American people—particularly those born during or after that period—believed about the case.

Whipple, writing serenely about this crucial period, was a bit wrong in his dates, and in the method of arresting Hauptmann. He begins on September 15, a Saturday, when Hauptmann drove into the gas station; then he recounts the way the police "leaped into action" by tailing Hauptmann through the Bronx, watching "every activity, following him into shops and cafes. . . allowing him only a little more rope." He wrote: "Then, on the morning of Tuesday, September 18th, they struck." It was actually September 19, and the "tailing" was a myth of Whipple's imagination, which may be a clue to the accuracy of some of his other deductions.

During the questioning of Hauptmann by detectives, he was asked where he was on the night of March 1, 1932? On April 2, 1932? This sort of questioning of a man who has just been arrested and handcuffed, and probably thought it was on a federal charge of passing illegal currency, borders on the ludicrous. Yet Hauptmann's replies, dug from his memory at the time, were written into the record and used at the Flemington trial.

Hauptmann was taken to the old Greenwich Police Station, a run-down building used for traffic violators and later as a women's detention jail. Meanwhile his apartment was ransacked by detectives, floors pulled

135

up, walls pried open, the garage floor dug up, as they searched willy-nilly for clues, particularly for ransom bills.

One of the places inspected was the attic. As noted earlier, Detective Lewis Bornmann of the New Jersey police had leased the apartment just after Anna Hauptmann decided to take their only child, Bubi, and move to a friend's home. Her husband was in jail, and was about to be turned over to New Jersey authorities to stand trial for the kidnap-murder of Charles A. Lindbergh, Jr. He had been moved on September 22 to the Bronx where he was grilled by detectives. This was the time I first saw Hauptmann, when I went to the Bronx courthouse to write my first story of the Lindbergh kidnap case.

After Bornmann moved into the apartment, it will be recalled, he searched the attic for several days without turning up anything. Then he noted that some of the wood flooring in the attic had been sawed off, and revealed the missing piece that ultimately became "Rail 16"—the bit of evidence which Wilentz said he would "hang around Hauptmann's neck."

Another point of considerable significance turned up when Hauptmann was asked where he was on the night of November 26, 1933. He shook his head; how could he remember?

Was he not at a Greenwich Village movie house on that date? It was a Sunday. He immediately replied that this was his birthday, and therefore he was at home at a party for him, given by his wife, Anna, and a few friends. "I do not remember ever going to Greenwich Village."

The detective suddenly held a tightly folded gold bill before him, creased lengthwise and crosswise and then lengthwise again—in the form the lady in the ticket booth, Mrs. Cecile M. Barr, had received it from a man with a black hat pulled down over his forehead, a thin, triangular face and a pointed chin.

"Do you recognize this bill?"

Hauptmann did not reply at first, probably because

136

he did not understand what they were driving at.

"Do you always fold your bills like this?"

No. He carried them in a wallet, unfolded.

Had the police been engaged in an investigation, instead of hunting for "John," they might have pursued this reply a bit further. Until the summer of 1934 many of the Lindbergh gold certificates turned up by banks had been folded in this manner; after that they were flat, as if carried in a wallet. The date Hauptmann said he found the gold certificates left by Fisch in the shoebox was in August, 1934. On each bill recovered by police *after that date* there were marks left by water, and they were not folded tightly. This would indicate that the man who gave the five-dollar gold bill to Mrs. Barr in the Greenwich Village theater might not have been the same person who passed bills later. In other words, he was *not* Hauptmann.

The New York and New Jersey police were not trying to determine the guilt or innocence of a suspected criminal, however. They were trying to find him and turn him over to the prosecution with enough evidence to convict him. As Lieutenant Finn succinctly explained in a remark made to Dr. Dudley Schoenfeld and quoted in the latter's book, "This is the parting of the ways. You're a doctor and you're interested in saving people. I'm a cop and I'm interested in hanging him."

While the detectives were questioning Hauptmann, their colleagues were prowling through the Hauptmann apartment, while Anna, who had not yet moved from their apartment, looked on. They had ripped up flooring, scattered furniture around, until the place looked as if a wrecking crew had passed through. Finally Detective James Petrosino, examining Hauptmann's garage workbench, saw a board which he tore loose. In a narrow compartment behind the board were two bundles wrapped in newspapers. Petrosino lifted the bundles from the compartment, and took off the wrapping of newspapers. A thick pack of bills—evidently gold certificates—fell out. He called the other detectives, and they counted the bills: they totalled

137

$13,760—all part of the Lindbergh ransom money!

It appeared the police had what they were looking for, although not by any means all of it. They checked the bills against the Lindbergh list, and with about $5,000 previously recovered from bank tellers it amounted to $18,860 of the total of $50,000 paid to the extortionist "John" in St. Raymond's Cemetery.

This was September 20, the day after Hauptmann was arrested. The bundles of bills were taken to the Greenwich Police Station, and Hauptmann was asked why he had lied about the gold bills he had. He shook his head; he hadn't lied. The bundles of bills were produced. Hauptmann still showed no signs of shock, possibly because he had already figured the police would find his cache of hidden money.

"This is Lindbergh ransom money," they told him.

He still shook his head. He knew nothing about any Lindbergh ransom; the money really was not his. It had been given to him by Isidor Fisch, his friend and business partner, who left the previous December for Germany.

One of the detectives remembered the name "Fisch." Several letters from him had been found in Hauptmann's apartment. He was asked to explain how Fisch fitted into the picture. Had he left the money with Hauptmann?

Bruno nodded. He explained Fisch's dealings with him in the fur trading business, since Fisch was a furrier; and he had also invested for Fisch in the stock market, in which Hauptmann had some success. They had made some money, and when Fisch went to Germany he gave Hauptmann a shoe box and told him to hold it for him. Hauptmann placed it on a shelf in a closet and forgot about it until a heavy rain, dripping down a vent-pipe, had soaked the box. He took it down from the shelf, figuring it contained letters and other papers; instead, it was filled with gold certificates.

Hauptmann said he knew Fisch owed him about $5,000 and he felt justified in taking some of the bills and cashing them in. He had been doing that for several

138

weeks, since he found the shoe box.

George Waller noted in *Kidnap* that it thus became important for the police to confront Hauptmann with the East Side storekeeper who had reported on March 1, 1934, that he had been tendered a ten-dollar gold certificate which was listed as Lindbergh ransom money. This was *before* Hauptmann said he found the shoe box stuffed with gold certificates, and was therefore important. There is no police record of the confrontation, although it must have occurred. Waller, as noted previously, later listed the storekeeper as one of the witnesses to be called to testify at the Flemington trial. But he was not called.

Police must have brought the storekeeper to identify Hauptmann; and since he was not called to testify at Flemington, the inference to be drawn was that he had not identified Hauptmann!

Waller did not mention the East Side storekeeper again in his book; yet he must have wondered at this omission. However, he had apprently committed himself—as had Whipple—to recording only what was in the police records and news accounts of the trial.

It would seem apparent at this point that Wilentz was indeed drawing the noose around Hauptmann's neck, but a loose fitting noose, which included possibly perjury in the testimony of several witnesses; highly controversial and in some cases faked evidence; shifts in the State's theory of the kidnapping, from a gang to a lone kidnaper!

And it included a stipulation on the part of Defense Counsel Reilly that the body found on Mount Rose Heights was the Lindbergh baby, when every bit of factual evidence—if Lindbergh's casual identification and Betty Cow's less-than-expert testimony about the baby's clothing is excepted—supported the theory that it was *not* Lindbergh's son whose body was found.

In this atmosphere of fact and fiction, of conflicting stories and confused circumstantial evidence, the trial was begun at Flemington courthouse, New Jersey, on Wednesday, January 2, 1935.

Part Three

THE
TRIAL

12

The Parade of Eyewitnesses

Samuel J. Foley, the Bronx district attorney, agreed with New Jersey State Attorney David Wilentz that no effort should be spared to move Bruno Hauptmann legally from New York to New Jersey. The reason was quite simple: In New York Hauptmann could only be tried for extortion; in New Jersey, where a crime of murder had supposedly occurred, he could be tried for both kidnaping and murder.

Public opinion, that mercurial element of justice, literally hungered for the murder trial. Most people wanted revenge for the dastardly crime committed against the nation's current hero. The logical target of revenge was Bruno Richard Hauptmann.

Foley went through the motions of preparing his case on the extortion charge, knowing the prisoner would soon be handed over to Jersey justice. He brought a parade of witnesses who, as George Waller naively noted, "testified to the *prisoner's* threatening demands in letters for fifty thousand dollars." Actually, no one had proved that the prisoner made these demands. It could as easily have been Isidor Fisch, Max Hassel, or perhaps J. J. Faulkner.

In preparing for the New Jersey trial, James Fawcett, Hauptmann's original chief defense counsel, had made a motion for a disclosure of evidence upon which the prosecution would rely. This is a legal nicety over which the prosecution and defense regularly wrangle. The judge decides what is relevant and what is not. In this case, Judge Thomas W. Trenchard, later trial judge, dismissed eleven of the twelve disclosures asked for by the defense, stating that they were already in the grand jury indictment; the twelfth—placement at the scene of the crime—was admitted as a necessary element of the case.

By the time the New Jersey trial began on January 2, 1935, Wilentz found it necessary to place the eyewitnesses on the stand to testify to Hauptmann's presence at the scene of the crime. Due to the largesse of the New York *Journal* Edward J. Reilly had by this time become chief defense counsel. The *Journal*, it will be remembered, had convicted Hauptmann in the press before he went to trial at Flemington, and was ready to pick up the tab to see that justice was done.

There were a number of people who told police they thought they saw a man who looked like Hauptmann in the area surrounding the Lindbergh home. Charles Rossiter, a salesman, swore he had seen him near the Princeton airfield the Saturday night prior to the kidnaping, which was on the following Tuesday. However, Rossiter turned out to be a man dismissed from jobs for supposedly stealing money, and was not a witness to be relied on.

Amandus Hochmuth, who was eighty-seven years old, had said he had seen Hauptmann in a car near the Lindbergh estate about noon the day of the kidnaping. According to Hochmuth there was a ladder in the back of the car, in three sections. Alan Hynd, in his research to help Mrs. McLean write her story, "I am Still Investigating," found that Hochmuth was almost totally blind, on welfare in New York where he gave two Bronx addresses to establish his residence, but lived in Hopewell.

Governor Hoffman called Hochmuth into his office in December, 1937—a year and a half after Hauptmann was executed—to find out who should collect the reward offered by the State for the conviction of the Lindbergh kidnaper. Hochmuth was told to sit in a chair and identify a silver cup filled with flowers. He first said it was a woman wearing a flowered hat. Apparently realizing he had made the wrong guess, he said it was a bowl of fruit.

When Hoffman began to question Hochmuth about his testimony at the trial, he seemed unable to remember which story he told at the trial. He first told police he saw Hauptmann in a car that slid into a ditch; later he said the car had almost gone into the ditch. Fearful that he would not share in the reward, he concocted a third story. "When the baby was killed, on March first, before that I saw a fellow hanging on the bridge—this is the first time I have mentioned this. We have a good many Germans coming into the neighborhood, and I said, 'Are you looking for a job?' I could see he was German and I spoke German to him and I said, 'I am from Hamburg,' and he said he was from Saxony. I said, 'What is your name?' and he said, 'Hauptmann.'"

This did not get Hochmuth much of the reward, yet the story he told on the witness stand at Flemington was one of the eyewitness accounts that sent Hauptmann to the electric chair.

The story told by another eyewitness, placing Hauptmann near the Lindbergh home, was even more spectacular. Millard Whited, a Sourland mountain man, lived about a mile from the Lindbergh estate. Corporal Wolf, one of the first State troopers sent out to check the neighborhood around the Lindbergh house the morning after the kidnaping, had interviewed Whited. In his report he said no one had any information about suspicious men in the area. Later Detective Horn told Governor Hoffman he distinctly remembered visiting Whited's home, and Whited did not mention seeing any suspicious person in that neighborhood prior to the kidnaping.

When Whited was called to testify at Flemington, he said he knew everyone in that neighborhood, and a couple of weeks before the baby was kidnaped he noticed a stranger. He saw him again a week later and identified him as Hauptmann, who was in the courtroom. Later he said he saw his picture in a newspaper the day after he was arrested and told the police.

At this point Whited's story becomes bizarre. The police immediately took him to the Bronx to confront Hauptmann. "It's the same man,' he said.

It is now necessary to go to the record. Governor Hoffman, in his investigation after Hauptmann's conviction, but before his execution, wrote:

> A former state police trooper told me where I might look in the state police files and find a statement taken from Millard Whited, to the effect that he had never seen any suspicious persons in the vicinity of the Lindbergh home before March 1, 1932. I found this statement taken by the state police themselves—on April 26, 1932—less than two months after the crime—setting forth the fact that this Sourland Mountain woodsman, of questioned reputation had then denied he had ever seen anyone who might have been identified with the crime.

Two years later Whited was taken to the Bronx where he specifically identified Hauptmann as a man he had seen near the Lindbergh estate. His testimony at the Hauptmann trial follows, under cross-examination by Lloyd Fisher.

> Mr. Fisher: How much money were you paid for testifying in the Bronx?
> Mr. Whited: None.
> Mr. Fisher: No expense money paid?
> Mr. Whited: Expense, yes.
> Mr. Fisher: How much expense money?
> Mr. Whited: I was took over there and my dinner.
> Mr. Fisher: Nothing for your day's work?
> Mr. Whited: No.

This was under oath. Governor Hoffman on February 22, 1936—six weeks before Hauptmann was executed—ordered Whited brought to his office at the

State House in Trenton, and with Assistant Prosecutor Anthony Hack of Hunterdon County, Lloyd Fisher, defense counsel, and a member of the New Jersey state troopers present, he questioned Whited, again under oath. Whited admitted he had been paid "about $150" and had "hollered" for $35 a day before he agreed to go to the Bronx. Fisher questioned him further.

Mr. Fisher: Now, Millard, in the trial you testified. You were asked if you got any money or not, and you said all you got was being taken to New York for dinner.

Mr. Whited: I know it.

Mr. Fisher: Did you lie about it?

Mr. Whited: I absolutely thought that was my business what I got out of it.

During the questioning, Whited was asked if he had been told by police he was entitled to part of the reward. He said, "Yes, about a third."

Whited's explanation of his change in testimony was that the New Jersey police asked him to keep secret the knowledge that he had seen a suspicious stranger—whom he later identified as Hauptmann at the trial—near the Lindbergh place two weeks before the baby was kidnaped.

There were other eyewitnesses but none who could definitely identify Hauptmann. The testimony of Amandus Hochmuth and Millard Whited placed Hauptmann at the scene of the crime.

The witnesses who swore they could recognize Hauptmann's voice as that of "John" of the cemeteries were equally impressive. They were primarily Condon and Lindbergh, although John Joseph Perrone, the cab driver who took the note to Condon, was also a key witness. Condon's odd switches in statements and testimony, in which he first said he would know "John" if he heard him, then refused to identify Hauptmann as "John" with a weird explanation, and finally testified that "John" was Bruno Richard Hauptmann, has been covered. But Lindbergh's testimony presents a problem, particularly to those who knew him as Slim Lindbergh, a daring aviator whose moral habits were not only incorruptible, but implacable.

It will be recalled that Lindbergh's testimony before the Bronx grand jury, made under oath, described "John" as having a "distinct foreign accent." When asked later, he said he could not say "positively."

"I remember the voice very clearly, but it would be difficult for me to sit here and say I could pick a man by that voice."

On the witness stand at Flemington he said, of the time at St. Raymond's Cemetery when he waited in the car for Condon's return, "I heard very clearly a voice coming from the cenetery, to the best of my belief calling Dr. Condon."

He was asked if he heard any words.

"In a foreign accent, 'Hey, Doctor!'"

He was asked how many times he heard the voice. He had testified before the Bronx grand jury that he first heard the voice say, "Ay, Doctor!" and later, "Hey, Doc!" At the Flemington trial he said, "I heard the voice once."

"Since then have you heard the same voice?"

"Yes, I have."

"Whose voice was it, Colonel, that you heard saying, 'Hey, Doctor?'"

Lindbergh looked directly at Hauptmann.

"That was Hauptmann's voice."

He had first heard the voice more than two years before; he testified shortly afterward that it would be "difficult" to pick a man by that voice. Yet two years later he picked out the man—whom he never saw in the cemetery—by that voice!

It is understandable why the public accepted Lindbergh's statement as positive identification. He was a national hero, and a bereaved father. Unless one studied all the records and transcripts in the case, there would be little doubt about it. Hauptmann was "John" of the cemeteries, and although nothing but circumstantial evidence linked him to the kidnaping and the murder of

Lindbergh's son, he was automatically regarded as guilty of both.

But what about Lindbergh? He was three hundred feet from "John" when the latter called, "Hey, Doctor!" He had not heard the voice before that night. He had not heard it for more than two years afterward. When Hauptmann appeared in the courtroom in Flemington, he testified without hesitating that the voice of "John" was the voice of Hauptmann.

And what about Wilentz and the other members of the prosecution staff? Wilentz had studied the record; he knew what Lindbergh said before the Bronx grand jury. Were the moral principles of the prosecution at such a low ebb that Wilentz would ask a question of Lindbergh that would force him to lie just to get a conviction? Possibly Wilentz himself can best explain the moral structure of his case against Hauptmann.

On December 5, 1972, when Harold Olson went to see Wilentz at his office in Perth Amboy, New Jersey, he and Wilentz discussed the question of identification—not of Hauptmann, but of the body found on Mount Rose Heights above Hopewell.

According to Olson Wilentz said, "The defense should have used the lack of true identification (of the body) in defense of Hauptmann, but the defense never did."

The reason, of course, was Edward Reilly's stipulation that the defense would not contest any claim that the body found on Mount Rose Heights was not the body of Lindbergh's son.

Wilentz knew the importance of this stipulation. He might have felt that if the defense chose this route, there was no reason why he should refuse it. But Judge Trenchard was not in the same position. He was in court presumably to see that the defendant's rights were protected. Permitting the chief defense counsel—who was in court because the New York *Journal* had agreed to pay his fee—to waive identification of the body was not conducive to protecting those rights.

It may not have occurred either to Wilentz or Judge Trenchard that this conbination of shaky evidence —Hochmuth and Whited placing Hauptmann at the scene of the crime, Condon and Lindbergh identifying him by his voice—might send Hauptmann to the electric chair for a crime he may not have committed. However, it is an obligation of a court as well as the prosecution to see that justice is done, and the peculiar distinction in American law permitting an adversary system to rule relations between prosecution and defense does not justify their action. The need for justice, regardless of whether or not a conviction is obtained, should have weighed something in the balance in the Lindbergh case, and it did not.

Many whose testimony would have had a significant bearing on the outcome of the case were not called to testify: John Hughes Curtis, whose affidavit said he could identify John, a member of the gang supposedly contacted by him, as Hauptmann, offered to testify and was refused; Dr. Philip Van Ingen, who examined the baby ten days before it was kidnaped and found it was twenty-nine inches in height whereas the body found on Mount Rose Heights was four-and-one-third inches taller, was not called to testify; the East Side storekeeper who remembered the man who gave him a ten-dollar Lindbergh ransom bill, was not called.

One may ask, why the defense did not call them. The answer probably was Reilly, the chief counsel, coupled with the ineptness of the entire defense staff, and even the lack of funds. Fisher failed to ask a Treasury agent, Frank Wilson, about the unexplained deposit of $2,980 in Lindbergh gold certificates by J. J. Faulkner when he was on the stand explaining how Hauptmann's cache of $14,600 was found.

One witness, John Joseph Perrone, who delivered the last note of the kidnapers to Condon, was asked to identify Hauptmann as the man who gave him the note. He stepped from the witness stand, touched Hauptmann on the shoulder, and said, "This is the man."

"You're a liar," Hauptmann said, in a voice not easily heard.

Reilly asked Judge Trenchard to put Hauptmann's reply in the record; Judge Trenchard refused.

During early phases of the investigation Perrone had given a description of the man who gave him the note that caused detectives to suspect it was Willie Krippendorf, who sailed for Germany a few days after the ransom was paid. Later he told police it was Henry Liepold, a friend of Condon's son-in-law, Ralph Hacker, who committed suicide. Still later he said he had been sitting in a police car and recognized a man who walked into Carl Geissler's Madison Avenue florist shop and gave him a ten-dollar gold certificate from the Lindbergh ransom list. Geissler had been suspected by Lieutenant Finn of being one of the kidnap gang, and his signature was found to be identical with that of J. J. Faulkner.

Perrone was not questioned at the trial about these incidents, which were matters of police record; instead, he was asked to identify Hauptmann in the courtroom. Again, why didn't the defense lawyers question him? Probably because they were not privy to the police record in the Lindbergh investigation, particularly those parts not consistent with the lone kidnaper theory, which were not released until Governor Hoffman asked for them. Nor was the public, who read avidly the accounts of the trial, aware of these records. But Wilentz was!

13

Hard and Soft Evidence

The hard evidence presented at the Flemington trial consisted chiefly on the ladder found seventy-five feet from the nursery window, and various footprints, one below the nursery windows, another inside the nursery, and others along the path where the ladder lay.

The soft evidence consisted of fingerprints and handwriting, all checked by avowed experts on the State's payroll, and contradicted by other experts testifying for the defense.

The fingerprints have been discussed; their primary importance seemed to be that none matching Hauptmann's was found—on the ladder, in the nursery, or even on ransom notes. But the fingerprints of a baby were found on toys and the crib after being raised by Dr. Hudson's silver nitrate process. They were kept in police files at Trenton until 1975, after which they mysteriously disappeared. They might have confirmed Harold Olson's claim that he was Lindbergh's son.

On January 22, 1936—the fifteenth day of the trial—Wilentz called Detective Lewis J. Bornmann to the witness stand. It will be recalled that Bornmann rented the apartment at 1279 East 222nd Street, the Bronx, formerly occupied by Hauptmann and his wife and child. The purpose was to investigate every nook and cranny and dig out whatever evidence was available. There was little available until Bornmann, by accident or design, found a board in the attic floor which ultimately was found to match "Rail 16" of the alleged kidnap ladder.

This was on September 26, a week after the arrest of Hauptmann. Bornmann said that after having searched the apartment for several days, he finally found a section where the floorboard had been cut away.

As a matter of plain logic, it did not make much sense for Hauptmann to have ripped out a section of his attic floor to find a board to use on the jerry-built ladder, when he could have gotten a similar piece of wood from a lumber yard. The attic floorboard would have constituted a calling card for the police to pick up, if he intended to use the ladder to kidnap the Lindbergh baby. At the time, however, the police had little to go on in linking Hauptmann to the crime, and rigging the ladder as evidence probably showed the most promise.

More information on the so-called kidnap ladder will be discussed in a later chapter, covering Governor Hoffman's investigation and the work of Lieutenant Robert W. Hicks, Washington criminologist, who was retained by Mrs. Evalyn McLean and Governor Hoffman to reopen the case in 1936 just before Hauptmann was executed.

However, the record of the trial is interesting in itself. Lieutenant Bornmann explained his discovery that eight feet of wood had been removed from the attic floor.

Wilentz called Arthur Koehler, the wood expert, who followed a trail to South Carolina and back to New Jersey, New York, and Connecticut to find a match for the wood used in "Rail 16." Bornmann accompanied him.

Koehler testified that the ladder was sloppily build by a man who had "no love of wood." The tools used to build it were not sharpened, the chisel cut too deeply, and it was sawed imperfectly. Hauptmann had been portrayed as a skilled carpenter, capable of cabinet work. This was hardly the work of a skilled craftsman. Frederick Pope, one of the defense counsel, objected to using the ladder as evidence; it had not been connected in any way with Hauptmann, it had been moved from New Jersey to New York and back again, handled by almost everyone in the investigation by both States. It had even been altered.

Judge Trenchard at first said he would defer admission of the ladder until its connection with the kidnaping had been substantiated. Wilentz called Lieutenant John Sweeney, who had tried out the ladder at the nursery window and found it fitted. Judge Trenchard, after listening to Sweeney's account, which proved only that the ladder might have been laid against the wall to the nursery window, finally found the link he had been looking for: Amandus Hochmuth!

Pope again objected to introducing the ladder. George Waller, whose acceptance of the prosecution's case goes beyond the limits of human credulousness, said in *Kidnap*: "Pope summoned up a show of force for his final point against the tiresome ladder. 'There is no connection between this ladder and the defendant on trial. No one had suggested that this ladder was ever in the possession of the defendant here on trial. No one has suggested that he had anything to do with building it. It is immaterial, irrelevant, and we submit that it should not be introduced in evidence.'"

Judge Trenchard asked Pope if he had "overlooked the testimony of the old gentleman, Mr. Hochmuth, to the effect that on March 2, 1932, he saw the defendant in possession of the ladder."

Judge Trenchard may not have known that Hochmuth was almost blind from cataracts, or that he was collecting double welfare in New York by listing two addresses when he lived in New Jersey. But even the most cursory investigation by Schwarzkopf must have revealed that. An investigator, on June 29, 1932, had reported on Hochmuth: "Health very poor, partly blind." Alan Hynd, a writer who was among the few who questioned the Hauptmann verdict, investigated

153

Hochmuch, and reported that on August 4, 1932 another investigator had noted in Hochmuth's file: "Frail, failing in eyesight due to cataracts."

This was the man on whom Judge Trenchard relied in ruling on the admissability of the ladder. "I feel constrained to admit this ladder in evidence, and it will be admitted."

Koehler resumed his testimony. Waller, who seemed to have a faculty for penetrating minds, described in *Kidnap* how Koehler sat in court, awaiting Judge Trenchard's decision, watching Hauptmann's hands— "the hands of a careless carpenter, with scant feeling for the wood he used—the hands that crudely fashioned the kidnap ladder." This appeared to be the basis on which Koehler, the wood expert, decided that Hauptmann was guilty.

Koehler noted in his investigating trip to North Carolina to trace the "Rail 16" wood, that the ladder was "amateurish," evidence that its maker was a "poor carpenter." Yet Hauptmann's reputation among those for whom he worked was that of a skilled craftsman. This might have led investigators to question whether or not he built the ladder; but no such thought appeared to have occurred to David Wilentz.

Koehler explained, in considerable detail, how he had finally traced the wood for "Rail 16" to the National Millwork and Lumber Company in the Bronx.

Scaduto offers an interesting theory on the question of who built the ladder. He quotes Whipple, whom he mistakenly calls a "police reporter," in *The Lindbergh Crime:*

> The known customers of National Millwork and Lumber Company were then thoroughly investigated and one by one eliminated from the case. . . .At this point a reporter made the logical suggestion that every automobile license application from within a certain well-defined zone of the Bronx be examined for comparison with the ransom notes. Such a search was

conducted. Of thousands of such documents on file, all but 480 were eliminated, and there remained only forty-eight possible suspects by the end of 1933."

Scaduto suggested that the known customers of the lumberyard, and the licenses issued to drivers in that area, must have included Hauptmann. He was a known customer of the lumberyard, and had an automobile. Was he cleared of all suspicion? Had his name been on either list, he must have been under surveillance, and he was not picked up! Yet after he was arrested, his signature on the license was declared by the State's handwriting experts to be the same as those on the ransom notes. Scanduto asked in *Scapegoat*, "Is it possible Hauptmann did not fit the description of 'John' in 1933, and Condon revised his description a year later to fit the man who'd been arrested?"

One of the bits of hard evidence the State expected to use was a board taken from a closet in the nursery of the Hauptmann apartment. Inspector Henry Bruckman had found it inside the closet. Actually, he backed into the closet to see it. This was about four days after Hauptmann had been taken into custody, and the police in spite of their intensive search had found nothing and seemed to be reduced into going into odd places. Bruckman had noticed the board had some writing on it, hardly distinguishable in the unlighted closet. The words were finally made out: "2974 Decatur." A second line had been written underneath: "S DG 3-7154." It was Condon's telephone number—Sedgewick 3-7154, the old number, before he changed to an unlisted number to avoid telephone calls during negotiations with "John."

This telephone number was used with great effect by the police investigators and at the trial. Yet it must have been obvious that Hauptmann, assuming he was "John" of the cemeteries, would hardly jot down Condon's telephone number in an unlighted closet, where it would be difficult to see, when he had no telephone in his home and the nearest phone was a pay station a block away, where there was a telephone directory which contained Condon's listed number.

Yet this evidence was presented at the first New York hearing paving the way for Hauptmann's extradition to New Jersey. Hauptmann was so completely confused when shown the board and the numbers that he said he must have been reading about the Lindbergh case and Condon's part in it, and he wrote Condon's telephone number on the wall! He said, "I must have written it —it is my writing." He had also jotted down other things on the door to the closet, but these were figures written in plain view when the door was swung open. Condon's number was almost impossible to see.

After the Flemington trial, Condon said, "To this day I cannot bring myself to accept the written telephone number and address in the kidnaper's closet."

According to Scaduto, it was not Hauptmann's handwriting. In *Scapegoat* he says Murray Bleefield, who was indicted with Ellis Parker in the Paul Wendel case— of which more will be written later—told him that a newspaper reporter, Tom Cassidy of the New York *Daily News,* wrote the number on the wall, emulating Hauptmann's handwriting, just to stir up a fresh story on the kidnaping case!

Hauptmann himself may have furnished the best answer. When Governor Hoffman visited him in his cell at Trenton, while awaiting execution, Hauptmann had pointed to testimony by Inspector Bruckman in which he told of finding the board.

"This man lied!"

"I wanted to ask you about that," Governor Hoffman said. "You did admit that it was your writing, didn't you? And it was Condon's telephone number."

"That is one of the things they did to me! A few days after my arrest, Annie and the child could not stand it in the house. The baby could not sleep because of the police. . .so they went to relatives. Now I can see that it was the wrong thing, for the police could manage to do what they wished. . . .When everything is mixed up, the police bring me a board on which there is some writing. They say the board is from a closet in my home. When I look at the writing, it looks like mine and I say it must be mine, because often it is my custom to write down things, like many carpenters, on pieces of wood. But then they tell me it is Condon's telephone number and the number of his house. Dear God, if I had done that—that number I had written—and knew what it was, would I have been stupid enough to tell the police? No! I would say I had never seen it before!"

The soft evidence consisted of handwriting and fingerprints. These were among the most controversial in the prosecution's case, subjects of continuous wrangling between experts for the State and the single expert for the defense. It is unnecessary to dig deeply into this phase of the State's evidence; merely scratching the surface will indicate the uncertainty, even among the experts, with the exception of Albert S. Osborn who was not uncertain about anything.

Osborn, the State's chief handwriting witness, wound up his testimony by stating that his analysis of the similarities of Hauptmann's handwriting with the ransom notes, conceded writings such as auto license applications, and requested writings which the police asked him to write, was "irresistable, unanswerable and overwhelming."

Several handwriting authorities have since taken exception to his estimate. Samuel Small, a professional penman, told Governor Hoffman during his post-trial investigation that Hauptmann "could not possibly have been the writer of the ransom notes." Hoffman said Small had told him Osborn's testimony conflicted with Osborn's own writings on the subject. Osborn had first suggested to the New Jersey police, when he was retained as a handwriting expert, that they prepare several messages on different sheets of paper and ask the accused man to reproduce the writing. The messages would contain certain words, syllables and letters which would reveal that the writer had written the ransom notes.

Small told Hoffman that Osborn himself had said a man could not disguise his way of writing. "In a lifetime of painstaking effort, a man cannot change the way he was taught to write." He showed Hoffman enlargements of Hauptmann's writings, and sections of the ransom notes exhibited at the trial.

"The shadings are different, downstrokes and upstrokes. Every letter has a different characteristic. The smartest criminal in the world couldn't do that." Small had asked the Governor for permission to appear before the New Jersey Board of Pardons, when Hauptmann's appeal was to be heard, and was told that would be impossible since no additional testimony would be heard.

"Do you mean that your state will send to the chair a man who could not possibly have written those notes? It isn't a question *if* Hauptmann wrote those letters; it is a question whether he could write them."

Osborn had sorted out, from various sources, indications of Hauptmann's lack of familiarity with the English language, which he detailed: writing the word "boat" as "boad" in the last note from the kidnapers; transposing "n" and "g" as in "singature"; hyphenating "New-York." He prepared a handwriting test sheet on which matters of spelling and writing style were embodied in the text. This was dictated to Hauptmann, who wrote down each paragraph as dictated.

Osborn ound that in each case Hauptmann had presumably *disguised* his writing. Osborn explained to the jury that this indicated Hauptmann was dishonest; he had partly disguised his hand.

Hauptmann, in his interview with Governor Hoffman, said, "Right after my arrest I had to write. I did not know at the time why they wanted specimens of my writing. If I had any idea, then I would not have let them dictate to me to write down mistakes. Of course I make mistakes in writing. Still, not such blunders as were dictated to me. They took out of my writing those things which looked like the ransom note. In the note found in the baby's room they found only one little word, 'is' that they say looked like mine.''

Hauptmann had been asked to write according to the text of the test paragraph. He had been awakened time after time and asked to write again. It is possible that he was tired. Osborn interpreted this as an effort to disguise his handwriting.

Theo Bernsen, a European writer covering the Hauptmann case, told Anthony Scaduto he had discussed the matter of Hauptmann's writing with an expert on translating English and German attached to the German embassy in London. He showed his enlarged photographs, presumably the kidnap notes, and was told that these were not written by a German who had been taught English, but by a "man who thinks in English and is trying to write Germanic.''

"The grammatical errors show it clearly, the attempt to make a Germanic construction by a man who thinks in English. He particularly stressed the word "boad'' which Osborn and the others claimed was German. In German it is written with a 't'—'boot'—and it is not possible a German just learning English would make that mistake.''

Small, in discussing this with Governor Hoffman, pointed to sections of Osborn's books on handwriting, noting that a person cannot *disguise* handwriting; yet at the Flemington trial, in direct testimony and under cross-examination by Reilly, Osborn had said of the ransom notes, "I think they are all disguised, all the ransom notes.''

Apparently Reilly had not boned up on Osborn's previous views on the subject, or on his earlier testimony. However, John M. Trendley, whose credentials as a handwriting expert were similar to Osborn's, said in testifying for the defense, "It would have been absolutely impossible for Hauptmann to have written the ransom letters."

Later a handwriting expert from Clearwater, Florida, Hilda Schaffer, who had examined the ransom notes during the trial at Flemington, wrote to Governor Byrne of New Jersey that the ransom notes had been forged and showed "overwritings" indicating that someone had tampered with them to make them appear like Hauptmann's writing. She said Hauptmann could not have made the overwritings himself, because they were done with a different blend of ink and at a much later period than when they were left in the Lindbergh nursery, sent through the mail, or delivered to Condon.

Seven other handwriting experts were retained by the State to prove Hauptmann had written the ransom notes, including Clark Sellers of Los Angeles, a leading authority on handwriting. He concluded his testimony by saying, "Bruno Richard Hauptmann might as well have signed his name to all the ransom notes." Trendley apparently was the only expert the defense could afford, and the jury presumably accepted the prosecution's views by a vote of eight-to-one.

J. Vreeland Haring was a consultant for the prosecution, and in addition to his fee, he wrote a book, *The Hand of Hauptmann,* published by the Hamer Publishing Company of Plainfield, New Jersey. The publisher said it was "the only book of its kind in the English language." Haring sought to prove by an analysis of the handwriting that Hauptmann was guilty, so probably it was.

The battle of experts in the handwriting field was overshadowed by fingerprint experts, probably due to the lack of visible fingerprints on the ladder and in the nursery, and the startling discovery when Dr. Erastus Mead Hudson finally raised the fingerprints with his new silver-nitrate process, that none of them matched

Hauptmann's!

Dr. Hudson was consulted by the New Jersey police shortly after the Lindbergh baby was kidnaped. He offered his services when he first heard that there were no fingerprints found on the ladder or in the nursery. Trooper Frank Kelly had dusted everything, including the kidnapers note, and found nothing.

The new raising process was applied, and it produced several hundred fingerprints. By the time the police had Hauptmann in custody and had taken his fingerprints, Dr. Hudson was already being declassified as a consultant, but he was still interested in the case. He inquired of the New Jersey police whether any of the fingerprints he had raised on the ladder matched Hauptmann's. He was told, "No."

"Well, gentlemen, you must have the wrong man."

Mrs. McLean, to whom Dr. Hudson told this story, noted that after that he was discarded as a consultant.

According to Mrs. McLean, Dr. Hudson was extremely interested in the absence of any fingerprints in the nursery. Betty Gow had said she touched the crib when she leaned over to see if the baby was there on the night of the kidnaping. Why were her fingerprints not found on the crib?

"Dr. Hudson was a most level-headed man, with no ax to grind," Mrs. McLean said. "He said there was not the slightest doubt in his mind that the case had not been completely solved."

The manner in which the fingerprints—or lack of them—had been kicked around in the New Jersey police records, and the apparent indifference of defense counsel to this aspect of police bungling, was by no means the most significant phase of the fingerprint situation. As noted earlier, Dr. Hudson's process had raised fingerprints on several toys handled by the Lindbergh baby, and on the crib itself. He was called by the defense to testify, and under direction examination by Frederick Pope, he said, "Major Shoeffler of the state police phoned me and asked if I would come down to Hopewell and see if it is possible to get some finger-prints of the Lindbergh child; so I went down there and I remember I demonstrated at the time the silver nitrate process on wood, and then applied the silver nitrate process to some of the little books and things, and we found some of the fingerprints of the baby on those books. . . .So that day, I think it was a Monday, we spent the morning in developing fingerprints on little blocks, toys and various things.''

These were the fingerprints of Lindbergh's son which were kept in the New Jersey police archives at Trenton until 1975, when they mysteriously disappeared. What is even more remarkable is the curious reticence of the FBI to disclose from its records what happened to the photo-static copies of the fingerprints of the Lindbergh child they had been given. On January 15, 1938, Col. Mark Kimberling wrote to FBI director John Edgar Hoover stating: ''We have in our files finger print impressions taken from toys and other objects found in the nursery of the Lindbergh home, which are thought to be those of the Lindbergh child. . . .For the purpose of protection against the possibility of a fake attempt to prove identification, we believe it advisable not to release these prints to anyone.''

The fingerprints would be almost unassailable proof of the identity of anyone claiming to be the Lindbergh baby. Was Colonel Kimberling aware, at this time, of questions concerning the identity of the child's body found on Mount Rose Heights? If he was, he should have spoken up before he ordered the current shot through Hauptmann's body. The baby's body, identified by Colonel Lindbergh as his child, was the basis of the murder charge against Hauptmann, the *corpus delicti.*

Dr. Hudson, during his earlier association with the New Jersey state police, before he had in a sense ex-communicated himself by saying the police ''had the wrong man" in Hauptmann, had been given the kidnap ladder to examine for fingerprints. As previously noted, there were several raised fingerprints—about a hundred or more—most of which were identified as those of state troopers or detectives.

He was shown the kidnap ladder during the Flemington trial, and after examining it carefully, he noted that he had found a single nailhole in one of the rungs of "Rail 16."

On cross-examination, Wilentz said, "Are you willing to stake all your testimony on there being only one nailhole?"

Pope objected to the question, and Judge Trenchard sustained him. Koehler, the wood expert, had taken a photograph of the ladder showing *four* nailholes. Pope made the point in direct examination of Dr. Hudson that the ladder had been passed from the New Jersey police to the New York police, and back again, and that Dr. Hudson had examined the ladder *before* it was turned over to Koehler.

This was a matter of extreme importance. In George Waller's *Kidnap* he mentioned that during the investigation, after Hauptmann was arrested, Koehler decided that if the beam, from which the eight-foot section used to make "Rail 16" in the kidnap ladder had been pried, showed four holes that matched the four holes in "Rail 16," it would be proof that the section had been taken from the attic floor. He took Detective Bornmann—the man who discovered the missing board in the attic—with him, and they carefully measured the nailholes.

Dr. Hudson's testimony left only two possible conclusions: Either the doctor was wrong in saying he had seen only *one* hole in the ladder when he first examined it; or Koehler and Bornmann were tampering with the evidence, making four nailholes in "Rail 16" instead of one.

When Dr. Hudson said he had first observed that "Rail 16" had *only one* nailhole, Wilentz had quickly asked if he was willing to "stake all your testimony" about there being only one nailhole at the time he examined the ladder, and this question—meaningless in itself—was stricken from the record. Shortly afterward Wilentz produced a photograph which showed *four* nailholes. He said this was taken *before* Dr. Hudson saw the ladder, and asked the doctor if he would "admit you were mistaken." Dr. Hudson glanced at the photograph, apparently puzzled, shrugged his shoulders, and said, "I would say yes."

This is the only time this critical difference of opinion came up. The prosecution did not pursue it, and neither did Reilly. In view of the fact that much of the evidence produced by the State was rigged, it was not impossible that Wilentz' photograph was taken *after* Hauptmann was removed from the apartment, and *after* Bornmann had located the board in the attic floor. The question was never asked, and of course never answered. Dr. Hudson was a mild man who had offered his services first to the state police and later was called by the defense to testify. He was evidently puzzled by Wilentz' photograph, which he did not identify as to the time and place where it was taken; and the New York doctor would have had no reason to question it.

The matter was not given much importance by George Waller, and none by Sidney Whipple. Yet it was a point on which Kohler's entire testimony hung. If the ladder had been tampered with, and Dr. Hudson's first testimony indicated that it might have been tampered with, the link between the ladder and Hauptmann was shattered. The ladder had placed him at the scene of the crime!

As a final filip to the ladder testimony, William Bolmer, a Princeton graduate, was called by the defense. He said he operated a service station about four miles from Hopewell, within the general area of the Lindbergh home. About a quarter past one o'clock the morning of March 1, 1932—the night before the kidnaping—a man driving a Ford truck had driven into his station for gas. The car had a make-shift looking ladder fastened to the running board, and there was a woman in the car. Frederick Pope turned toward Hauptmann.

"Stand up, Mr. Hauptmann." Then, to Bolmer, "Is that the man?"

"Positively not."

Wilentz, cross-examining the witness, asked, "Did you ever report this to New Jersey authorities?"

"I did not."

"Why not?"

"I didn't recognize the description of the kidnap ladder, and in the picture I saw it was extended. The ladder I saw on the truck was nested, one part within another. I didn't think it was the same ladder and I didn't want to make a fool out of myself talking about something I didn't know anything about."

Pope on redirect examination, asked Bolmer what his opinion was, now that he had seen the kidnap ladder. Bolmer said it was the same ladder he had seen on the Ford. Wilentz tried to get Bolmer to say it might have been a Dodge, not a Ford. Bolmer was quite firm; it was definitely a Ford.

Bolmer's testimony might have been taken as of more importance than that of Hochmuth and Whited, who saw no suspicious strangers the day of the kidnaping, but were able to remember seeing a man they identified as Hauptmann two-and-a-half years later. It provided an eyewitness, not involved in the case, who said someone other than Hauptmann was near the scene of the crime, with a ladder identified as the kidnap ladder.

It was allowed to pass into the limbo of unexplained things in the Lindbergh case.

14

The Ransom Money

The source of the ransom bills, which Hauptmann had tried to get rid of after he found them in August, 1934, was traced to Isidor Fisch, a German furrier who had been a partner of Hauptmann's since early in 1932. At first Fisch was suspected of being "John" of the cemeteries; later the lookout at the Woodlawn and St. Raymond's Cemeteries. Whatever he was, Fisch was the man Hauptmann said left a shoebox filled with gold certificates with him when he left for Germany on December 6, 1933.

This was the story on which Hauptmann relied in his explanation of how he got the money, and that the New Jersey prosecution labelled a "Fisch story." Hauptmann said he placed a shoebox Fisch gave him on a shelf in a kitchen broom closet without knowing it contained gold bills.

The police traced Fisch through the German police, and found he had come to America in 1925 with Henry Uhlig, who lived with him in the rooming house where some of Hauptmann's friends lived: Carl and Gerta Henkel, and Hans Kloeppenburg. Hauptmann said he became acquainted with Fisch in March or April of 1932 and they formed a partnership, Fisch dealing in furs and Hauptmann playing the stock market while working as a carpenter.

Fisch had applied for a passport to return to Germany on May 12, 1932—the day the body supposedly of the

Lindbergh baby was found on Mount Rose Heights. He did not leave, however, until December of 1933. A few days before he sailed he had a party at Hauptmann's apartment and left the shoebox which he asked Hauptmann to keep for him. Hauptmann said he assumed the contents of the shoebox was papers.

A number of conflicting stories were told about the box, and it may be well to report what Mrs. McLean had to say about it in the story she wrote for *Liberty* magazine, published in September, 1938. She had asked Lieutenant Robert Hicks, who investigated the Lindbergh case for Governor Hoffman and was also retained by Mrs. McLean for the same purpose, to lease the apartment formerly occupied by the Hauptmanns and subsequently by the New Jersey state police. She wrote:

You probably remember the shoebox containing the money, which Hauptmann said his acquaintance, Isidor Fisch, gave him to keep while Fisch went to Germany, and which Hauptmann said he placed on a shelf high in the closet, where Mrs. Hauptmann in the normal course of her household duties wouldn't come across it. All right. Let me tell you something about that shoebox.

After the New Jersey State police had been in the Bronx apartment for some time, following Hauptmann's arrest, it was pointed out that Mrs. Hauptmann must have been blind not to have noticed the shoebox on the shelf, because it was at eye level. Mrs. Hauptmann had been unable to explain this, insisting that while she had occasion to go into the closet many times, she had never seen the box. She kept repeating, after her husband's arrest, that the closet shelf seemed *lower* than it had been before, but nobody paid much attention to her.

Examining the closet, Lieutenant Hicks decided that the walls had been painted within about a year. He applied chemicals to the paint, and what did he find under the outer paint but marks where a shelf had once been—many inches *above* where the shelf was when the

State Police got through with the apartment. When Lieutenant Hicks placed a shelf at the point where the markings were, and then placed a shoebox on the shelf, it was not possible for anyone to see the box unless standing on something."

Mrs. McLean offered no explanation of this. She said she was stating the fact as it was reported to her. But she asked: "If one thing in the Hauptmann apartment was tampered with, is it not reasonable to suppose that there might be something in the charge that other evidence was altered, too, in order to make it fit more nearly into the sudden and unexpected charge that the Lindbergh crime was a one-man job?"

The other evidence that may have been altered was the attic floorboard sawed from the floor to create "Rail 16" of the kidnap ladder, which Detective Bornmann observed after police had searched the attic exhaustively for several days. If Hicks story is true, the New Jersey police were guilty not only of altering evidence on the shoebox, but very possibly of rigging the strongest circumstantial link between Hauptmann and the kidnaping of Lindbergh's son—the so-called kidnap ladder!

It was this realization of how much tampering with the evidence had been done by the New Jersey police, when they occupied the Hauptmann apartment, that aparently caused Hauptmann to say to Governor Hoffman, when asked about the Condon telephone number found in a closet in his home, "That is one of the things they did to me!"

When Wilentz, who may or may not have been aware of the shift in levels of the shelf, asked Hauptmann on cross-examination whether he told his wife, Anna, about finding the shoebox full of money, he said, "No."

Wilentz expressed astonishment.

"You didn't tell your wife?"

"No."

The prosecution made a great deal out of this apparent dereliction on the part of a faithful husband who had said he "shared everything" with his wife—which would have included finding the money.

Turning to Mrs. McLean's investigation in 1938, she said she asked the Rev. D. G. Werner, an Adventist minister who had been Hauptmann's spiritual advisor in the period after he was arrested, to come to Friendship House in Georgetown. Among other things, she asked Werner why Hauptmann had not told his wife about finding the money.

"It was a Sunday morning when Richard discovered the money," the pastor said. "Mrs. Hauptmann was out with the baby. Contrary to the picture of the Hauptmann household as presented by the newspapers, Hauptmann was not a stern, masterful husband whose words caused his wife to tremble. If either deferred to the wishes of the other, Richard deferred to Annie's. As a matter of fact, Annie was a very excitable woman and Richard told me he would often hide things from her to keep her from being upset.

"Well, that is exactly what happened that Sunday morning when Richard found the money in the closet. He was afraid to let his wife know about it, for if he couldn't explain the presence of the money himself—and he couldn't—how would he explain it to her? So he hid it in the garage to avoid family trouble."

As Mrs. McLean noted, the statements of Dr. Werner are not to be regarded as the word of a man of God who might be "likely to place trust where it should not be placed." In fact, the Adventist pastor had at first believed Hauptmann was guilty, and it was only after Hauptmann had explained "in such simple yet logical fashion" many of the points made by the prosecution, that he became convinced of Hauptmann's innocence. Mrs. McLean said in her story: "Hauptmann's explanations to him (Dr. Werner) struck me as having more of the ring of probability than did many of the points brought out by the State at Flemington.''

There is another point in Mrs. McLean's interview with Dr. Werner that had a bearing not only on the finding of the Lindbergh extortion money but on the New Jersey police operations while they were in Hauptmann's apartment. Hauptmann had stated in his testimony as well as to Dr. Werner that there were several things Fisch had left in his apartment. The inventory of the Department of Justice on the contents of his apartment showed various records—including statements of profits and losses in Hauptmann's dealings with Fisch—which he referred to in his testimony, but which had mysteriously disappeared.

Again, there is no reason to suppose Wilentz, the prosecutor, was aware of New Jersey police tampering with the evidence.

During Wilentz' cross-examination of Hauptmann there was a growing feeling that Hauptmann was more bewildered and puzzled by the questions put to him. As an example, Wilentz showed him an accounting of expenses by Hauptmann and his wife during a trip to California with Hans Kloeppenburg, in which there appeared the word "boad.''

"Did you write that?''

Hauptmann said, "Yes.''

Wilentz asked if it were true, then, that Hauptmann had not learned to spell "boat'' with a "t'' instead of a "d'' eight years before, as he previously testified. Hauptmann was silent for a minute, then he shook his head. He said he had not realized that the paper he was shown was an accounting of a trip to California; he had simply been puzzled by the spelling of "boad'' instead of "boat.''

Wilentz asked him if he did not recall that on April 2, 1932, he had given Dr. Condon a note in which the "Boad Nelly'' was mentioned in exchange for $50,000?

"Me? Fifty thousand dollars!''

Wilentz merely said, "Yes, you recall that that was Dr. Condon's testimony," and moved on to the next question.

For one who already believed Hauptmann was guilty, this exchange would have tended to prove he was guilty; but for one who was not predisposed to believe him guilty, it would merely have meant that he was puzzled by the question. The possibility that the word "boad" was the result of more police tampering with the evidence probably did not occur to Hauptmann, and apparently did not occur to Reilly, the Chief Counsel for the Defense. As noted by Theo Bernsen, the expert on German-English translations, Germans do not spell "boat" with a "d."

Earlier in cross-examination, Wilentz had showed Hauptmann the receipt from the kidnapers which Condon said he had received from "John" in St. Raymond's Cemetery. He pointed to the words:

"The boy is on Boad Nelly it is a small boad 28 feet long. . ."

Wilentz asked, "You come from Saxony, don't you?"

Hauptmann said he did.

"In Saxony they use a 'd' instead of a 't,' don't they? In 'boad' instead of 'boat,' and things like that?"

"Sometimes, yes."

"And you spelled the word 'boad' as 'b-o-a-d' because that is the way they would spell it in Saxony?"

Hauptmann shook his head, and said, "In Saxony they might pronounce it with a 'd' but they would spell it with a 't.'"

This was a direct refutation of what Wilentz later tried to show: that the word was spelled by Germans with a "t" rather than a "d," as in the note from "John." It coincided with what Theo Bernsen had said. Waller, in *Kidnap,* paid no attention to this exchange. He wrote: "The prosecutor swung over to a new line of attack."

It is not the purpose of this review to discuss George Waller or the writing of *Kidnap;* his motives are his own, and are not grist for this mill. But the casual way in which he refers to situations that on closer examination might offer fairly convincing evidence that the prosecution was using every known tactic to convict a man who may not have committed the Lindbergh crime, is little short of appalling.

Wilentz again shifted his attack when he asked Hauptmann whether or not he recalled that he had given Condon a note in St. Raymond Cemetery, which included the spelling of "Boad Nelly" in return for $50,000 ransom, and Hauptmann said, "Me? Fifty-thousand dollars!" Wilentz moved on to another line of questioning.

This may have been courtroom strategy but it was a long way from being forthright. The spelling of "boad" instead of "boat" was an important part of the testimony given by Dr. Condon, Osborn and the other handwriting experts. It bore on the basic question of whether or not Hauptmann had written the kidnap notes. It was Osborn's contention that he wrote them, and John M. Trendley's contention that he could not have written them—a point later affirmed by Samuel Small, a professional penman, in a discussion with Governor Hoffman.

Wilentz throughout his cross-examination of Hauptmann accused him of lying, at one time remarking, "My God! don't you tell anybody the truth?"—a comment that was stricken from the record.

Wilentz was not above shifting his own position. When the trial opened, he described Hauptmann's exit from the house, carrying the baby. When the ladder broke, he said the child was probably killed when its head struck the side of the house during the fall from the ladder.

At the close of the trial he said, "Certainly he stilled

the little child's breath—right in that room! The child did not cry when it was. . .yanked from the crib! The pins were still left in the bedsheets. Yanked and its head hit against the headboard—must have hit!. . .Still no outcry. Why? Because there was no cry left in the child. Did he use the chisel to crush the skull? Is that a fair inference? What else was the chisel there for? To knock the child into sensibility right there in that room!''

This change in theory seemed to be no impediment to the State's prosecution of the case, any more than the change from a gangster kidnaping to a lone kidnaper, a complete reversal of the original State's position. Most of the early evidence had been predicated on the gang theory: Condon's report of someone yelling, *"Statto citti!''*—Italian for "Shut up!"—for example. This did not fit in with Wilentz lone kidnaper theory, and was never mentioned by the prosecution. Nor was it mentioned by Reilly.

These changes were perhaps the weakest link in the prosecution's case; but the strongest part of the case—one which the defense could not challenge—was the general belief by the man in the street that Hauptmann was guilty!

The trail of the ransom notes was strewn with evidence of a gang. Mrs. Decornille's report that a well-dressed woman in gray had tried to pass a Lindbergh ransom bill in her pastry shop; the deposit of Lindbergh gold bills by J. J. Faulkner; Curtis' dealings with gangsters—which he later said included Hauptmann; none of these things were mentioned at the trial. The lookout at St. Raymond's Cemetery was not mentioned by Condon or Lindbergh. It did not fit the prosecution's theory of a one-man job.

What is perhaps most disturbing—more than the failure to call key witnesses, such as the East Side storekeeper who took a ten-dollar Lindbergh bill from a man he said he would recognize if he saw him again, or the vapid way in which George Waller and Sidney

Whipple accepted these incidents—is the moral vacuum in which the prosecution itself seemed to exist. It is one thing to be swayed by largely circumstantial evidence that a man is guilty; it is another to use rigged evidence, dishonest or distorted records, eyewitness testimony that is palpably false, just to convict a man who may have had nothing to do with the crime with which he was charged.

It is also one thing for the public, during the time of the trial, to accept what was laid before it; they were not investigators, and had no access to police reports. But Waller says he spent years researching the Lindbergh case. Why did he not pursue the loose points, track through police records the strange links between J. J. Faulkner and Carl Geissler and Willie Krippendorf and Leo Rodel that finally led to Condon's son-in-law, Ralph Hacker?

The newspapers of that day had for the most part accepted Hauptmann's guilt. The New York *Daily News* headlined Martin Sommers' stories: "Bruno's Fisch Story Hit" and "Kidnap Ladder Linked to Hauptmann's Home." Sommers wrote of Koehler, the wood expert: "The one and only great detective of the Lindbergh case took Bruno Richard Hauptmann's own tools and turned them against him. . . .When he had finished, Hauptmann appeared betrayed as the builder of the fatal kidnap ladder by his own tools." This was not true, but it sold newspapers.

Writing about the same material many years later, however, would seem to impose an obligation on the writer to look more deeply into the evidence and testimony of the trial, question unsubstantiated statements, trace the origin of clues. Otherwise all that remains is a digest of police records and news stories. It may be this is all Waller intended, but an investigative reporter should do more.

As a case in point, Department of Justice experts checked each of the ransom notes sent to Lindbergh and found fingerprints on several. They did not match

Hauptmann's after he was arrested, and were therefore disregarded. No one had touched these letters after they were first opened; they might have furnished evidence that would have led to someone other than Hauptmann, but since they did not match Hauptmann's fingerprints, they were discarded! This may not have been known to those reporting the trial; but it must have been known to a later investigator. He should have asked, Why ignore these clues?

Returning to the trail of ransom money, Reilly had announced during direct examination of Mrs. Bertha Hoff, who said she met Isidor Fisch at a farm in November, 1933, near Flemington, New Jersey, that it was the intention of the defense to tie Fisch into every aspect of the case in which Hauptmann had been identified: "that the man who jumped over the cemetery wall was Isidor Fisch, that the money was handed to Isidor Fisch, that Isidor Fisch from that date on approached many persons in New York trying to dispose of this money. I am going to trace every connection of Isidor Fisch with this money until he left on the steamer. . . .I am going to trace everything to show that Isidor Fisch, and not this defendant, received this money from Dr. Condon and tried to dispose of it. . ."

Unfortunately for Hauptmann, Reilly did not do what he had promised. He brought on witnesses whose credibility was questioned, one of whom had been in an insane asylum, another who had a criminal record. Hauptmann asked Lloyd Fisher, "Where are they getting these witnesses? They're hurting me! Tell Mr. Reilly he has got to find out if the witnesses are honest, good people."

The real trail of the ransom money—the lady in gray in Greenwich, Connecticut, the deposit made on May 1, 1933 by J. J. Faulkner, the various Lindbergh ransom bills passed in New York stores—was not actually raised by the defense and only casually mentioned in the trial. Even Mrs. Cecile Barr, the ticket seller at the Greenwich Village movie house who identified Hauptmann as the man with cold blue eyes, a thin face, and a pointed chin, who had tossed a tightly folded Lindbergh ransom bill at her, was not challenged, although Lieutenant Finn's report said she described the man as "apparently an American."

Whether Reilly's failure to provide a strong defense was due to ineptitude, his avowed belief that Hauptmann was guilty, or—as some writers suggested—his devotion to the New York *Journal* which paid most of his fee, obviously cannot be determined at this date. But there is every evidence that Hauptmann's defense was never properly handled, the vulnerable points in the prosecution's case—the rigged evidence, changed versions of testimony, changes in theory of the case, failure to call key witnesses—were not effectively challenged.

Add to this the stipulation made by Reilly, as to the identification of the body found on Mount Rose Heights, which barred the defense from challenging the proof of the *corpus delicti,* there can be little doubt that this in itself resulted in a miscarriage of justice. But it did even more: it effectively removed the opportunity for a child who had lived to identify himself as Lindbergh's son unless he could do this through matching fingerprints.

Claims based on likenesses would be largely unprovable, and would be painful reminders to the parents of the child they had lost. This may be the best explanation of Lindbergh's hasty identification: he firmly believed his son was dead and wanted no aftermath. His willingness to change his testimony on recognizing the voice of "John" of the cemeteries may have been due to a desire to protect his wife from further pain.

This explanation is a bit harder to accept, since a man's life was at stake—a point that will be discussed in the concluding chapters.

15

Final Hours of the Trial

The parade of closing witnesses for the defense was a dismal affair. Much of the information necessary for a proper defense—records of the investigation by the New York and New Jersey police—was not available to defense counsel. It was not until Governor Hoffman ordered these records released that they became available; and this was too late to help Hauptmann. As a matter of fact, many of these records are still being withheld.

One defense witness, Mrs. Anna Bonesteel, offered some testimony that should have been of interest. She operated a restaurant at the Yonkers ferry, across from Alpine, New Jersey. She said she knew Violet Sharpe, the Morrow maid who killed herself. She said Violet Sharpe had come into her restaurant the night of March 1, 1932 about half-past seven, carrying a gray blanket. She seemed quite nervous, and a quarter to nine she left the restaurant and jumped into a car that stopped outside.

During the informal investigation of Violet Sharpe by Joe Dunninger and myself, I talked with Mrs. Bonesteel, and she gave me some interesting information which she did not mention in her testimony at the Flemington trial. She also knew Red Johnson, the sailor friend of Betty Gow; he came into her restaurant quite often on his trips to and from New Jersey. He never came in with Violet Sharpe, although Mrs. Bonesteel said that when she came in the night of the kidnaping there were two men with her, and she was unable to identify either.

Miss Sharpe, it will be recalled, left the Morrow home on the evening of March 1 to meet Ernest Miller. There were two companions, Elmer Johnson and Katherine Minners, who testified that they spent the evening at a roadhouse in Orangeburg, New York, just across the New Jersey border. According to Mrs. Morrow, Violet served dinner and was last seen about a quarter to eight, an hour before Mrs. Bonesteel said she left her restaurant at the Yonkers ferry. The timing of her departure from the Morrow home would seem to preclude her being in the restaurant.

However, Mrs. Bonesteel might have been wrong about the date; it could have been February 29, in which case it would leave open the possibility, raised later by Harold Olson, that the baby had been injured earlier in an accident near Hopewell involving the Lindbergh car. This will be discussed in Part V of this review.

In this case, Violet Sharpe might have been involved, either as a participant or informant, and may have committed suicide when she heard—rightly or wrongly—that the baby was dead. The question of an earlier accident was never raised; Wilentz merely tried to destroy Mrs. Bonesteel's credibility by showing her a picture of Violet Sharpe.

Questions relating to Violet Sharpe, as well as to Red Johnson, Ollie Whately, and others in the Lindbergh-Morrow melange will be discussed in the concluding section; the point to be made here is that the trial testimony never reached into any part of the Lindbergh case where the facts or suspicions turned up were not consistent with the State's theory, or theories—since more than one was involved—that the kidnaping was a one-man job.

The defense of Bruno Hauptmann, on the other hand, had no investigation to pursue until Hauptmann himself was arrested, and had neither means nor money to backtrack over the trail already followed by a bungling police force and a conviction-hungry prosecution.

If anything was needed to climax the miscarriage of justice, it was the final charge to the jury by Judge Thomas W. Trenchard. Even Lindbergh seemed startled by the uninhibited bias of the judge's statement. George Waller, in an effort apparently to ease the effect of Judge Trenchard's charge upon the minds of people who were not aware of the general public hostility toward Bruno Hauptmann a quarter of a century earlier, writes: "It was Judge Trenchard's duty to make the road (for the jurors) clear. New Jersey law granted him a good deal of freedom in framing his charge. Many states held a tight rein on the judge; in their courts he served solely as a guide to the law's technicalities. But New Jersey followed its honored ancestor, English law. . ."

How closely it followed English law is a matter for a more learned critic than myself, and perhaps also for Waller to determine. But Judge Trenchard's admonition to the jury was possibly the most specific example of Jersey justice in a trial which *Editor and Publisher* described as "degrading the administration of justice."

He began with "the defendant is presumed to be innocent, which presumption continues until he is proven guilty." After reviewing the testimony, he noted that the testimony of Dr. Condon was called "inherently improbable" by the defense lawyers who said it should be rejected.

"But you will observe that his testimony is corroborated in a large part by several witnesses whose credibility has not been impeached. . .Is there any doubt in your mind as to the reliability of Dr. Condon's testimony?"

Concerning the switch from a gang to a lone kidnaper theory, he said, "The argument (of the defense) was to the effect that it (the kidnaping) was done by a gang, with the help and connivance of one or more of the servants of the Lindbergh or Morrow households. Now do you believe that? Is there any evidence in this case to support any such conclusion?''

Concerning Amandus Hochmuth, the half-blind old man who lived in New Jersey and drew double welfare payments from New York, Judge Trenchard said, "As bearing on the question of whether or not the defendant was present at the Lindbergh home on March 1, 1932, you should consider the testimony of Mr. Hochmuth. Mr. Hochmuth lives at the entrance to a lane that goes up to the Lindbergh house. He testified that on the forenoon of that day, March 1, 1932, he saw the *defendant* (italics mine) at that point driving rapidly from the direction of Hopewell. . .that he had a ladder in the car, which was a dirty dark green. Do you think there is any reason to doubt the truth of that statement?''

The Judge had nothing to say about the testimony of William Bolmer, the Princeton University graduate who did *not* identify Hauptmann as the man who drove into his gas station early in the morning of March 1, in a green Ford—not a Dodge. Hauptmann was usually identified as driving a dark green Dodge, and was in a blue Dodge when he was arrested.

Bolmer had also testified the ladder, strapped to the running board of the Ford; this testimony was not challenged by Wilentz, and yet it was ignored by Judge Trenchard.

Speaking of the entire defense testimony, he said, "The testimony produced by the defense I shall not attempt to recite in great detail. It should be given consideration by you and given such weight as you think it is entitled. . .''

On the fundamental question of what happened to the ransom money, Judge Trenchard made no comment on the strange deposit of $2,980 in ransom bills by J. J. Faulkner. The only mention of that transaction was the brief cross-examination of Treasury Agent Frank Wilson by Lloyd Fisher. Wilson admitted that the

James M. Fawcett,
Hauptmann's original attorney.

Edward J. Reilly, "The Bull of Brooklyn."

Justice Thomas W. Trenchard.

David T. Wilentz,
Attorney General
of New Jersey.

Treasury Department had followed up the lead but never found Faulkner.

Judge Trenchard's only comment on the ransom bills was, "You will consider, as bearing upon that question (of the disposition of ransom bills) the fact that a record of the serial numbers of the ransom money was retained. Now, does it not appear that many of the ransom bills were traced to the possession of the defendant? Does it not appear that many thousands of dollars of ransom bills were found in his garage, hidden in the walls or under the floor, and others found on his person when he was arrested, and others passed by him from time to time?"

"Not *does* it appear, but does it *not* appear! This was like asking, Have you stopped beating your wife?

Judge Trenchard's final remarks on the ransom money concerned Isidor Fisch.

"The defendant says these ransom moneys were left with him by one, Fisch, a man now dead." To emphasize this point, he paused; then leaned forward. "Do you believe that?"

Damon Runyon remarked, after Judge Trenchard had finished his charge to the jury, "He has just strapped Bruno in the electric chair!"

Judge Trenchard completed his charge to the jury at about a quarter past eleven in the morning of February 13, 1935. Shortly after ten o'clock that night Sheriff John Curtis came for the prisoner. Hauptmann's face was dead white when he entered the courtroom. The Associated Press had already sent out a false flash that the jury had found Hauptmann guilty and "recommended life imprisonment" due to mixed signals.

Fisher whispered to Hauptmann, "This is only the beginning, Richard. Don't make a sign."

The verdict was guilty, with no recommendation. That meant the electric chair. Judge Trenchard turned to Wilentz. "Do you wish to make a motion for sentence, Mr. Attorney General?"

Things were moving with the speed and precision of a

well-oiled machine. Wilentz arose and moved for "immediate sentence."

Judge Trenchard asked the defendant to arise, and said, "Bruno Richard Hauptmann, you have been convicted of murder in the first degree. The sentence of the Court is that you suffer death at the time and place and in the manner provided by law."

The mob that had gathered at the courthouse was still screaming "Kill Bruno!" when he was led through the door, handcuffed to two guards. Fisher's last word to him was, "Remember, it's only the beginning!"

Part Four

POST-TRIAL
INVESTIGATIONS

16

More "Unanswered Questions"

The end of the Flemington trial left far more questions unanswered than answered. In fact, none of the significant questions were answered. The New York *Times* said editorially: "The long trial at Flemington, the charge of the judge and verdict of the jury established a crime but did not clear away the mystery. . .The presiding judge told the jury that the State had been unable to present positive evidence identifying the prisoner at the time and place of the original crime, and that circumstantial evidence had to be depended upon. . ."

A summary of the evidence was written by Harold Nicolson, an English writer staying at the Morrow home in Englewood to write a book on Dwight Morrow. Lindbergh had been sitting with his wife and a few friends and heard over the radio, "You have now heard the verdict of the most famous trial in all history. Bruno Hauptmann now stands guilty of the foulest—"

Anne Lindbergh turned to her husband.

"Turn that off, Charles—turn that off!"

What passed through her mind was not revealed; but Lindbergh made a summation of the trial which undoubtedly intended to ease any doubts in his wife's mind as to Hauptmann's guilt. Nicolson wrote down what he said:

The handwriting testimony; the brilliant piece of detective work in tracing the ladder to the Hauptmann apartment; Condon's telephone number found in

Hauptmann's apartment; the prisoner's possession of the ransom money and the fact that he began to invest immediately after the $50,000 had been paid; recognition of Hauptmann's voice by Condon, Colonel Lindbergh and the taxi-driver, Perrone; and the fact that Hauptmann's alibis were all proved fraudulent. . .

A review of the evidence and testimony at the trial indicates that serious doubts existed on every one of the points made by Lindbergh:

Osborn's handwriting testimony was contradicted by John M. Trendley, and later by Samuel Small and the lady from Florida, Hilda Shaffer.

The "brilliant piece of detective work" by Koehler was nullified by simple logic. Would Hauptmann have ripped a board out of his attic floor to provide an inescapable clue to the commission of a crime? Or was it more likely that Bornmann and his fellow detectives provided the board?

The writing of Condon's telephone number in an ill-lighted closet, where it could not be seen, hardly needs any comment.

Possession of ransom money by Hauptmann could only be traced with any certainty about a month before he was arrested. His story that Isidor Fisch had given him the money, although labelled a "Fisch story" by Wilentz and in the newspapers, was as believable as the State's theory. The prosecution did not mention any ransom bills passed by people other than Hauptmann—such as the lady in Greenwich, Connecticut, or J. J. Faulkner.

The sudden increase in Hauptmann's investments offered only a circumstantial possibility if Hauptmann had possession of the money from April 2, 1932; otherwise it was of little importance.

The linking of Hauptmann's voice to that of "John" of the cemeteries was inherently suspect, and becomes even more so when the changed testimony of Condon and Lindbergh is considered.

The so-called fraudulence of Hauptmann's alibi witnesses depends on whose ox is being gored. Witnesses who said they saw Hauptmann at the Fredericksen bakery where Anna Hauptmann worked on the night of the kidnaping were no less believable than the testimony of Whited and Hochmuth, one a liar and the other half-blind.

Nicolson wrote that Lindbergh's summation was to alleviate the uncertainty of Anne Lindbergh and Betty Gow; and the question arises: Why were they uncertain?

Anne Lindbergh had been in court when she was asked to testify concerning the clothes worn by the baby the night he was kidnaped. At times she had looked at Anna Hauptmann, and one reporter noted that she had smiled. When Anthony Scaduto visited Anna Hauptmann in an Atlantic Coast city, sometime in the early 1970's, he reported her saying, "I think what Mrs. Lindbergh said was the truth. My heart went out to her. In the courtroom I was thinking, 'Someone took her baby, and here is my husband on trial, who had nothing to do with it—' and still my heart goes out to her."

It is quite possible that Lindbergh's effort to protect his wife from the direct impact of the trial may have been one reason for his revised testimony on the recognition of "John's" voice, which he heard once in the cemetery two-and-a-half years before, and was able to recognize as the voice of Hauptmann in the Flemington courthouse. This would hardly explain his willingness to send a man to the electric chair on such shabby evidence.

What appears more probable, in the light of the generally accepted view that Hauptmann was guilty, was Lindbergh's determination to see Hauptmann punished, regardless of any qualms he might feel about changing his testimony. He saw in Hauptmann the kidnaper and murderer of his son; it was unlikely that he would have hesitated to use any method to see that he paid for his crime, which was not only against the law

188

but against Lindbergh himself.

Lindbergh was a strong-willed man. He was a close friend of Colonel Breckinridge, and also of Colonel Thomas G. Lanphier, two men who represented extremely conservative political positions, and this probably rubbed off on Lindbergh.

Lindbergh must have recalled what he said, under oath to the Bronx grand jury shortly after the kidnaping. He could not say "positively" that he could "pick a man out by that voice." When he confronted Hauptmann in Foley's office, wearing a disguise, he said nothing. Three months later, in Flemington courthouse, he positively identified Hauptmann by his voice!

There are other factors that lead to the suspicion that Lindbergh's testimony should be questioned. He failed to state to the Flemington jury that he saw a third man at St. Jerome's Cemetery, a significant omission since it would have jeopardized the State's theory that only one man participated in the extortion scheme. If his only purpose in changing or omitting parts of his previous testimony was to save Anne Lindbergh from further agony, he chose an extremely callous way of doing it, since his testimony, in the minds of many people, sent Hauptmann to the electric chair.

Many questions, developed later in a study of the facts and testimony, were not actually presented in the trial at Flemington. Lindbergh accepted the statement of the police that Condon's telephone number was written on a board in an unlighted closet. This might have been excused; the reporter who later said he wrote the number did not surface until several years afterward. But there is much less excuse for Lindbergh accepting other evidence. He sat in the courtroom day after day, and listened to all the evidence. He must have questioned Hauptmann's using a board from his own attic to make "Rail 16" of the ladder; yet he cites this as one of the convincing links of circumstantial evidence!

The passing of gold bills from the Lindbergh ransom

list was well known to Lindbergh. Did he wonder how the lady from Greenwich, Connecticut, or the mysterious J. J. Falkner, had come into possession of the bills?

Wilentz became quite sarcastic in his cross-examination of Hauptmann's alibi witnesses, yet he never proved that such key witnesses as Gerta Henkel, Karl Henkel, Hans Kloeppenburg, and Christian Fredericksen, in whose bakery Anna Hauptmann worked, were in any sense "fraudulent," as Lindbergh stated.

The most important of the unanswered questions was the identification of the body found on Mount Rose Heights. Lindbergh established that identity by the briefest examination; he looked at the teeth and one foot. The body was badly decomposed and hardly recognizable. Did Lindbergh later follow up this identification by checking on the measurement by his pediatrist, Dr. Van Ingen, and the county coroner, which showed a four-and-a-third inch discrepancy?

Lindbergh undoubtedly was prepared to say the corpse was his son when he first saw it. He had no reason not to when he made the original identification. But he had two and a half years to ask himself whether or not the body was really his son! He must have had access to Dr. Van Ingen's records, and the report of Dr. Mitchell, the coroner of Mercer County. If so, he would have noticed the disparity in measurements of his son and the body found on Mount Rose Heights, as well as the overlapping toes.

Was he so indifferent to these facts that he neglected to follow up on them? Lindbergh's training as an aviator, his attention to precise details, and his clear and logical intelligence would belie this explanation.

Much of this will be explored in the concluding chapters; yet it is pertinent to remark at this point that his mind could have become so fixed in the belief that his son was dead—presumably at the hands of Hauptmann—that he no longer considered any alternative possibility. He threw the whole weight of his belief that Hauptmann was guilty behind the effort to exact punishment from the man who he believed had kidnaped and killed his son. If there is added to this his devotion and desire to protect his wife from the ravages of grief, it would explain why Lindbergh acted as he did, refusing to consider any alternative to Hauptmann's guilt.

What he very possibly did not realize at the time was that in adopting this adamant position, he was foreclosing a possibility that is the principal theme of this book—the possibility that his son was *not* killed during or shortly after the kidnaping! In refusing to consider the reports brought to him by John Hughes Curtis, in assuming that the so-called confession of the Norfolk shipbuilder was a hoax, he cut off what could have been an important source of information, as he had earlier in abandoning the New Haven search.

In tracing the twelve-year search of Harold Olsen, the Connecticut computer salesman, whose ancestry is clouded with uncertainties, several possibilities will emerge which may cast a new light on the events of March 1, 1932 and the unanswered question: What really happened to the Lindbergh baby?

Meanwhile we can return to the events that followed the Flemington trial and the imposition of sentence by Judge Trenchard, which occurred immediately after the jury's verdict came in—almost as if the judge feared the jury might retract the verdict and wanted the whole matter settled as soon as possible.

Lloyd Fisher's last words to Bruno when he was led from the courtroom were, "Remember, this is only the beginning."

It was the end of Edward J. Reilly's association with the case, however. He submitted a bill for $25,000, and after some consultation with the other attorneys and Hauptmann, Anna Hauptmann wrote a letter telling him he was fired. Fisher, Pope, and Rosecrans were left to carry the appeal to New Jersey's highest court.

The appeal was filed on February 21, 1935. Judge Trenchard had set the week of March 18 for the execution, and it was necessary to file a transcript of the testimony by March 12. Carrying out the sentence was delayed automatically until the Court of Appeals heard the case. Throughout the summer of high court considered the appeal, and on October 9 the court sustained the jury's verdict. A week later a second delay in carrying out the sentence was ordered when defense counsel petitioned the United States Supreme Court to review the case.

During the spring, summer, and early fall Bruno Hauptmann sat in his jail cell in Trenton, near the electric chair, with plenty of time to consider the alternatives—to admit guilt and ask for a reduced sentence, or fight to the bitter end.

About this time two events occurred: Governor Harold Hoffman of New Jersey, after a long talk with Hauptmann in his jail cell, decided to ask for a stay of execution to permit a post-trial investigation; and Paul H. Wendel, a Trenton lawyer, confessed he had kidnaped the Lindbergh baby! The first event occurred in December, 1935; the second was on March 27 of the following year.

17

Governor Hoffman's Interview

Early in October, 1935, after the Court of Appeals had rejected Hauptmann's petition for a new trial, Col. Mark O. Kimberling, warden of the State prison at Trenton, walked into Governor Hoffman's office at the State Capitol and said, "Governor, Hauptmann has asked to see you."

The Governor, a middle-sized, rather plump man, then thirty-nine years old, said, "Me see Hauptmann, Mark? What for?"

"I don't know. He keeps asking for you."

Hoffman, in his own record of his investigation, says he had believed at the time that Hauptmann was guilty, that the jurors at Flemington had returned a fair verdict. But Hauptmann's request that the Governor visit his cell nagged at him. What particularly disturbed him was a remark made by Ellis Parker, the chief of detectives of Burlington County, a friend of Hoffman and regarded as the dean of detectives in New Jersey— the "country detective" who had displayed in more than forty years of public service an uncanny ability to ferret out the guilty in hundreds of criminal investigations. The previous Governor, A. Harry Moore, had asked Parker to investigate the Lindbergh case, and shortly after Hauptmann's arrest, Parker said to Hoffman, "Harold, they've got the wrong man!"

Parker later produced the confession of Paul Wendel, and Parker and his son and three others were sent to jail after Wendel repudiated his confession—which will be discussed in detail in the following chapters. This served to render Parker's opinion a bit dubious. But at the time he spoke to Hoffman, the Wendel affair had not occurred.

Hoffman, acting partly on Parker's comment, decided to visit Hauptmann in his jail cell, thus unleashing a storm of public abuse by those who believed in the jury's verdict, and some undesired approbation by those who did not believe Hauptmann was guilty. Between these extremes there was a considerable number who thought Hauptmann was involved in the extortion scheme, but did not believe he had carried out the kidnaping alone. This view was probably expressed as well as possible by a friend of Evalyn Walsh McLean, the Washington lady who had been bilked of $100,000 by Gaston Means. He was Nugent Dobbs, a former Assistant Attorney General of the United States. Mrs. McLean, in a discussion at Friendship House, had asked Dobbs, "Are you completely satisfied that the Lindbergh case is completely solved by Hauptmann's conviction?"

"No, I am not."

She asked what Dobbs thought about the Hauptmann trial.

"It wasn't a trial. It was a courtroom lynching."

Mrs. McLean telephoned Governor Hoffman asking if he would meet Dodds; he said he would. After consulting with Hoffman, Dodds talked with Lloyd Fisher, and as a result it was agreed he would carry the Hauptmann appeal to the United States Supreme Court. Dodds and Fisher had several meetings with Hauptmann in his jail cell. Later he reported on these meetings to Mrs. McLean.

"Let me tell you one thing Hauptmann said when I talked with him, one thing more important than anything else that passed between us. I talked about the case, considered some points on which to base legal action, and found him apparently bewildered and confused. But when I was about to leave, he said, 'Mr. Dodds, if you do not believe I am innocent, you can do me no good at all, and you might as well stop right now!'"

There is much in Governor Hoffman's report on his own interview with Hauptmann that appears to bear on this point. He had received a telephone call from Charles Curtis, former Vice President of the United States under Herbert Hoover.

"Governor, are you looking into this Hauptmann case?"

Hoffman said he had not been particularly interested; the jury had returned its verdict and it was sustained by the New Jersey Court of Appeals. The matter would shortly come before the Board of Pardons, of which Hoffman was a member.

"I think," Curtis said, "there are a lot of funny things about that case. I've read a lot of the testimony, and it doesn't seem to me he was adequately represented, or that he got a very fair deal." It was at this point that Curtis advised Hoffman to see Mrs. McLean.

Governor Hoffman began to think over what had happened. He knew Evalyn Walsh McLean and the story of how she was fleeced out of $100,000 by Gaston Means, who claimed he had returned the money while driving across the Potomac River bridge. He also recalled how another man, Jafsie Condon, had left Lindbergh sitting alone in his car and taken $50,000 into a Bronx cemetery to hand to the mysterious "John," over a graveyard hedge.

It suddenly struck Hoffman that both stories were somewhat similar, except that one sent a man to the Federal prison at Leavenworth and the other made the teller of the tale a public benefactor. He began to think more seriously about visiting Hauptmann in his jail cell.

It occurred to the Governor that Hauptmann's request to see him might also mean that he had thawed.

He had been portrayed in newspaper accounts as a man with nerves of steel, of infinite coldness, who would never crack. Perhaps, as he faced almost certain death in the electric chair, he had decided to tell all.

He called Colonel Kimberling.

"Mark, I'm coming down to see that fellow. Will tonight be O.K.?" Kimberling said it would.

Hoffman called Mrs. Anna Bading, for many years secretary to Ellis Parker, and asked her to meet him within an hour at the office of Colonel Kimberling, to take notes. There was considerable speculation later about this meeting. Mrs. Bading was portrayed as a mysterious woman wearing a trenchcoat who accompanied Hoffman to Hauptmann's jail cell, as if he were displaying the convicted killer to society women. As Hoffman explained later she wore Colonel Kimberling's coat because she was at a party dressed in formal attire when the Governor called, and she said, "Governor, I simply can't walk into the cell dressed like this!"

If Hoffmann had expected an admission of guilt, he was disappointed. He found Hauptmann sitting on his cot, and sat down beside him. The prisoner was in a blue-gray shirt, and dark prison pants. On a table were a bible, several books on philosophy, pictures of his wife and son, and a paper-covered set of volumes containing all the testimony taken at the Flemington Trial. Hauptmann turned toward the Governor, looking straight into Hoffman's eyes, and said, "Guv'ner, why does your State do to me all this? Why do they want my life for something somebody else has done?"

Hoffman remarked that the jury had found him guilty.

"Lies! All lies! Would I kill a baby? I am a man. Would I build that ladder? I am a carpenter!"

Hoffman was quickly convinced that he would hear no confession, no appeal for clemency, or terms of a proposed bargain. Hauptmann's "most earnest plea" was for the use of a lie-detector.

"Why won't they use on me that? And on Doctor Condon? They have too some kind of drugs. . .why don't they use on me that drug? And on Doctor Condon use it, too."

Hoffman's first interview increased the doubts in his mind. As he wrote: "Here was no cringing criminal pitifully begging for mercy, but a man making a vehement claim of innocence, bitter in his denunciation of the police and the prosecution and their methods. And bitter, too, in his excoriation of his former chief counsel, Reilly."

Hauptmann seemed to echo the words of former Vice President Curtis, "Could a man do for dollars what Reilly has done to me? Only once, for about five minutes, did I have a chance to explain my case to him, really. Sometimes he came to see me, not often, for a few minutes. How could I talk to him?"

Hauptmann's opinion of Reilly, incidentally, was shared by his sister, Mrs. Emma Gloeckner. When I first interviewed her in her West Hollywood home on July 8, 1935—while Hauptmann's first appeal was being considered in New Jersey—she seemed bitter against all lawyers.

"After my brother's trial I went to New Jersey and talked with the attorney's about certain things which did not come out in the trial. Mr. Fisher said that all the defense lawyers had agreed the child found was not the Lindbergh baby, but when this came up Mr. Reilly, then the chief defense counsel, stood up and said the defense would stipulate it was the Lindbergh baby.

"The other lawyers walked out of court. Why didn't they tell the judge that it was not the wish of my brother or the other lawyers? When these lawyers came before the New Jersey Supreme Court (Court of Appeals) they were asked why they did not raise objections to these things, and their answer was, 'Mr. Reilly was the chief counsel.' Were they not there to protect my brother's interests?''

In a later statement which Mrs. Gloeckner made when I visited her with Vincent Marco, her attorney, on the night Hauptmann was to be executed, she was even more vehement.

''I do now know the law, and Richard did not know. But I know people want the truth, and there were facts that did not come out at the trial, facts which would have shown my brother was not guilty. My brother was tried in newspapers, and when he came to court everybody heard only one side. His lawyer should have seen to it that other evidence was known, but instead they quarrelled.''

These remarks, of course, were from a person vitally interested in Hauptmann's case and were made on the evening of Hauptmann's execution. The last cry of a despairing woman who believed her brother was a victim of a newspaper trial and a frame-up, and saw no hope of saving him from the electric chair.

During the interview with Hauptmann, Governor Hoffman found out certain things which probably prompted him to try to reopen the case.

''Why did they take from me all my shoes? When I was arrested they took, among many things, all my shoes. What for I could not imagine, but now I have found out. Because they have a footprint. . .''

He had studied the transcript well; he spoke of the smaller footprint which Corporal Wolf has described and which evidently was that of Anne Lindbergh.

''But there was, too, a footprint of a man, who, according to the prosecutor, climbed the ladder to get to the unfortunate child. It was to me a riddle, for, said the prosecutor, it was many feet and all soft earth from the window to where the ladder was found—how could it have been but one footprint? Why did they not produce at the trial the impression of which they cast a mold? Why? They cannot say my footprint has become larger or smaller! So, too, in the graveyard where Doctor

Condon swore he gave to John fifty thousand dollars. My shoe certainly did not fit. Why did they not produce the plaster model that was made? Does anyone think these footprints have been held back out of pity for me? Oh, no. For me, no pity!''

He continued talking, switching to fingerprints.

"Is it not true that in every case when a person is arrested they take fingerprints? So they did with me. A few days after two New Jersey State Police came to me and wanted further prints. I told them these had already been taken. These men replied that the ones they took were not clear enough, so they take about six sets. Then one or two days later they come again saying there were still several spots not plain enough. They took also the side of my hand, and especially the joints of the fingers and hollow parts of my hand.

"At the trial, when my counsel asked about finger-prints, the prosecutor say simply, 'There are no finger-prints.' If that is so, no fingerprints on the ladder, on the letters, on the window, in the room, why would they want so many of my fingerprints? I can only think they have fingerprints, but they are not like mine, so they say they have none.''

He mentioned Dr. Mead Hudson.

"He took many fingerprints from the ladder, but there were nowhere any of mine. The jury would not believe this expert because he would not say anything to convict me.''

Hauptmann became sarcastic in his analysis of the evidence.

"They invent another story. They say I have worked with gloves. Is this not a worthless lie? Because since in that room they found no other fingerprints—not of the parents, or the child's nurse or other servants—can this statement be possible? It is even said Mrs. Lindbergh and the nurse, Betty, pulled down the window which was stuck, but there were no fingerprints on the window frame. Do the parents, when they go into the room to take joy in their child, and all the servants, also wear gloves?''

It was on the basis of Hoffman's first interview with Hauptmann that the Governor decided to re-investigate the case, a decision for which he was pilloried in the press. Even George Waller, writing a quarter of a century afterward, expressed the opinion that Hoffman's decision was politically motivated. In *Kidnap* Waller hardly touched on the interview with Hauptmann, although he devoted a dozen pages to the departure of the Lindberghs for England.

In Governor Hoffman's report of the interview, he remarked on the number of times Hauptmann returned to the subject of the ladder.

''Is it not unbelievable that to make one support for the ladder, out of six, I would have from the floor in my own house tear up one of the boards? This is what they call 'Rail 16.' In the first place, it had in it some large knots which alone would prevent a carpenter from making a ladder of it. It is not altogether a ladder— it is a wooden rack. Its construction shows it did not come from the hand of a carpenter, not even a poor one.''

Anna Bading's transcription of Hauptmann's words may have infused some Germanic inflections into the text, but his meaning was quite clear.

''It was said to the jury, by experts, that it came from my house. Whether it really came from my house I do not know, but I make responsible the persons who were there after my Annie left the house.''

Hauptmann arose from the cot and stood before the Governor.

''Listen,'' he said. ''Wilentz says I am a smart criminal. He says on these hands I must have worn gloves, because there are no fingerprints. He says on these feet I must have worn bags, because there are no footprints. If I was a smart criminal, if I would do all those things, why would I go in my own house and take

200

half of one board to use for one piece of the ladder—something that always would be evidence against me? If I wanted to make a ladder, could I not get around my yard and my garage all the wood like that I would need? I have lots of boards like that. Besides, only about one block from my house is a lumber yard where for a few cents I could buy such a board."

Hauptmann seemed particularly bitter when he denounced Koehler, the State's wood expert, for having improvised his testimony. He noted that the grain of wood and the marks of the cutting saw could be found on thousands of feet of lumber shipped from the Dorn mills in South Carolina to lumber yards in the North.

"Why would the jury believe Koehler?. . .I know why!" His eyes wandered to the electric chair, covered with white cloth and in range of his vision. "The poor child has been kidnaped and murdered, so somebody must die for it. Is the parent not a great flyer? And if somebody does not die for the death of the child, then always the police will be monkeys. So I am the one who is picked out to die."

Hauptmann's words may have been simplistic; but they struck many of the points which Hoffman, who now had studied the case, had begun to suspect. They were the same questions asked by Mrs. McLean, and later by others who had studied the case. Was the entire story told at Flemington? There was the matter of Lindbergh ransom bills that were passed by people other than Hauptmann. He arose again from his cot, and picked up the transcripts of the trial testimony, with many of Hauptmann's markings in the margins.

"Guv'ner, if you have been a man who was picked up with some of the Lindbergh money—even though that money has passed through ten hands before it came to you—I think some of these men would prove from your writings that you were the one who has written the ransom letters."

The Governor's report told of Hauptmann's

201

explanation of his relations with Isidor Fisch, which corresponded with the story he told at the trial. He said he met Fisch in March or April of 1932 at Hunter's Island. Fisch said he was interested in the stock market and said he was in the fur business, and suggested a partnership. They carried on transactions for more than a year, selling the furs and reinvesting the profits. Then Fisch grew more sickly, and decided to return to Germany.

"He asks me when he goes to Germany if he can leave with me some of his belongings."

Hauptmann said he agreed, and went to Fisch's room and took two satchels. Fisch said there was not much in them, "only old stuff," and suggested Hauptmann put them in his garage. Then at the farewell party, before Fisch left for Germany, he brought a cardboard box and asked Hauptmann to keep it until he came back from Germany.

"I thought maybe in the box were some things he forgot to put in the satchels, maybe papers and letters, so I put the package on the upper shelf of the broom closet."

At this time neither Hauptmann nor Hoffman knew what Mrs. McLean later revealed: that the closet had been repainted and the shelf moved to a lower position, where it could readily be seen by Mrs. Hauptmann, during the time Lieutenant Bornmann and New York detectives were in the apartment.

"Even up to that time (before he was arrested) I had not thought of the little box, but three or four weeks before I got arrested it has been raining and the water comes into the broom closet and I run across the box soaking wet. When I look I find it is full of money. I say to myself, 'That is where Isidor's money has gone!' What he has saved he has put in gold certificates to be safe. I put it in a pail and took it to my garage, where I dried it and hid it, like the police found it, except for the few bills I have spent. I did not put it in the bank because with gold certificates I think I should have trouble."

He recited the incident at the gas station, when he passed one of the Lindbergh bills.

"Could I have known that money was the Lindbergh baby money? No! How could any sensible person think that? Was it not testified at the trial, and truly so, that to the gasoline station man when I gave the bill, 'I have a hundred more like that'? Would I say that if I knew that these bills maybe could take my life some day?"

Hauptmann also had something to say about the mysterious J. J. Faulkner.

"Why don't the police keep on looking for the man Faulkner, who deposit nearly $3,000 of the Colonel's money? Why is it just me they want for the death of the poor child?. . .Why do they try to prove I have spent $50,000 when only maybe $15,000 has been found?"

Hauptmann's bitterest comments were reserved for Jafsie Condon. He told Hoffman that Condon occupied a small shack as a real estate office on City Island, where Hauptmann and his friends went three or four times a week, during the summers of 1932, 1933, and 1934. To reach his real estate office, Condon had to pass the Dixon boathouse, where Hauptmann kept a canoe. Hoffman wrote: "Hauptmann could not conceive that three full seasons could have passed, with both Condon and himself frequenting this place so continuously, without an identification."

He quotes Hauptmann as saying, "How could anybody believe that when Doctor Condon was looking all over the country for 'John' who he now says is me, without coming face to face with me?"

He referred to Condon's statement at the trial that once he was riding on a bus and saw "John" and jumped off the bus, but could not catch the man.

"When 'John' was walking along the street he was on top of a bus, yet on City Island nearly every day he would not see me and pick me out as 'John.' If I was the kidnaper and I got the money from Doctor Condon, would I not know, too, that the Doctor was in City Island many, many times? And would I not have stayed away from City Island because I would have been afraid of being identified by Condon?''

Hauptmann appeared to be quite confused about many of Condon's statements, and about certain phrases of the prosecution's case—which, indeed, was confusing to many who studied the events of the trial. But he was not confused about Condon's role, according to Hoffman's account. He told about Condon's visit to his cell during the time he was held in Hunterdon County Jail.

"He said if I know anything I should confess, because if there was no connection between the money and the kidnaping I would clear myself and himself. He said the police were treating him roughly. But he never said I am the fellow. . ."

This statement, if the account is true, will have some importance in a review of the various theories of the Lindbergh case in the concluding chapters. Condon's role in the Lindbergh case, always mysterious, becomes less so if the theory that he was somehow involved in the extortion plot is considered. Hauptmann's discussion with the Brooklyn schoolteacher, reviewed in the latter light, becomes more significant.

Condon's statement, after he left Hauptmann's jail cell, that he would "not testify against that man" was more than revealing. It enlarges on the possibility that Condon was picked in advance by the extortionists, who knew him, and knew his penchant for publicity and his desire to be regarded as a citizen who reveled in "good works.''

Hauptmann, under Governor Hoffman's questioning, disclosed his own version of practically every accusation the State had brought against him. The Governor later wrote:

I could not answer many of Hauptmann's questions. I, too, was to start on a trail rough with bitterness and censure, searching for answers to the same questions— and some others that were beginning to form in my mind.

I, too, was to feel some of the futility of the search, to sense that indefinable, mysterious force threatening to destroy any one who dared to question that the Lindbergh crime had been solved and that full and complete justice had been meted out to all participants.

Governor Hoffman left Hauptmann's jail cell, not necessarily convinced of Hauptmann's innocence, but committed to pursue the investigation in the belief that there was more to the story than had been disclosed at the Flemington trial.

18

The Post-trial Investigation

Most of the vocal public—newspapers, radio commentators, politicians, and, of course, George Waller, who researched the case many years later—held to the view that Governor Hoffman's role in the Lindbergh case was politically motivated. He was a Republican, and David Wilentz, who would probably run for the Governorship on his record of having convicted Hauptmann, was a Democrat.

From the day Hoffman first indicated he would like to reopen the Lindbergh case, and when he subsequently reprieved Hauptmann on January 16, 1936, for a period of thirty days to permit time to complete the investigation, he was hounded by those who wanted the case bottled up and forgotten.

He said he had never expressed the belief that Hauptmann was innocent or guilty. The jury had made that decision, and it was on their own conscience. But he added that in the face of "carping criticism, misstatements, rumors, and even threats" he had followed the dictates of his own conscience and judgement. As Governor of the state, he would use his full power to see that ultimate justice was done—and this could only be through keeping Hauptmann alive until all questions had been resolved.

He noted that the American Bar Association, meeting in Los Angeles, had appointed a special committee to investigate the conduct of the Hauptmann trial, and except for certain passages which condemned the Governor's "interference" and "deplored" his "search for publicity," the report was "almost a textbook for the conduct of my own investigation." It condemned the conduct of the trial, castigated the press for making the proceedings a "madhouse of publicity" and stated in conclusion that a fair trial under such conditions was impossible.

Hoffman's investigation was more specific. He listed, in a letter to Colonel Schwarzkopf, as head of the state police, the points on which he wanted further investigation:

First, there was Dr. Condon. The Governor had received an affidavit from a source he declined to reveal —evidently a State Trooper—declaring that after Condon had failed to identify Hauptmann as "John" at the Greenwich Street police station, he had been told that if he did not say positively that Hauptmann was "John," he would be indicted as an accessory after the fact. Was this true?

Second, there was the question of Isidor Fisch. Hauptmann had left several letters in his apartment from Isidor's brother, Pincus Fisch, written to him after Isidor died in Germany. These were listed in the Department of Justice inventory of what was left in the Hauptmann apartment, and might have helped Hauptmann establish part of his case. But they were not produced by the police at the trial. Why not?

Third, there was the ladder. Kohler's testimony, which Wilentz said he would use to "hang the ladder around Hauptmann's neck," was of value only if Hauptmann had taken a length from the attic floorboard used for "Rail 16," and there was considerable doubt about this. The evidence may have been tampered with by the police. Was this true?

Fourth, the testimony of the handwriting experts produced by the prosecution was subject to serious challenge; the original letter from the kidnapers had not been adequately investigated, and other evidence was so conflicting—depending on which side produced the testimony—that the entire matter should be reviewed.

Other questions were even more specific:

Had the police tried to identify the man who said "*Statto citti!*"—"Shut up!"—when "John" was talking to Condon on the telephone?

Who was the Italian woman who spoke to Condon at the antique sale, telling Condon to meet her at the Tuckahoe station? Had the police followed up on this?

Condon had reported to police that he was offered a $25,000 bribe to say Isidor Fisch was "John." This happened when Hauptmann was in jail, so it had to be someone else. Had the police followed up on this?

Why had the State changed from a gang theory of kidnaping—to which not only Condon but Lindbergh and the police originally agreed—to a lone kidnaper theory?

Hoffman summarized this line of questions with a question. "Is Dr. Condon, whose word was so greatly relied on by the prosecution, to be believed when he says, 'I am still convinced that more than one person is involved in this crime?'"

As a final point, Hoffman referred to J. J. Faulkner, who had deposited $2,980 in Lindbergh ransom money. Why had the search for him been abandoned?

After studying these questions, Schwarzkopf telephoned Wilentz and found he had received a similar letter. Wilentz' reply was quite simple. Hauptmann, and Hauptmann alone, was guilty of the crime. All other questions were irrelevant.

Wilentz' reply to the Governor's letter—which was not only unresponsive, but as political as anything the newspapers and other critics had said was Hoffman's motive—did not deter Hoffman from pursuing his investigation. He called in Lieutenant Robert W. Hicks, the Washington criminologist, to carry on further inquiries. Mrs. McLean had retained Hicks for the same purpose, and persuaded him to lease the apartment formerly occupied by Hauptmann, and later by Bornmann, the New Jersey detective.

Hoffman meanwhile issued a brief to Schwarzkopf detailing more explicitly what questions he wanted answered, and stressing the fact that John Hughes Curtis, the Norfolk shipbuilder, had been tried and convicted on the ground that he was in touch with a gang of kidnapers and had impeded the forces of law enforcement by his interference. How did the State answer that one?

The Governor mentioned to Schwarzkopf that he understood Curtis had been brought to Philadelphia by New Jersey police—since Curtis seemed to be allergic to Jersey justice—who tried to persuade him to admit that the "John" of Curtis' dealings was not the same as Hauptmann, which Curtis refused to do. Was this the reason that Curtis' affidavit, stating that he had recognized "John" as Bruno Hauptmann, was not used in the trial? Because it did not fit into the lone kidnaper theory?

Hoffman also asked Schwarzkopf a very significant question. "Was the State right when they obtained a conviction of Curtis based on obstructing justice after having contacted the gang of kidnapers, or was the State right in prosecuting Hauptmann as the lone wolf? The prosecution had to have been wrong in one of these instances. . . .Would it not be desirable to make further inquiry into this very important issue, on which some significant conflicts in testimony seemed to exist?"

What, for example, happened to the state police inquiry into the case of Violet Sharpe? Was her suicide coincidental, or she was involved in the crime, as Inspector Harry Walsh had indicated, and as Schwarzkopf himself had stated during the early investigation? If they still felt the same way, why had the prosecution persisted in the lone kidnaper theory?

Hoffman was born in South Amboy, New Jersey, an

area hard by the Democratic domain of Mayor Frank Hague of Jersey City. He entered political skirmishes when he was twenty-five and cut his political teeth in one of the toughest arenas—a Republican running for office in a Hague-dominated district. Two years after winning the South Amboy mayorality race he ran for Congress and won. He was elected Governor of New Jersey in 1934 in the face of a Democratic landslide that swept the country.

It was hardly likely that he would permit his questions on the Hauptmann case—there were nineteen of them—to be answered by David Wilentz' statement that "only Hauptmann" had committed the Lindbergh crime.

The Governor's first visit to Hauptmann had been on October 16, 1935, and it was the following December 6 before his visit became known publicly. In spite of this, the New York and New Jersey newspapers accused him of seeking publicity in his visit to the convicted killer of the Lindbergh baby. Even the Perby Amboy *Evening News,* a paper on which he had once worked as a reporter, accused him of "impropriety."

On December 7 Hoffman issued a statement to the newspapers explaining the reasons for entering the case. "The case of Bruno Richard Hauptmann is one with which the dimensions of American justice will be measured by all Americans and by the world. . . . There have been countless rumors in circulation, some alleging the existence of evidence not presented at the trial. If the defendant in this case is guilty beyond a reasonable doubt, he must pay the penalty demanded by the law. If he is not guilty, he should not be punished."

The point immediately raised was that the jury had found him guilty, so why "interfere with the orderly processes of law?" It was a ticklish point, but Hoffman had read the transcript of the trial carefully, and he had requested reports not previously made public—police records of the questions asked of Condon, Whited,

Hochmuth and others. He was convinced the complete story had not been told, and in some respects had been suppressed at the Flemington trial.

"I had no funds to conduct an investigation," he wrote later. "It had cost over a million dollars to put Hauptmann behind the bars awaiting death, but I did not have a single dollar of state funds available."

On December 13, after the Supreme Court had ruled against his appeal, Judge Trenchard set the date of Hauptmann's execution, for the week of January 13, 1936. A few days later while in Washington on state business, the Governor called on Mrs. McLean at Friendship House. She told him her telephone call to him had been prompted by a gathering at her home of several United States Senators, and "according to Mrs. McLean they were unanimous in agreeing that the trial had not been fair and the solution was not complete." She had persuaded former Vice President Curtis to make the call that first stirred Hoffman to action.

"They told me that Governor Hoffman wouldn't dare go into this matter, and I said, 'Well, if Governor Hoffman won't, I'll go to the President!'" She added something that Governor Hoffman later said he had almost forgotten.

"You will recall, Governor, that I called you and warned you that my friends had said the case should be investigated, but that anyone who had nerve enough to do this would ruin his political future."

This turned out to be a prophetic statement, but it is doubtful at the time that Hoffman realized this. What is of curious significance is that this threat from various not clearly defined sources has persisted to this day. This point will be discussed in detail in the following chapters in which Harold Olson's twelve-year search to find out whether or not he is the supposedly dead Lindbergh's son repeatedly came up against blank walls and several vague threats if Olson persisted in his search.

Two days before Christmas of 1935, Hauptmann filed a petition before the last tribunal of hope—the New Jersey Court of Pardons, of which Hoffman was a member. On January 11, 1936, the Court of Pardons refused to grant his appeal for reduction of his sentence to life imprisonment, and Colonel Kimberling set the date of execution for January 17.

Hoffman notes in his written record that on the date set for execution—later delayed by the Governor's thirty-day reprieve—not a single person who had been in the Lindbergh home at Hopewell on March 1, 1932, when the baby was abducted, were still in the United States. He listed them:

The butler, Oliver Whateley, had died in a Princeton hospital.

Betty Gow, the baby's nurse, was in Scotland.

Elsie Whateley, the butler's wife, was in Wales.

The Lindberghs had left the United States for England on the SS. *American Exporter* a few days before Christmas.

In addition, Mrs. Elizabeth Morrow, the baby's grandmother, was in London, and Violet Sharpe, the maid in the Morrow home, had committed suicide.

Even Dr. Condon had left the country with his daughter, Myra, for a vacation in Panama. Hoffman writes of this:

> Just a week before Bruno Richard Hauptmann was slated to die, the newspapers and radio brought the word that Doctor Condon—Jafsie, who had thrust himself into the Lindbergh case; Jafsie of the Bronx, who had contacted the kidnaper through an ad (actually a letter) in a neighborhood newspaper; Jafsie of the safety pins and sleeping suit; Jafsie who had talked with John on a bench in the Woodlawn Cemetery; Jafsie who had handed the $50,000 over a hedge at St. Raymonds; Jafsie who had finally identified Hauptmann and sent him on his way to the chair—had suddenly sailed with his daughter for Panama.

On the night of January 15, two days before Hauptmann was scheduled to die, Hoffman and Wilentz met in the Hotel New Yorker in New York City. The Governor expressed his reasons for wanting to delay the execution. In his summary of the investigation which he later wrote for *Liberty*, he said:

> I gave him (Wilentz) frankly my appraisal of the value of the State's identification witnesses, the things I considered as evidence that should have been presented, the position in which I had been placed by misrepresentation.
>
> There were some things I could not tell him, facts that will be given later in this series; but I gave him what I felt then to be the important reasons why the man should be permitted to live, and the investigation, with all the resources of the police, continued.

The attorney general outlined the principal points of the prosecution's case: the Condon telephone number on Hauptmann's (apartment) door, "admittedly written by him;" the "b-o-a-d" spelling of the word "boat" in the ransom notes.

"Even assuming that the State's principal identification witnesses might have been untruthful, he felt there was sufficient evidence to warrant conviction," Hoffman wrote.

Hoffman noted that this evidence would support "only the crime of extortion." Even if unanswerable, the evidence would not put Hauptmann at the scene of the kidnaping and murder.

The Governor's account offers an interesting study of the working of Wilentz' mind. His entire prosecution was predicated on the accusation of Hauptmann murdering the Lindbergh child; without that proof Wilentz could not have obtained a conviction under New Jersey law. Yet he was willing to say that even without the identification witnesses, placing Hauptmann at the scene of the crime, he could have secured a conviction!

No more explicit statement could have been made that the Flemington trial was a courtroom lynching fomented by the newspapers and radio coverage, confirming the opinion of *Editor and Publisher,* as well as many notable legal minds, that it was a "degradation" of the American system of justice.

It was at this point that Wilentz' real motivation became apparent. Hoffman quotes him as saying, "Then why in hell doesn't he tell the truth?"

What if he was telling the truth!

Hoffman and Wilentz agreed upon a plan. Hoffman would talk to Anna Hauptmann, offering her an opportunity to save her husband from the electric chair by persuading him to tell all. This, in effect, was an admission by the attorney general that the trial had not brought to light all the facts. In fact, it was an admission that prosecuting the case was unfounded.

The way in which this plan was carried out, along with Nugent Dobbs' comment to Mrs. McLean in which he quotes Hauptmann saying, "Mr. Dobbs, if you do not believe I am innocent, you can do me no good at all!" presents possibly the most convincing substantiation of Hauptmann's claim that he was framed.

When Governor Hoffman called on Mrs. Hauptmann at the apartment she had leased in Trenton, he said, "Mrs. Hauptmann, tomorrow is the day when, under the law, your husband is to die. I want to help him, but he has not been telling me—or anyone else—the truth."

Mrs. Hauptmann screamed, "No! No! No! That isn't so! Richard did tell the truth!" She suddenly clenched her fists and began to beat on the Governor's chest. "Listen to me, Gove'nor, listen to me!"

Hoffman had agreed with Wilentz the night before that "getting the truth" was as important as Hauptmann's life—to "learn how this unknown Bronx carpenter could have obtained the information that the

Lindbergh family would be in Hopewell, for the first time, on Tuesday night (March 1, 1932), how he could have known about the unlocked window, the broken shutters, the layout of the nursery, how he could have executed the astounding feat of scaling that rickety ladder—climbing to the window after balancing himself on the top rung of that ladder, thirty inches below the window ledge, how he could have skillfully avoided disturbing the stein on the window sill, the toy on top of the suitcase, the suitcase itself.

"It was important to learn how Hauptmann, if it was Hauptmann, could have carried the baby, alive or dead, out of its crib, otherwise undisturbed, and on through the window. It was vitally important to learn how, with his bundle, he could have closed the window after leaving the note upon the window sill, how he could have fallen from the broken ladder without leaving the imprint of his body upon the soft earth, why he would have stopped, under the circumstances, to carry the telltale ladder seventy-five feet away from the house.

"It was important to know how he could have eliminated all fingerprints from the nursery, the ladder, all the ransom notes, how he could have disguised his footprints. It was important to learn how, for two years, he could have baffled the best police brains in the country until he was picked up through the chance precaution of a gasoline-station attendant; how he could have disposed of $35,000 of ransom bills—as they 'proved' he did at Flemington—without any of these bills, long in circulation, being picked up in any of the banks or by the Treasury Department. . ."

The answer is, of course—as Hoffman must have expected—that an unknown Bronx carpenter could not have done these things. Only the one-track mind of a New Jersey prosecutor, obsessed by the conviction that Hauptmann was somehow guilty, could have rationally entertained this series of impossible happenings, and believed he did them alone.

Hoffman continued with his account of his meeting with the wife of the convicted prisoner, "Things look bad for your husband. Everyone believes he is guilty. There is only one way in which he can save his life."

"What way is that?"

The Governor told her of his meeting in New York with David Wilentz, the prosecutor and state attorney general. "He thinks it is important, and I do, too, to get the whole story of how this happened. If your husband committed this crime—"

"He didn't! He didn't! I tell you—he couldn't do it!"

Once again she tightened her fists, and seemed to attack the Governor again. He waved to her to sit in a chair. Then he explained that nobody believed Hauptmann's story about how he came into possession of the Lindbergh ransom bills.

He promised that he and Wilentz would go before the Court of Pardons and ask for a reduction of his sentence to life imprisonment, which would be granted by the court, providing Hauptmann told the whole story. His next words, he said, brought her shrieking from her chair. He said, "You must go to the prison this morning. You must tell your husband he can save his life. You must tell him you want him to tell the truth."

"No! No! No! I couldn't do that! He would turn his back on me. He would think that the last one in the world to know he is innocent should think, too, that he has committed this crime."

She stopped; her eyes were red from crying, a woman —as Hoffman wrote—"who was either telling the truth that burned deeply in her heart, or was staging a scene that would dwarf any of the great actresses that had appeared on the American stage."

"My husband has only a few hours to live! Could I do that to him—make him think that I, like that judge— like that jury—believe, too, he would kill a baby? Would I make Richard think that I, too, have believed those lying witnesses who for money would send a good

216

fully did Wendel adhere to the state's theory of a lone kidnaper. The document described in a rambling way how Wendel had taken Lindbergh's son from his crib, crawled down the ladder and taken the baby to an apartment in Trenton. When Wendel returned, after a brief trip, he found the child was ill.

After several days had passed, he returned one day and found the baby had fallen out of the crib, fractured its skull, and was dead. One weak point among many in Wendel's account, was his story of having taken the body back to the area near the Lindbergh estate and buried it in a shallow grave. The body was badly decomposed when it was found, and, as previously noted, was four-and-a-third inches longer than the Lindbergh baby, and probably had been embalmed.

The confession had two important results, however. First, it threatened to delay Hauptmann's execution. Wilentz realized this, and promptly sent a wire to Ellis Parker in Burlington asking him to arrest Wendel and deliver him to Trenton, the State's capital. Second, and more important, it tied Isidor Fisch, the man Hauptmann said gave him the Lindbergh ransom bills, to Paul Wendel.

In justice to Wilentz, it should be noted that at the time of the trial, he probably did not know of the possible connection of Wendel and Fisch. Nevertheless, he had an opportunity to learn of it during the period immediately after the trial, when Hauptmann was in his cell awaiting execution.

During the trial, it will be recalled, Joe Dunninger and I found Karl Henkel in an apartment in the Bronx; and he told us that Isidor Fisch had been a regular attendant at the spirit church of Peter Birritella, across the street from where Henkel and Isidor Fisch lived.

Chris Cunningham, of the United Press, who was with Dunninger and me, asked Henkel if he knew that Fisch and Hauptmann were friends, and he said, "Yes, we were all friends." He then added, "Fisch was a strange sort of fellow. He lived in the house where I lived. He attended the church (the Rev. Birritella's spirit church) and said it was very interesting.''

It was at the church, according to information supplied Dunninger and me by Professor Victor, the Harlem spiritualist, that Isidor Fisch, Violet Sharpe, Ollie Whateley, and possibly Condon and J. J. Faulkner met occasionally. Years later Anthony Scaduto provided some corroboration of this account when he wrote in *Scapegoat* that Murray Bleefeld, Ellis Parker's aide, had told him: ''Isidor Fisch at one time was represented by Paul Wendel, when he was a lawyer in Trenton in a case that's on the record. . . .Isidor Fisch and Paul Wendel were connected.''

Later Bleefeld said, ''I'll show you the meaning of the connection between Wendel and Fisch. Paul Wendel gets the money from old man Condon (in St. Raymond's Cemetery). Nobody but Paul Wendel. He has the money now, but in a year or so the gold notes are called in by Roosevelt. Now if I was your lawyer, representing you in a narcotics case and got you off, and I knew you were capable of certain criminal acts, what would I do?''

According to Bleefeld's story, Wendel told Fisch he had some counterfeit money and asked Fisch if he could sell it for him. Fisch said he could, and asked for samples. When Wendel brought the money to Fisch, he recognized them as gold certificates; and since the numbers of the Lindbergh ransom notes were printed in the newspapers, Fisch probably identified them as Lindbergh bills. He did not tell Wendel that he recognized it as hot money—not counterfeit money—and made a deal to pass some of them. When Fisch had to produce clean money for the Lindbergh bills, he said to Wendel—according to Bleefeld—''Get lost, you bum—this is kidnap money!''

Wendel could not go to the police, so he got lost and Fisch had the hot money. He turned it over to his friend and partner, Hauptmann, and told him to hold it while he went to Germany. Before he died in Germany, he urged his brother, Pincus Fisch, to write to Hauptmann, which he did. The letters fell into the hands of the police, so Hauptmann was left without corroboration of his story.

This entire account might be passed off as fiction, the results of an overactive imagination, except that many parts of the story fitted into what was known. The extent to which they fitted will be discussed in the final chapters of this review.

Shortly after Wilentz sent the wire to Ellis Parker, a Mercer County detective, James Kirkham, reported to County Prosecutor Erwin Marshall that Wendel was with Ellis Parker. Marshall had recognized the name of Paul Wendel as a man indicted for embezzlement in New Jersey; Wendel meanwhile was brought to the Mercer County line by Parker to be turned over to the police, and the old warrant alleging embezzlement was served on him. Wendel had a copy of his confession when he was arrested and after reading it, Detective Kirkham put it in his pocket.

When Wilentz, accompanied by Schwarzkopf, arrived at the county jail, he shook hands with Wendel and asked him if his confession were true or false. Wendel said, "False, of course."

He said he knew nothing of the kidnaping of Lindbergh's son; he had been forced to sign the confession through fear of a mob that kidnaped him. Wilentz asked Wendel to tell him what happened; Wendel complied. He had been staying at the Hotel Stanford on 32nd Street in New York when a man came to his door and said, "De Louie wants to see you." It was the name of a New Jersey detective in Trenton; Wendel, thinking that the embezzlement charges had finally caught up with him, left with the man and was taken to Brooklyn where he said he was tied up and locked in a cellar.

After two weeks in captivity, he said, during which he

was asked to confess to kidnaping the Lindbergh baby, he gave in and signed the confession. He was taken to Mt. Holly, New Jersey, to a house he recognized as that of Ellis Parker, the Burlington County chief of detectives. According to Wendel's story, Parker warned him that he had fallen into the hands of some underworld characters, who got his confession and dumped him at Parker's house.

After several days in Parker's home, Wendel said he was persuaded by Parker to agree to the confession, plead insanity, and throw himself on the mercy of the court. Parker also mentioned, according to Wendel, that he was a close friend of Governor Hoffman; they both agreed there were unanswered questions in the Lindbergh case and Wendel would be protected.

Wilentz and Schwarzkopf listened to the story; it was probably more fantastic than the stories told at Flemington, but Wilentz apparently was not thinking of that. He felt this would delay Hauptmann's execution. He finally told Wendel they had better have his story in writing. Meanwhile a number of newspapermen were at the jail, demanding details.

The following day, Sunday, March 29, headlines in the New York and New Jersey papers screamed the news that Paul Wendel, a disbarred New Jersey lawyer, had confessed to kidnaping and killing the Lindbergh baby! On Monday, March 30, Lloyd Fisher appeared before the New Jersey Court of Pardons and asked for a stay of execution until the Wendel matter had been cleared up. By midafternoon the Court rendered its verdict. Fisher's plea was denied.

Wilentz felt this was the end of the case; Hauptmann would die in the electric chair on April 1. He had asked Hauptmann to "tell the truth"—a statement that must have burned in his conscience, since it indicated that Wilentz himself did not know *all* the truth—and Hauptmann had said he had nothing more to tell. Wilentz returned to his office in Trenton, and a telephone call from Erwin Marshall, the prosecutor of Mercer County, informed him that this was not the end. The Mercer County grand jury had met and its foreman, Allyne Freeman, had advised Marshall that Wendel's confession had made it necessary for the grand jury to determine whether to indict him for the kidnaping and murder of the Lindbergh baby!

Wilentz pondered a bit, and wondered whether the fine hand of Governor Hoffman could be discerned in this action. More probably, it was Parker. The grand jury had stipulated that the County prosecutor, Marshall, should not present the case, since he had publicly stated that he gave no credence to Wendel's confession. The only witnesses asked to appear were Ellis Parker, his son, Ellis Parker, Jr., and his secretary, Mrs. Bading.

Wilentz had several arguments on his side. According to Wendel's confession, the baby had died in Trenton, the county seat of Mercer County, but the kidnaping had been in Hunterdon County, so the Mercer grand jury could not indict him for that crime.

When Mark Kimberling, warden at the Trenton prison, heard of the action of the grand jury, he was in a quandary. It was a few minutes before eight, and preparations had been made for Hauptmann to be strapped in the electric chair. The people authorized to be present—newspapermen, officials, and others who had won the right to see Hauptmann die—were all there and ready to go down to the death chamber. He put in a call for Marshall, and found he was not even invited to the grand jury room. Finally Allyne Freeman, the foreman, telephoned. The grand jury had instructed him to ask for a forty-eight-hour postponement of the execution, while it figured out what to do about Wendel's confession.

Lloyd Fisher went to Hauptmann's cell, where two ministers were praying—the Reverend Werner, a Seventh Day Adventist, and the Reverend Matthiesen, a

Luthern, although Hauptmann did not belong to either church—and advised him of the forty-eight-hour reprieve. Hauptmann arose from his knees, his face ashen, and said, "This must be good news!"

The delay also brought some hope to Anna Hauptmann, in her apartment in Trenton.

On April 1, the grand jury in Trenton decided to drop the Wendel case. Those concerned wanted to know why. The answer was they had no bill of complaint, no warrant. It turned out Detective Kirkham had put the document in his pocket when he met Wendel at the county line, and had forgotten about it!

Wilentz finally cut through the red tape. He sent Kimberling a message announcing that Bruno Richard Hauptmann must be executed in accordance with the sentence imposed on him by Judge Trenchard, and that Governor Hoffman had no authority to grant a reprieve. At five o'clock in the afternoon of April 3, Governor Hoffman was still considering a petition by Lloyd Fisher for a reprieve, and telephoned Wilentz to come to the Governor's office. A hundred Trenton policemen and State troopers had gathered outside the prison forming a ring around the walls; more than a thousand citizens crowded as close as possible, some of them shouting imprecations at Hoffman, but most were silent.

There were four men in Cell 9: Hauptmann, Fisher, and the two ministers. The Reverend Mathiesen handed Fisher a paper on which Hauptmann had written his last statement:

I am glad my life has ended in a world that has not understood me. Soon I will be at home with my Lord, so I am dying an innocent man. Should my death serve for the purpose of abolishing capital punishment—such punishment being arrived at only by circumstantial evidence—I feel that my death has not been in vain. I am at peace with God. I repeat, I protest my innocence of the crime for which I was convicted. However I die with no malice or hatred in my heart. The love of Christ has filled my soul, and I am happy in Him.

Fisher went to the warden's office. He was told that at half-past seven Governor Hoffman had called and said there would be no further reprieve. He was now without power to grant another stay. Fisher asked the warden if he would stay the execution until Saturday night, the end of the week when Hauptmann was to die. Kimberling said, "No."

It was a quarter past eight. Kimberling turned to the witnesses assembled in his office, and said that if Hauptmann indicated that he wanted to confess, he would do everything in his power. But the rest—the newspapermen, physicians and others who had been invited to see Hauptmann die—must remain silent.

Robert Elliott, the executioner, had been testing the current into the chair, and it was this that led the Associated Press to announce Hauptmann's execution in a flash over their wires before it occurred. They had apparently tapped the wiring to the electric chair. The United Press had no such tap; they announced it on time.

At 8:44 Kimberling nodded to Elliott. The executioner spun a wheel which sent the electric current through Hauptmann's body. At the third spin of the wheel, he was pronounced dead.

On the night Hauptmann died, I was in Los Angeles, and spent the early evening at the home of Mrs. Emma Gloeckner, his sister, in West Los Angeles, with Vincent Marco, the attorney she hired in the hope of freeing her brother. After going back to the United Press office to flash the execution of Hauptmann on the Los Angeles city wire and the slow wire, I returned. Mrs. Gloeckner and her 23-year-old daughter, Mildred, were in the parlor of her tiny apartment, dry-eyed but bitter.

"Tell your people in New York to ask Mr. Wilentz

and Dr. Condon how they spent the night," she said. "My brother is dead—they cannot torture him more. But find out how Mr. Wilentz slept, will you?"

After a few seconds, she said, "When I was in New Jersey visiting my brother, he told me a very strange thing. He said, 'Emma, when they kept talking to me up in the Bronx (September 22, 1934) they asked me again and again what I had done with the baby. Why did they ask that, if they knew already that the baby was dead and where it was found?'"

This was a question that never was answered. Mrs. Gloeckner said Fisher and all the defense lawyers had agreed that the body found near Hopewell was not the Lindbergh baby, "but when this came up in court, Mr. Reilly stood up and said the defense would stipulate that it was the Lindbergh baby."

"Why was not Mr. Curtis, the man who was convicted because he contacted the kidnapers, brought to court to say whether it was my brother. The jury should have known what Mr. Curtis had to say."

She was silent for a while—a tiny, worried little woman. Her daughter continued to stroke her hand. Then she said, "Too many questions were never asked at the trial—evidence that could have proven my brother innocent. My brother is now dead, but these questions will not go away. Some day they will be answered."

It is not likely that her prophetic words will ever be answered in their entirety; most of those who might have answered them, including Hauptmann, are now dead.

One man, however, is not dead: David T. Wilentz. At the last report, he was still living at his home in Perth Amboy, New Jersey.

And the one question that will not die until it is answered. What really happened to the Lindbergh baby?

The Lindbergh case had not taken its full toll with Hauptmann's execution. Almost a month after Hauptmann died, the Mercer County grand jury had turned the matter over to District Attorney William Geoghan of Kings County, New York, in which the Bronx was located. Geoghan presented Wendel's story to the grand jury, and five men were indicted: Harry Bleefeld, who owned the house where Wendel said he was held captive; his son, Murry Bleefeld; Ellis Parker, Jr., son of the Burlington County chief of detectives, and two helpers, Harry Weiss and Martin Schlossman.

A sixth indictment was added: Ellis Parker, Sr. Governor Hoffman refused to sign the extradition papers, holding that the entire prosecution was politically motivated. Wendel took his charges to the United States Attorney General, and after studying the case, a federal grand jury indicted both Parkers, father and son, for conspiracy under the newly enacted Lindbergh law. Attorneys for the two argued that both Parkers were convinced that Wendel had kidnaped the Lindbergh baby, and had acted in the only way open to them. The jury found them guilty but recommended leniency.

Both went to prison in Lewisburg, Pennsylvania. On February 14, 1940, Ellis Parker, Sr., died in prison of a brain tumor; eighteen months later Ellis Parker, Jr., was released. Murray Bleefeld was also released after serving part of a twenty-year sentence for kidnaping; and it was he who provided Anthony Scaduto with the original information on which *Scapegoat* was based.

In the closing chapters of this review, an effort will be made to answer at least two of the many unanswered questions in the Lindbergh case, to the extent that an answer is now possible: First, what was the real motive behind the kidnaping of Lindbergh's son, and second, what really happened to the Lindbergh baby?

Part Five

SEARCH
FOR
IDENTITY

20

The Cardinal Error

Many errors, omissions, and certainly mistakes in judgment were made by the New Jersey police and by the Federal Bureau of Investigation that allowed the Lindbergh case to drag on for many years. There were two errors at the very inception of the case, however, so fundamental—and so obvious—that one wonders why they occurred. The first was the immediate assumption that the kidnaping of the Lindbergh baby and the extortion of ransom money were part of a single conspiracy; the second—and possibly the most significant—error was the hasty identification by Lindbergh himself of the body found on Mount Rose Heights as that of his son.

There was every possibility, from a legal as well as a criminological viewpoint, that the identification of the body should have been approached separately, as a matter of primary importance, if only to make it a rounded subject for later scientific analysis. When the trial of Bruno Hauptmann was shifted from New York to New Jersey where the crime took place it became even more important to establish the *corpus delicti*.

Nevertheless, David Wilentz, about to run for Governor, and Colonel Schwarzkopf, chief of State Troopers who wanted to become Attorney General, not only persuaded them to treat both cases the same but to accept the uncertain identification of the kidnaped baby. If they had not done so, it might have resulted in the entire case being thrown out of court. Indeed, this might have occurred if it had not been for the bias of Judge Trenchard, the power of a one-sided press and the ineptness of defense counsel.

The second error was linked to the first. If the body found on Mount Rose Heights was not that of the Lindbergh child—a question that was foreclosed by Reilly's stipulation that it was—the principle question was left unanswered: What really happened to the Lindbergh baby? If it was not killed near the kidnaping scene, where was it? This brings up a point that will be explored in this section of the review: not only the question whether Lindbergh's son is still alive, which has been regarded as a subject for crackpots and amateur sleuths, but a legal question involving the issue of paternity.

In following this point, it becomes necessary to review the history of Harold R. Olson's search for his own identity. Olson has disclaimed any rights to the Lindbergh estate, in a letter to Superior Court Judge S. J. Fukuoka, probate judge on the Island of Maui where the estate was probated. He wants no part of any inheritance. He merely wants to prove or disprove his Lindbergh parentage, and as noted earlier was psychologically hostile to the notion that he might have been Lindbergh's son. The idea that he was the son of Capone was equally obnoxious. His real purpose was to determine his roots.

The story of Harold Olson might be rejected on the ground that it borders on what is commonly accepted as the lunatic fringe were it not for an amazing series of coincidences, supported by the disclosure of a number of facts. The story might have been relegated to such uncertain areas as ESP and clairvoyance when it is added that it also involved 15 psychic readings by Edgar Cayce, the Virginia Beach mystic, who was asked by Lindbergh's aviator friend, Thomas Lanphier, to trace the kidnaped baby by psychic means.

A closer study of the New Haven investigation, mentioned briefly in the first chapter of this review, should

231

indicate just how close Lanphier and the FBI came to solving the Lindbergh kidnaping. The New Haven search, which the FBI decided was of "no value," was not revealed to the press or radio. It was mentioned later by Governor Hoffman, but at the time it occurred it was known, as far as can be determined, only to the FBI, Lanphier, and by extension to Lindbergh and Breckinridge; to David Kahn and his friend, Grove Seely; and to the associates of Edgar Cayce. Details of the search might have been regarded as pure fiction, or lost in the limbo that buried so many elements of the Lindbergh case—including the baby's fingerprints—had not the voluminous FBI reports contained proof that it actually took place.

In the fall of 1972, Olson was talking with Tom Valentine of the National Tattler. Valentine, an experienced reporter of Chicago gangland activities and also of psychic phenomena, told Olson about the readings by Edgar Cayce, given on March 9 to 25, 1932, at the request of Major Lanphier, who was then a Vice President of Transcontinental Air Transport (TAT), known as "The Lindbergh Line," which later became TWA.

Lanphier, on the urging of David Kahn, a member of Cayce's Virginia Beach group, had asked Cayce if he would attempt to locate the Lindbergh baby through psychic readings, a form of clairvoyance. This was March 8 or 9, 1932, and was agreed to by Lindbergh. A few days earlier Mary Gerrita, the Harlem psychic, and her common-law husband, Peter Birritella, were interviewed by Breckinridge and Schwarzkopf at Princeton Junction, so Lindbergh was not averse to using psychic sources in the search for his child.

The kidnaping was described to Cayce, and he was asked to trace the movement of the baby, giving the exact location at the "present hour"—which was March 9, 1932—and "describe the surest way to restore the child unharmed to his parents."

Left, the baby with mother Anne Morrow Lindbergh.
Sara Olson and Harold. Note the boy's turned-in foot.

Cayce was in a trance during the reading. He told of the baby being removed from the room, carried by a man with another man waiting. He did not say how the child was taken from the room, but it was lowered to the ground and taken to a car. The car drove away and "now we find there are some changes in the manner of transportation. . . .Another car is used." They headed northward toward Jersey City, through a tunnel and across New York City into Connecticut to the region of Cordova.

The location of the house where Lindbergh's son presumably was held was even more exactly described. The Cordova section was on the east side of New Haven and could be reached by following a route along Adams Street, turning right at a shingled house two tenths of a mile from the end of Adams Street, numbered 473. The baby was held in a brown house, formerly painted green, on Scharter Street, the third house from the corner. Cayce also mentioned red dirt on the paving.

Lanphier went to New Haven, enlisting the services of the FBI. According to FBI reports, they found no Adams Street or Scharter Street, nor was there a Cordova section in or near New Haven.

On March 12, 1932, they called Virginia Beach and asked for a more exact directions. Cayce seemed a bit testy when they asked for a more particular description of the Cordova section, which he later spelled Cardova. When they asked through what channels Scharter Street might be located, he said, "By going on the street, seeing the name on it. That's the way we see it!"

Asked if there were any marks on the street, he replied, "If the name's on it, that's a right good mark!"

In the earlier session, on March 9, he had referred to three men and a woman who were guarding the baby. Later he named two of these as Madge Beliance and Meglo, which he later changed to Megleo.

Cayce was asked, "Who guards the body (of the baby)?"

234

He replied, "One woman and three men who are now at home."

He was asked what means should be used to communicate with the kidnapers without harming the baby?

He replied, "Someone who may make arrangements, or agreements, for the release or return without injury to the body."

"Is it possible to get the names of these people?"

At this point Cayce mentioned the name Meglo, later referred to as Megleo. The FBI agents were having some trouble with names; in the Keith summary they had confused Kahn with Cayce. They should have had little trouble placing Megleo, however. Paul Maglio was then a prominent member of the Capone mob, and in 1932 he was head of the Capone operation in New Haven. He later returned to Chicago and was known as Paul (the Waiter) Ricca.

In Special Agent Merrick's report, dated March 18, 1932, he spelled Megleo as Magelo. He said they had checked the post office and consulted the City Directory. Apparently there was no Magelo in New Haven.

Several of the FBI reports, which did not become available until 1977, indicated they were having some trouble deciding what might be the purpose of their search. There was indication Capone was interested in finding the baby, so E. J. Connelly, special agent in charge of the New York office, wrote in his report of March 21, previously quoted, that he expected soothsayer Kahn to lead them to Capone, citing Kahn's connection with Albert Pick of Chicago.

Apart from confusing Kahn, a respectable head of a New York furniture manufacturing firm associated with the Pick Industries of Chicago, with soothsaying and fortune telling—which Connelly assured his superiors he "did not, of course, in any way believe"—he seemed to feel that the reason for the New Haven expedition was to trace Kahn to Chicago's bootlegging business.

He said in his report, "In view of this situation (indications that the trail led back to Chicago gangsters) there might be a well-worked out shrewd plan of contact" which might lead ultimately to Capone and "eventually to the child."

As a matter of fact, Connelly and Lanphier already had the contact in the person of Paul Maglio, or Paul Ricca, who must have been known to the FBI since he later became a member of the Belt-Buckle Brigade, gangsters who wore a gold belt-buckle to signify their status as a member of the inner-circle in the Capone mob. Cayce's reading should have told them that they were dealing with Capone through Maglio, or Ricca, not through Kahn as a soothsayer. As a matter of interest, Maglio, or Ricca, became the head of Capone's Chicago operations and died October 11, 1972, the year Olson first heard of the Cayce readings.

In Cayce's reading of March 9, he was asked what forces could be put in motion leading to a return of the Lindbergh baby. His reply was, "There are already *many in motion.*" (italics mine)

These comments appeared to be aimed directly at Capone, but they were not picked up by the FBI. Cayce gave a number of clues at the readings on March 9 and later on March 12, but none seemed to strike a spark of enlightenment. It is possible agents of the FBI were not aware of them; Lanphier was the only one present at the first reading. For example, on March 12 Cayce was asked, "Was Red Johnson, a friend of the Lindbergh nurse, involved?"

He replied, "Involved, as seen."

"Was the nurse (Betty Gow) involved?"

"Not directly."

Information gathered later indicated that Red Johnson might have been involved. He was arrested for questioning. But the decision that Cayce's readings were of no value eliminated this possible clue.

Cayce had mentioned Megleo as "the one to be dealt with directly. . .the leader of authority of the group—

Megleo.''

He also mentioned a man named "Serceio," who made telephone calls "from the bar," apparently to Colonel Breckenridge. Later, when Olson visited New Haven in 1972, he decided Serceio, whom Cayce described as a comedian, might be Frank Markutzi, who played the Catskill vaudeville circuit and also the Taft Hotel. It is quite possible he was trying to arrange communication between Capone's mob and Lindbergh.

Cayce also made an interesting answer to a question about communications.

"There are many channels through which contacting may be done. These are the ones that are acquainted best with the nature of racketeering. . .would be the channel. These individuals are part new, partly *not* new, to such rackets—see? That is, one who has been in the employ of such a one—the others entirely new."

This might have aroused the interest of the FBI agents, but it did not. It could have been interpreted in several ways, possibly referring to Mickey Rosner, the ex-bootlegger who had been selected by Lindbergh as a go-between. Or it could have referred to Paul Maglio, or Paul Ricca, the "leader" of Capone's New Haven group. With an obtuseness that seems almost unfathomable, the FBI chose to ignore this clue.

Several of the reports of the New Haven search were signed by Special Agent Leon Turrou, who will be remembered as the agent who accompanied Jafsie Condon to the Greenwich Police Station where Hauptmann was taken after his arrest, to identify him. He was unable to do this, telling the police—and Turrou—that Hauptmann looked "like a brother" of "John" of the cemeteries, but definitely was not "John." Turrou knew this; and he must have known that Condon later identified Hauptmann as the man he knew as "John." This was at the trial, when Condon was under oath.

As a slight digression from the New Haven expedition, on January 24, 1977, in response to a letter Olson had written him sending Anthony Scaduto's

237

book, *Scapegoat,* Turrou—then living in Paris—wrote Harold Olson that Hauptmann was "guilty as hell." He based this conviction in his letter on the fact that Hauptmann had some of the Lindbergh ransom money. The purpose of this digression is to present an example of what has been called policeman's mentality—a single-track mind with a single objective.

In point of fact, Hauptmann's possession of the Lindbergh ransom bills might have linked him to the extortion scheme but they certainly were not proof that he kidnaped and murdered the Lindbergh baby. In a later letter, Turrou refers to Isidor Fisch as an "imaginary story," and in a subsequent statement to United Press International he said Scaduto's book was "made up of innuendoes, speculation and conjecture" —apparently not realizing that the New Jersey prosecution's case at the Flemington trial was based on innuendoes, speculation and conjecture.

Had Turrou exercised the talents of an investigator, either at New Haven or in assessing Hauptmann's guilt, rather than the instinct of a policeman, he would have dug more deeply into both subjects and perhaps come up with some useful ideas. He might have directed the search to Capone's New Haven gangsters.

It is difficult at this point to assess reasons for the failure of the New Haven investigation to produce results, in the form of a contact with Al Capone's gang. Neither Lanphier nor Lindbergh were trained investigators; and Lindbergh, although guided by Breckinridge, was running the show. The FBI may be faulted for its policeman's mentality—its refusal to look at more than one side of a problem. Perhaps it should have utilized its widespread sources of information; it was aware of Capone's interest in getting the baby back to its parents as a means of getting himself out of jail, but it does not appear to have occurred to the FBI to act on the possibility that Capone's scheme might have included kidnaping the baby in the first place.

Whatever the reasons for failure might have been, the

results were obvious: the FBI blew its chance. Efforts of Capone's lieutenants to contact Lindbergh's representative were fruitless, and Capone went to prison. The opportunity for a deal—if one was possible—was lost.

Several years later Hugh Lynn Cayce, the eldest son of the psychic, wrote a book called *The Outer Limits* in which he included an explanation of some of the lost persons cases his father had failed to solve. Among these he mentioned the Lindbergh case. He wrote: "In the. . .most famous kidnaping case of our time, the Lindbergh child, Edgar Cayce seemed to have been completely inaccurate."

He noted the request for a reading made by Lanphier. The suggestion was given Edgar Cayce that he trace the Lindbergh baby giving "the exact location at the present hour (March 9, 1932), describe the surest and best way to restore the child unharmed to its parents." Hugh Lynn Cayce then added: "The reading indicated the baby was removed from the bedroom by a man about 8:30 p.m. Another man took the baby. There was a third person in the car. It was further stated that the child was taken to a house in a mill section near New Haven. A section called Cardova was mentioned. Scharter Street was spelled out and the house was described as a 'two-story shingle building.'"

A second reading was given on March 10, still referring to Cardova as the section where the house was to be found. Further attempts were made to locate the area, which was described by Cayce as "including the manufacture of leather goods, shoes, boots and saddles." Adams Street was mentioned again; there was a "shingled house numbered 473." A third reading on March 12 gave the same information.

The explanation in the book by Hugh Lynn Cayce may have been merely an account of certain failures of his father; the Lindbergh case may have been described to conform with the accepted public record.

Harold Olson refused to accept the book's account of

the failure of Edgar Cayce. After talking with Tom Valentine in Chicago, he obtained a summary of the readings. They included, as noted above, references to Meglio as the leader, Serceio, and also Madge Beliance as the nurse.

Olson reasoned that the directions given by Cayce may have been due to a misunderstanding of the words he used. A man in a trance might pronounce indistinctly. He and his wife, Angela, decided to go to New Haven and check on Cayce's readings. According to an account written by W. C. Rockwell, a veteran reporter writing features for the *Suburban News* of Shelton, Connecticut, who accompanied them on the trip to New Haven, it required about an hour for Olson to accomplish what Lanphier and the FBI failed to accomplish in a week.

Olson was able to locate a densely built up mill section in East New Haven—now called East Haven—which corresponded to the east side of New Haven in Cayce's readings.

He talked with James Kilmartin at the Kilmartin Chevron Service Station in East Haven, and asked him if he knew of any section of East Haven or its environs that sounded like Cardova. Kilmartin said there was a Dover section across the Connecticut River from New Haven. Olson then asked if there was an Adams Street, or a name that sounded like it. Kilmartin suggested Chatham Street, pronounced Chattam. Olson, his wife, and Rockwell then went to Chatham Street, found a shingled house with the number 73. They turned right from a point two-tenths of a mile from the waterfront end of the street, and found a store building.

The street on which this building is located is now known as Maltby Street. The number is now 109, but the location is precise. It was in a ramshackle condition when Olson first saw it in 1972. The name "Scharter Street" which Cayce mentioned does not appear on any New Haven map, but even though it was spelled out in Cayce's reading, it is quite possible that it was confused with Adams Street as similar to Chatham, or the name was changed to Maltby Street.

The confirmation of the location of the house described forty years earlier by Edgar Cayce had been made, even to the shingled house on the corner, two-tenths of a mile from the end of Chatham Street. Olson decided to get some additional information. Cayce had said in his reading of March 12, 1932, that manufacturers in the area made shoes, boots, saddles and the like. This was still true.

Olson talked with several people and went into a neighborhood candy store. He asked the proprietess if she knew who had lived at 73 Chatham Street years earlier. She told him someone named "Maglearo." This name was strikingly familiar to the name "Meglo" mentioned by Cayce.

When Olson pressed the woman for details, her husband glowered at her and she refused to give any further information. However, she did refer him to a woman, Jenny Bertozzi, who lived about three blocks away and had been in the neighborhood a long time.

Olson went to see Mrs. Bertozzi, a woman in her mid-seventies. He also met her children and gave them the Cayce readings to look over. Mrs. Bertozzi's son recognized their former home in Pick Alley, within 20 feet of 109 Maltby Street from the Cayce description. They had lived there in 1932. Mrs. Bertozzi remembered that a Mrs. Herkler (sic) had lived in the top apartment at 109 Maltby Street. A local rumor at the time was that Mrs. Herkler was caring for the Lindbergh baby and that her husband had gone to Germany. Mrs. Bertozzi also recalled that a house-to-house search for the Lindbergh baby was conducted by the local police, and babies' diapers were removed to check the sex of the children.

Mrs. Bertozzi told Olson that Mrs. Herkler had children living and with her help he was able to locate

1. Paul Magleo lived in the top apartment of 73 Chatham Street.
2. 109 Maltby Street. Mazie Hertler lived on the third floor, leaving April 28, 1932—the day she was notified her husband was dead in Germany.
3. 80½ Peck Alley where Mrs. Gaetano (Jennie) Bertozzi lived.
4. 76 Peck Alley, a two-family residence. Mrs. Jennie Panico had a goat in the yard and barn. Edgar Cayce

mentioned goats in the yard. The other resident: Mrs. Adelaide Smith.
5. Mrs. Panico's barn.
6. The Quinnipiac River goes into New Haven Harbor. Atlantic bootleg boats anchored in this dock area.
7. Leather goods were made in this building, according to the two Bertozzi children who used to go there and watch.

Mrs. Herkler's sister Catherine who lived in Orange, Conn. When Olson asked Catherine Herkler about her sister's children, he was told, "I'm not supposed to talk about that." However, she did finally tell Olson that Bill Herkler and his sister Mary lived in Middletown, Conn. and another sister Catherine Herkler Rook lived in West Reddington, Conn.

Olson looked up Mary Herkler's address in the phone book and drove to Middletown. Mary invited him in and asked, "Do you remember meeting my mother?"

"Where?"

"In Rhode Island."

It was at this point that Olson recognized Mary Herkler as the daughter of the woman who had encountered him the day after his wedding and told him that she had cared for him as a child and he was the Lindbergh baby. Mrs. Herkler and Mrs. Hertler were one and the same.

Mary remembered her mother had always proclaimed Hauptmann's innocence, but did not have any first-hand knowledge of the Lindbergh case. And she did not know if, in fact, her mother had cared for the Lindbergh child.

The trip to New Haven, to check on the strange reading of Edgar Cayce, was, in a sense, the turning point. The coincidences were becoming more than coincidences. There were too many to be ignored.

Before proceeding to the next phase of Harold Olson's search for identity it might be useful to emphasize certain points.

When the Lindbergh baby was kidnaped, Capone was in jail, ready to serve an eleven-year sentence for income tax evasion. He immediately offered his services in the effort to recover the baby. But in Capone's case, the *quid pro quo* was quite definite: if he returned the baby the authorities would have to agree to let him out of prison!

Olson believed during the first years of his search for his own identity that the Capone organization was involved in the kidnaping.

At the time Olson went to New Haven to follow up Edgar Cayce's remarkable reading on the Lindbergh case, he had spent over five years trying to establish his personal identity. He only partly believed he was Lindbergh's lost son; and at that time he didn't want to believe any of the story. This was in 1972. When I talked to him later at his home in Westport, Connecticut, he told me he had resisted the notion that his parents were not his natural parents.

He was either forty-two or forty-four years old in 1972, depending on whether his age is based on his birthdate as Harold Roy Olson, April 8, 1928, or the date of birth of Charles A. Lindbergh, Jr., June 22, 1930. Twenty years before when his mother, Sara Olson, was dying of cancer, she had told young Harold that he was not her natural son.

I asked him why he had fought the idea; his answer was simple.

"I was like any other young person; I wanted to believe my parents were my own."

First, the psychic readings of Edgar Cayce are in no sense to be compared with the spirit-guided words of Mary Cerrita. Her statement to Breckinridge and Schwarzkopf, which she said came from spirits, could have as easily come from the kidnap or extortionist gang. Peter Birritella's church, across East 127th Street from the house where Isidor Fisch lived, was a veritable hotbed for many suspects in the Lindbergh case: Fisch, Violet Sharpe, Ollie Whateley, J. J. Faulkner, and Condon. The Harlem soothsayer, as Sidney Whipple called Birritella, might readily have transferred what he knew or heard from these people to Mary Cerrita by hypnosis.

Edgar Cayce's reading was through clairvoyance and probably telepathy. He was at Virginia Beach when the readings occurred, and not by the wildest stretch of imagination could even the most adamant non-believer in extrasensory perception, or ESP, have assumed that nine days after the kidnaping, Cayce could have arranged for information to be supplied on the street location of the house in New Haven where he said the baby was held.

The inability of Lanphier and the FBI agents to locate the street or the house might have resulted in Cayce's psychic readings being lost in the limbo of many dark secrets in the Lindbergh case. Hugh Lynn Cayce's verdict that it was a failure would have been accepted by believers and skeptics alike, had not Olson pursued the search forty years later.

Olson's findings at this point were by no means proof that the Lindbergh baby was being held in the house on Scharter Street. But his discovery of the location of the house, described by Cayce, the mention of Megleo as the leader of the kidnap gang, together with reports that a man named Paul Maglio had lived at 73 Chatham Street in 1932, cannot be dismissed as coincidence.

Nor could the address on Maltby Street—109—where Cayce said the baby was held, and where Mazie Hertler and her daughter lived, be dismissed as a coincidence.

With this array of "coincidences" and facts, some of which were supplied later in the FBI reports, Harold Olson began an intensified search for his own past.

The Lindbergh case itself had been wrapped in a blanket of uncertainty and confusion, and part of this may be attributed to Lindbergh himself. Alan Hynd, who assisted Mrs. Evalyn MacLean in writing her article in *Liberty*, wrote in *True Magazine* in 1949: "For a variety of reasons, the principle ones being the prominence, gullibility and stubbornness of the victim's father and the esteem in which he was then held, the Lindbergh kidnaping served to assemble under one tent the most notable congress of clowns, villains, screwballs, exhibitionists and other entertaining characters ever to perform in one arena except that of the Ringling Brothers."

21

Beginning the Search

Harold Roy Olson's earliest recollection of his childhood was in the town of Escanaba, Michigan, on the shore of Green Bay about fifty miles south of Lake Superior. An open waterway by Lake Michigan or a truck route to Lake Superior is the route to Canada. In 1932 it was a place where bootleg whiskey could be transferred from boats to trucks.

There is a red brick house still standing in which Olson lived or frequented as a boy. It was reputed to be headquarters for Al Capone's bootleggers, operating out of Chicago. According to information Olson has dug up, or remembers, it was once owned by Capone.

Olson recalled that as a boy in Escanaba he heard stories that might have led him to believe he was an adopted child. He had lived with these thoughts for years. In 1952, working for an advertising agency in New York, he received a telegram informing him that his mother was dying in a Michigan hospital. Earlier that year he had driven his mother to Escanaba, and she brought up the subject of his early life and his parentage. He told her he was quite happy with his present parents. When he arrived at the hospital in the fall of 1952, she seemed determined to reveal his parental background. All he remembers was the name Johnson, apparently of the Johnson bandage family company.

She had told him earlier that he had been taken to a hospital when he was a young child, and was about to have a brain operation when a nurse—possibly her sister, Ebba, or another sister, Karen—had taken him out of the hospital because she feared the brain surgery might affect him permanently.

Olson began to put these pieces of the puzzle together after his father died in 1967: the Cayce readings, which he had followed up in 1972, locating the house at 109 Maltby Street; the meeting with Mary, the daughter who told him her mother lived in the house; the curious mention of the Lindbergh name by a man at City Island and later by Mazie Hertler.

Was Mazie Hertler the link that connected him with the Lindbergh baby?

These questions began to mill through Olson's mind. By searching records of the Lindbergh kidnaping he was able to find certain signs of bodily similarities. The overlapping toes which apparently were ignored in the identification of the corpse found near Lindbergh's estate, yet were described in a newspaper report quoting Dr. Ingen as saying they were "curled in." Olson's own toes had the same configuration. There were other similarities.

Several reports of the Lindbergh kidnaping indicated the baby had suffered a fall, either when taken from the nursery in the Lindbergh home, or during the time it was held by the kidnapers. Did this account for the dent in the back of Olson's head? He had been given various explanations of the dent: a slipped forceps, or a fall. How did Mazie Hertler know about the dent?

Had brain surgery been performed on the Lindbergh baby—and if so, was this prior to the kidnaping? Or was the kidnaping contrived to cover up the brain surgery? These questions fairly tumbled through Olson's thoughts.

About this time he began to develop what might be regarded as a fanciful theory. He had found a story in the Hartford *Daily Times* of March 4, 1932 that told of

248

The red brick house on South 10th Street in Escanaba, owned by Al Capone. One of Olson's earliest memories is visiting this house.

a man named Alfred Denzler, who claimed his life had been saved by Anne Lindbergh when she found him bleeding on a road after an automobile accident near Hopewell.

Denzler had walked into the press room at Hopewell to tell reporters his story, and to offer to help the bereaved mother in any way possible. According to his account, he had been driving in the country near the Lindbergh estate when he lost control of his car and it crashed into a bridge near the Lindbergh home, leaving him bleeding on the road where he said Anne Lindbergh found him.

Certain things about Denzler's story seemed fishy to Olson. He located a Dr. Reginald J. Pierson in Jamesburg, New Jersey, whose father was reported to have operated on Denzler, when Mrs. Lindbergh and another woman brought him to Dr. Pierson's office. He showed Dr. Pierson the newspaper report of the accident. After reading it carefully, the doctor said he had no knowledge of such an accident. This was in May, 1976. Dr. Pierson said when his father retired he had destroyed his records. He added that his father might have taken care of Denzler, but in that case he would have known of it; he had no knowledge of his father having billed or received payment from the Lindberghs.

The accident apparently occurred several weeks before the kidnaping. By this time Olson's theory began to take shape. He suggested to Dr. Pierson that the Lindbergh child might have suffered a skull fracture in the accident, which could have been the result of the Lindbergh car having collided with Denzler's. According to this theory, the baby might have been taken to Hartford for brain surgery.

It was Olson's theory that the Lindbergh baby had been taken from the Lindbergh home several months before the kidnaping; that the baby was on its way to Hartford when it was snatched by members of the Capone gang; that the kidnaping itself had been faked possibly with the connivance of Ollie and Elsie Whateley and the baby's nurse, Betty Gow.

This theory does not in any way conform with many known facts in the Lindbergh kidnaping. The kidnaping itself was too well reported by the press to leave any possibility that it was a fake; and the distress which Anne Lindbergh recounts in her diaries—*Hour of Gold, Hour of Lead* and *War Within and Without*—is hardly compatible with Olson's effort to explain the Denzler incident by advancing the date of kidnaping. It may be noted, however, that in *War Within and Without*, Mrs. Lindbergh speaks of her "18-month-old-baby" when it was twenty months and eight days at the time of the kidnaping. She says it was "kidnaped from our first home near Princeton, in 1931."

Olson's Denzler theory is not consistent with any other facts in the kidnaping case; but it might be applied to an earlier accident which may have injured the child. Lindbergh, with his obsessive dislike of publicity, might have had the baby taken to Hartford for an operation. This would have fitted into Mrs. Hertler's comment in the Rhode Island incident, as well as Sara Olson's mentioning young Olson being taken to a hospital and removed by a nurse.

Extending Olson's fanciful theory even further, it might have triggered Capone's New Haven gang to try to kidnap the baby as a means of applying pressure to Lindbergh in getting Capone out of jail. In a sense, it would also explain Cayce's comment about Betty Gow and Red Johnson being involved. Violet Sharpe was accused of being an informer in the case.

The Denzler theory will be discussed in the closing chapters of this review. It may help explain Lindbergh's curious effort to cover up several aspects of the kidnap case, including discrepancies in his testimony at the

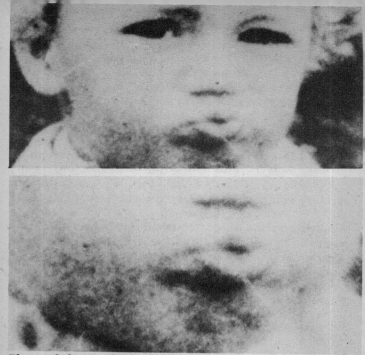

Photo of the Lindbergh baby. Note the scarred chin, possibly from an accident.

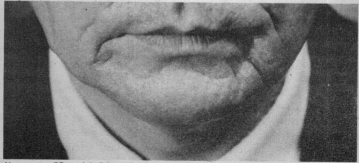

Scars on Harold Olson's chin.

Alfred Denzler, who was in the Hopewell accident prior to the kidnaping in which the baby may have been injured.

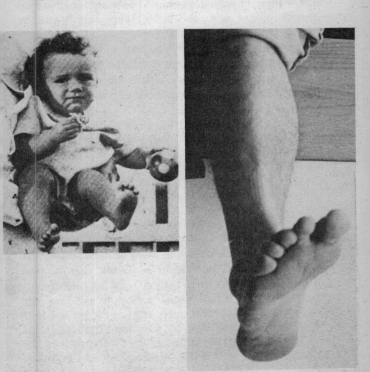

Harold Olson's right foot, with turned-in toes.

Hauptmann trial. It might also shed some light on the placing of the wrong body in the Mount Rose grave, hoping this might end the search for Lindbergh's son.

There was a rumor that a body had been found on Long Island which Lindbergh was called into identify; this will be discussed in the final chapter, but it was theorized at the time that the kidnapers had placed the body in a boat, hoping that its discovery would close further investigation of the case. Obviously it did not; and the two-and-a-half year search for "John" of the cemeteries, which ended with the arrest, conviction and execution of Bruno Hauptmann, did not close the books, either. There were already too many unanswered questions, including doubts as to Hauptmann's guilt or the fate of the Lindbergh baby.

There is also a question concerning Olson's actual age. A birth certificate filed in Escanaba showed that he was two years older than Lindbergh's son but he explained that he was not big enough to have fitted that birthdate.

"When I entered school I was only 42 inches in height and weighed 38 pounds," he said. His first grade teacher, a Miss Lind, said he was too young to begin school, and should be returned to kindergarten. He was six years old according to his registered birthdate, but only four years old based on the birth of the Lindbergh baby.

Bit by bit pieces were beginning to fall into place. It was evident that the Chicago gang of Al Capone had been involved in the kidnaping, however it took place. It was likewise becoming evident to Olson that he was getting closer and closer to establishing his identity.

One bit of evidence would definitely confirm the belief, which he was reluctantly coming to accept, that he was the kidnaped son of Charles Lindbergh; the fingerprints! If he could compare the fingerprints of the Lindbergh child, which Dr. Erastus Meade Hudson,

254

Harold Olson, noticeably smaller and younger than the other children, at graduation from kindergarten, 1934.

Olson after his confirmation, 1943.

Lieutenant Robert Hicks, and Mrs. McLean said existed at one time, with his own fingerprints, the evidence would be inescapable, one way or another.

It was noted earlier that Anthony Scaduto, in researching material for *Scapegoat*, said he had actually seen the box of fingerprints at the Trenton police archives, labelled "Lindbergh fingerprints"; and that among these were fingerprint photos that must have been those of the child. According to Dr. Hudson's story to Mrs. McLean, he had raised fingerprints of a child from toys and other objects in the nursery with his silver nitrate process.

Later Dr. Hudson said he had made enough samples of the baby so that "from the baby's books and toys, we were able to produce enough palm and fingerprints . . .to identify or disqualify, without dispute, any living Lindbergh baby that might be presented in the future."

Olson retained Glenn B. Miller, an attorney from Princeton, early in 1977 to help him obtain the fingerprint comparison. Miller said he would take Olson's case "with the understanding that I was not going to reopen the Lindbergh case."

Later, under the Freedom of Information Act, Olson obtained a letter from Mark Kimberling to J. Edgar Hoover, previously mentioned, in which he said the New Jersey police archives had "fingerprint files taken from toys and other objects" in the Lindbergh nursery, adding that to protect the Lindberghs from fake identification he did not want to release the prints, but that the New Jersey police would be glad to make comparisons of prints.

In his letter to William Sullivan, Olson noted that on Thanksgiving Day in 1975 Scaduto had called him and said that the previous day he had gone to the New Jersey police headquarters in Trenton and had personally seen the baby's fingerprints.

Olson said he "decided to take the bull by the horns"

and some months later, on a business trip to Trenton, he visited the Police Identification Headquarters, produced a copy of Kimberling's letter to Hoover, and asked to have his fingerprints compared with those of Charles A. Lindbergh, Jr.

Several months earlier, on May 5, 1976, Olson had written to Clinton L. Pagano, then superintendent of the New Jersey state police, asking for an official comparison of his fingerprints with those taken from the Lindbergh house by Dr. Hudson on March 13, 1932 and added: "You will find them in the building where New Jersey keeps the files of the Hauptmann case." He described the room: "a jail cell-barred door." He had evidently obtained this description from Scaduto who said he saw the fingerprints in 1975.

He received a reply from Pagano advising him that his request was "under review by the state police and in cooperation with the office of the New Jersey attorney general."

It soon became apparent to Olson that his request for identification had aroused more than official attention; it was more in the nature of suspicion. Why did he want a comparison? A positive identification of Olson's fingerprints with those of the Lindbergh child might open a Pandora's box of unanswered questions. In fact, it might force a reopening of the Lindbergh case itself!

The *Trentonian*, a newspaper published in Trenton, broke the story on Monday morning, June 13, 1977, that Olson, with his attorney, Glenn Miller, had asked for a comparison of the Lindbergh baby's fingerprints with his own, and was told the Lindbergh child's fingerprints had disappeared from the Lindbergh file in the police archives.

A state police lieutenant, Gordon Hector, explained that the baby's fingerprints were "unusable" and had not been closely guarded. He also revealed that another man, claiming to be the lost Lindbergh child, had surfaced. His name was Kenneth Kerwin; he had filed a suit contesting the Lindbergh will.

Ann Rinaldi, the *Trentonian* reporter, quoted Hector as saying the New Jersey state police are "convinced that the baby found was the Lindbergh baby."

The attorney general's office was at some pains to dilute the importance of the baby's fingerprints. She quoted Robert P. Martinez, assistant to Attorney General William F. Hyland, saying, "It was never established that there were a child's prints. We only saw prints of adults. Even if prints existed, they wouldn't establish anything. They could be the prints of another child who was in the room."

There was never any report of another child being the room; and Dr. Hudson had noted that fingerprints, taken from the baby's books and toys, would "identify, or disqualify, without dispute, any 'living Lindbergh baby' that might be presented in the future."

Rinaldi reported that Miller, asked about the reason for the fingerprint search, had said, "All the poor guy wants is to have his prints checked."

She finally wrote in her report: "All the prints are gone. Where? Nobody knows. More than that, those in charge aren't upset, don't think it matters. After all. . . that was a long time ago."

A year earlier, on March 20, 1976, Harold Olson had written Judge Samuel Fukuoka, of the Second Circuit Court on Maui, where Lindbergh had died and his will was being probated, disclaiming any intention of holding up the probate or sharing in any way in the estate. His letter stated that, if needed, he would "readily sign a waiver to that effect."

In the letter Olson noted that there was evidence that tended to prove the body found on Mount Rose Heights was *not* that of the Lindbergh baby, and explained why he was taking action in the case.

"It has been said that your court provides the only forum to (determine my identity) and that it will never exist again, and I would be remiss in not doing so." He included a set of his own fingerprints, and said the baby's fingerprints might be found in the New Jersey state police headquarters. He said they were in a box labelled "Lindbergh fingerprints" and included photos taken by Dr. Mead Hudson.

After being told by Olson of the missing fingerprints, Anthony Scaduto wrote Lieutenant Hicks in Washington, stating that "in or around December, 1975," he had been permitted to look through the Lindbergh file at the New Jersey police headquarters in Trenton.

"A trooper took me to what he said was the oldest barracks building on the grounds, and down in the basement was a Lindbergh case room, about 12 feet by 8, with prison type cell bars and a sign identifying it as a repository of Lindbergh materials. . . .The most vital part of the evidence I was able to find under the restrictions placed upon me was the child's fingerprints."

He described a row of five or six steel cabinets, and a number of cardboard boxes, pushed back toward the wall.

"Atop one of these boxes, in front of the larger boxes, was a smaller box about the size of a shoebox . . .loosely covered in brown wrapping paper. On top of that paper was written, 'Lindbergh case fingerprints.'

However long ago the case seemed in the minds of New Jersey state police or the attorney general's office, it would not appear too remote for fingerprint identification; and so the Lindbergh baby's fingerprints were conveniently missing.

22

The Strange Role of the FBI

Harold Olson had embarked on a search to determine who his parents were, but he suddenly found himself confronted with something akin to a conspiracy. Since his father's death in 1978 had written to many people, talked with others, and obtained correspondence of the FBI.

Three days after he learned that the fingerprints were missing, Olson wrote William C. Sullivan, once the third man in J. Edgar Hoover's FBI hierarchy, asking for help. Sullivan had retired, or been pressured into retirement, after he accused Hoover of authoring books and selling articles mostly written by subordinates on government time, and pocketing the proceeds.

He told Sullivan of his fruitless effort to have his own set of fingerprints compared with the Lindbergh child's, and enclosed several news reports, pictures of the body of the dead baby identified by Lindbergh as his son, and a fairly complete summary of his own background and reasons for believing he might be the Lindbergh child. Unfortunately, Sullivan could not help Olson; he was killed in a hunting accident later that year.

Olson decided to request all FBI files that mentioned him, under the Freedom of Information Act. He found to his considerable surprise several letters, including some written to him with notations not contained in the original, and a memorandum on Olson sent to the director by Special Agent in Charge of New York John

Malone, dated June 6, 1968. The document, which Olson later referred to as the "Malone memorandum," detailed the steps taken by the FBI to maintain surveillance over Olson.

The Malone memorandum, written in New York, was sent out as information for the Washington, Detroit, and New Haven bureaus. It noted that Olson, a social acquaintance of Special Agent Henry C. Ruda, "in the last few months has apparently been attempting to ascertain his identity and questions the identity of his parents."

The memorandum said:

Olson, in the enclosed and previous communications, has indicated that he received a skull fracture as a child and is attempting to ascertain how it occurred. He has questioned the identity of his parents and on occasion has theorized that he may possibly be the kidnaped Lindbergh child, or a child of Al Capone, both of whom he alleged formerly visited Escanaba, Michigan when he was very young.

He has indicated in a previous conversation that he has undergone psychiatric analysis at a New York hospital, and one of the enclosed communications, addressed to the Waupaca County Hospital, Wisconsin, indicates that an uncle, one Julius Carlson, was formerly a mental inmate.

Olson obtained a copy of the Malone memorandum on October 10, 1978. Five days later he wrote a letter to William H. Webster, the current director of the FBI, in which he mentioned the Malone memorandum and said he was "citing some facts so future material might be closer to the truth."

He said in the letter: "I never seemed to understand the presence of Ruda, but when I started my background investigation in the summer of 1967 Henry seemed to make more sense. . . .As it slowly dawned on me that I might possibly be the Lindbergh child, Henry was always there to discuss the matter and (was) thoroughly knowledgeable. . . .''

It also dawned on Olson that Ruda and the FBI were becoming curiously interested in the progress of his search for his own parentage. He noted at one point in his letter to Webster that when he suggested to Ruda that he ask those to whom he had made inquiries about his past to send their replies to Ruda, ''Henry said not to mention him because he would not be able to help me.''

''Is the Malone memo saying that Hoover (the FBI) had found the Lindbergh baby, kept it under tabs thru Ruda, and then when the baby decided to try and find itself, proceeded. . . .to destroy it?''

Olson enclosed a complete file of his visits to determine how he received the dent in his skull, and not for psychiatric analysis. He added: ''I never underwent psychiatric analysis at a New York hospital, or any other hospital . . . . For Malone to have used this against me, when I in good faith thought the FBI was in a position to help me, was just plain weak.''

He might have added a stronger word—an illegal invasion of privacy.

Malone also mentions Sara's brother Julius. ''He was placed in a mental hospital not because he was insane,'' Olson says, ''but as the result of a fight with a relative over my parentage.''

As a final point in the letter, Olson wrote: ''Hoover made one hell of a deal out of getting the Lindbergh baby fingerprints. On numerous occasions Hoover sent fingerprints to New Jersey for comparison with possible Lindbergh babies. This was long after the baby was accepted as dead. In the name of all that is sacred, why didn't Hoover or Malone or Ruda send Harold Olson's fingerprints to New Jersey for a comparison? Why didn't anyone for eight years tell Olson that there were prints?

"Over in New Jersey Col. Pagano says he has lost the Lindbergh fingerprints, after he took copies of mine!"

The inference seemed to be plain: Harold Olson was beginning to suspect that there was more than met the eye in the FBI's interest in his search. Why? The FBI had officially dropped out of the Lindbergh case on October 10, 1934. Hoover, through his connection with Evalyn Walsh McLean, had maintained an interest, however. Mrs. McLean had supplied him with a set of the Lindbergh baby's fingerprints obtained from Robert Hicks, the Washington criminologist retained by her and Governor Hoffman. In 1976 the director who succeeded Hoover, Clarence M. Kelley, had written to Olson, in a reply to a letter from him, stating that "the FBI cannot be of assistance to you."

Why all this surveillance over Olson's activities? Why was Ruda assigned to keep tabs on Olson, if it could not be of assistance?

During the period following 1972, Olson began to gather what he described as massive information concerning his heredity. He had virtually proved in his trip to New Haven that the house on Scharter street actually existed, as Edgar Cayce's psychic reading said it did, in spite of Hugh Lynn Cayce's statement that the reading was a failure, and Thomas Lanphier's inability to find the place.

He had also obtained evidence that Paul Megleo, the Capone lieutenant, had been in New Haven during the time of the kidnaping, and had gone to Chicago at the request of Meyer Lansky, who took over Capone's gang, and changed his name to Paul Ricca.

Olson reasoned that Megleo, working for Capone, had snatched the Lindbergh baby and was holding it in order to bargain for Capone's release from prison; and when neither the Department of Justice nor Lindbergh himself had agreed to that exchange, the baby became a

263

useless encumbrance.

Most of this could be regarded as a far-fetched theory, but Olson had other reasons for believing that he was gradually beginning to put together the story of the Lindbergh kidnaping. He had bought a copy of Anne Lindbergh's book, *Hour of Gold, Hour of Lead,* published in 1973 by Harcourt Brace; opposite page 196 there is a picture of Lindbergh's mother, Mrs. Evangeline Lindbergh, holding the baby. Its toes are distinctly revealed; the little toe on each foot *curved inward*.

The autopsy report on the body found near Hopewell, made by Dr. Mitchell, says: "The first toe of the right foot completely overlaps the large toe and the second toe of the right foot partially overlaps the large toe." The letter from Dr. Van Ingen, the baby's pediatrician, to Mrs. Elizabeth Morrow says he "especially noted that both little toes were slightly turned in and overlapped the next toe."

This difference possibly escaped the notice of newspapermen at the time; the baby's toes were usually referred to as overlapping. But in Olson's view, the differences were unmistakeable, as they were to Robert Hicks and even Dr. Van Ingen. The importance of this to Harold Olson was, of course, that his own toes curled inward, as did those of the Lindbergh baby!

Other incidents began to confirm in Olson's mind the belief that he was Lindbergh's kidnaped son. A brother, or foster-brother of Olson, in Escanaba, in 1968, had mentioned to Werner Olson, his uncle, and a member of Capone's organization, that Harold had been investigating the possibility that he was the Lindbergh child. The elder Olson had said, "The Lindberghs don't want him."

Again, in 1972, Olson says he met a sister-in-law of Mazie Hertler, the nurse who had felt the back of his head in Rhode Island. He told her of his effort to find out whether or not he was the Lindbergh baby, and she said the Lindberghs "didn't want him" and unless he expected to get some money out of his quest, to "forget it!"

It was then that he began to construct the theory that the kidnaping was separate from the extortion, and that the $50,000 extortion money was not the real reason for the abduction. If Capone's gang kidnaped the baby, that reason would have ended when Capone's offer of a trade of the baby for his freedom was refused.

Yet the FBI continued its interest in Olson, according to his story, for several years afterward—even after Lindbergh's death in 1974. What prompted this interest? He had disclaimed any desire to participate in Lindbergh's estate; and at any rate, this was a civil matter.

The probable reason was that the FBI, as well as the State of New Jersey, did not want the Lindbergh case reopened. There are several reasons why New Jersey would not want the controversy over Hauptmann's trial rekindled: the evidences of bungling by the police, the false and possibly perjured testimony by many of the State's witnesses, the growing belief that the conviction and execution of Hauptmann was a miscarriage of justice.

But what about the FBI's reasons, which under the language of our times might be labelled "security interests?" Why was the FBI involved? Olson, in his letter to William Sullivan, the former aide to J. Edgar Hoover who was eased out of the FBI, wrote: "All information I can get points to (the fact) that Lindbergh, from air mail flying days to the time he died, was an agent or cover or front for the American intelligence activities."

This seemed to add a new dimension to the Lindbergh case. Lindbergh had performed many services for American Intelligence, including informing the Narcotics Bureau of drug smuggling along Long Island

Sound and the New Jersey coast. He also worked with intelligence services in other ways. One was his trip to Japan and China in August and September, 1931, acting as a consultant for Pan American Airways and Transcontinental and Western Air (TWA), then known as The Lindbergh Line. He was reported to have been accused by the Japanese of taking pictures of their airfields and other sensitive areas. Anne Lindbergh, who accompanied him on the trip, does not mention it in *Hour of Gold, Hour of Lead,* nor does Walter Ross in *The Last Hero*, a biography of Lindbergh; but it was widely reported that Lindbergh was held in custody for a time while the Japanese tried to sift out his purpose in the visit to their country.

There was also the association of Lindbergh and Colonel Thomas Lanphier, who was also associated with the Coordinator of Information Office, later the OSS, headed by General "Wild Bill" Donovan. Lindbergh met Lanphier in 1927 at Selfridge Field in Michigan as an Army airpilot. It seems strange that Ross, who wrote a fairly complete biography of Lindbergh, hardly mentioned the trip to Japan and never referred to Lanphier!

There seemed to be a strong probability that the agencies connected with American intelligence were anxious to avoid any inquiry into Lindbergh's life—even after he died in 1974—apparently fearing that matters not connected with the kidnaping might be revealed by a reopening of the Lindbergh kidnaping case and the Hauptmann trial.

In addition to his problems with the State of New Jersey and the FBI, Olson was confronted with another mystery: the apparent desire of remnants of the old Capone gang to keep constant watch on him. This continued after he built his home at Westport, Connecticut, living there with his wife, Angie, and working as a successful salesman for a computer company in New

York.

According to Olson, he represented insurance that Meyer Lansky and others of the former Capone gang would never be held for the murder of the Lindbergh baby, on which there was no statute of limitations, as long as he was alive.

Harold Olson's story of his twelve-year search for his own identity is long and at times seems to ramble a bit; but under the skin it appears to hold together. He told me he was "95 percent sure" of his identity as Charles A. Lindbergh, Jr.; and from his other comments, that figure could be 99 percent sure.

What makes his story of absorbing interest in this review is the amount of factual material he has dug up, both as to the kidnaping itself and the evidence, largely circumstantial, which points to a new theory, or theories, of the Lindbergh crime.

Part Six

FACTS
AND
THEORIES

23

A Crime Without a Theory

As this review of the Lindbergh case grinds toward a conclusion—or what may be accepted as a reasonable conclusion, since it is apparent some questions will never be answered—certain aspects begin to stand out. Among these are two points raised earlier: The lack of any clearly defined theory by the police, the State of New Jersey, or those who for one reason or another were embroiled in the case; and secondly, the personality of the father, Charles A. Lindbergh, Sr., who from the very outset assumed full charge of the investigation —even to the point of threatening to shoot anyone who defied his arbitrary edicts.

The first aspect is revealed by a simple recording of what happened. From the first discovery that the Lindbergh baby was missing from his nursery in the Sourland Mountain retreat of the Lone Eagle and his family on March 1, 1932, to the death of Bruno Hauptmann in the electric chair on April 3, 1936, the case was a shambles of misdirected investigation, theories instantly arrived at and instantly changed without notice. The question of when and how the Lindbergh baby was killed—if he was killed—was never disposed of! The suicide of Violet Sharpe was never explained. Clues provided by Edgar Cayce from Virginia Beach were never followed up, until Harold Olson's search forty years later.

The second aspect—the personality of Lindbergh

himself—in a definite way involved the first. Lindbergh was always polite, always dictatorial. Perhaps the capsule description by Alan Hynd, previously quoted, offers the best explanation of the utter lack of a reasonable and consistent theory: "the prominence, gullibility and stubbornness of the victim's father." It may explain why the entire case has been wrapped in mystery, unresolved theories and general confusion.

Two examples illustrate this. First, the meeting in two Bronx cemeteries between the kidnaper, who should have known that the baby was dead—if he was—and an emissary of the father, and later the father himself, confronting each other and realizing that the body, dropped in a shallow grave as the kidnaper fled hastily from the scene, should have been found!

Secondly, the character of the father as furnished by Lindbergh himself. On the night of the kidnaping a note, presumably from the kidnaper, was found lying on a window sill in the nursery. Did the distracted father pick up the note, tear it open and read it? It could have furnished a specific clue. But no. With a calmness that later was described as "iron self-discipline" he let it lay for *more than two hours!* Nor did he permit anyone else to touch the note or open it. Two hours of waiting—while the kidnaper fled through the unguarded New Jersey countryside! Lindbergh kept this important clue inviolate until State Trooper Frank Kelly, the fingerprint expert, arrived to dust the note for fingerprints, with notable lack of success! As Judge Trenchard might have said, "Do you believe that?"

Believe it or not, it happened. The only logical reasons for this senseless delay were that Lindbergh knew what was in the note, or that he displayed an irresponsible and amateurish exercise of authority as the father of the victim. The latter was probably the most reasonable explanation, although the first was not impossible.

If there is added to Lindbergh's arbitrary exercise of

authority the "ghastly remembrance of police tip-stavery"—Harry Morton Robinson's word for "tipstaff," the badge of constabulary authority—on the part of the New Jersey police, which began an hour or so after the kidnaping and lasted for two-and-a-half years of police bungling, falsification of evidence, conflicts in testimony not only between witnesses but often by the same witness, plus judicial bias which ended in the execution of Bruno Hauptmann, the difficulties in reaching a reasonable solution will be apparent.

Americans as a rule treat national heros with sychophant adulation. They assume, as in Lindbergh's case, that knowledge of flying, together with stamina, stubbornness, and good luck that enabled him to cross the Atlantic alone in a small plane, in itself endows a man with strong morality and a lofty and impeccable character. The world today no longer seems to have new heroes, and it jealously guards those who have been heroes. Walter Ross noted in *The Last Hero:* "There are many bold men exploring frontiers in strange lands, at the bottom of the sea, in the air, on mountains as well as outer space. . . .They are not heroes, because the world no longer creates heroes, believes in heroes."

Lindbergh, as a man, fell considerably short of meeting all the standards of heroic expectations. He was given to senseless practical jokes, yet was obsessively reserved, personally retiring, a potential recluse. In addition to being a far-seeing genius in the field of aviation, and perhaps in other fields, he was virtually an amateur as an investigator. Even the New Jersey police, as inept as they were, regarded him as an interfering trouble-maker.

In order to bring an element of reason into the mish-mash of speculations and rumors surrounding the Lindbergh kidnaping case, it may be well to set down certain facts, either accepted as proved or, in the area of circumstantial evidence, proved beyond a reasonable doubt. These may furnish the framework for a solution, or at least a reasonable theory of the case.

The first fact of importance is the identification of the body found on Mount Rose Heights as Lindbergh's son. The difference in measurements between the body taken from the grave and the Lindbergh baby has been discussed, as well as the possibility that the body found in the shallow grave had been embalmed. There has also been reference to overlapping toes which presumably enabled Lindbergh to identify the body as his son.

There was one odd circumstance connected with the overlapping toes, however, that has not been previously mentioned.

In *The Last Hero,* written by Ross without Lindbergh's authorization, the author describes the identification of the body by Lindbergh according to the script. "He looked at the mouth, and counted the teeth. Then he looked at the foot with the 'overlapping toes.' He told Erwin Marshall, the Mercer County prosecutor, 'I am perfectly satisfied that it is my child.'"

The first edition of *The Last Hero* was published by Harper & Row in 1964. Lindbergh never enjoyed reading a biography of himself, but at the request of his publisher, William Jovanovich, he read this book. Then he produced a seventy-six page typewritten analysis of his book, which was turned over to Ross who made certain corrections. Ross said he did not have to make them; he had written the book with no help from Lindbergh and was under no obligation to change it.

There was a revised edition, however, published in 1976, two years after Lindbergh died. Ross made several corrections, based on Lindbergh's analysis; one is of particular interest.

In the original edition, Ross had written:

"He (Lindbergh) looked at the foot with the

overlapping toes.'' (italic mine)

In the revised edition, he wrote:

"He looked at the foot with the *turned-in* toes.'' (italics mine)

Harold Olson noted this difference. He referred to a picture in Anne Lindbergh's *Hour of Gold, Hour of Lead,* which plainly revealed the curled-in little toes on both feet—similar to the configuration of Olson's toes. The autopsy report by Dr. Mitchell states that the "left leg from knee down missing. The first toe of the right foot completely overlaps the large toe, and the second toe of the right foot partially overlaps the large toe.''

If Lindbergh had examined the right foot with care—and there is evidence that he did not—he would have noted that the first three toes were overlapping. He could not see the left foot, because it was missing. But the overlapping toes were sufficient for him to have doubted that it was the body of his son. What is the explanation? Did he identify the body by the most cursory examination, merely looking at the teeth? Did he assume that this was his child? Or did he *know* in advance that this was *not* the body of his son?

If he had looked carefully at the toes, he would have been aware that it was not his child. Nevertheless, his identification, coupled with that of Betty Gow, who examined bits of cloth, established the *corpus delicti*—the fact of the crime.

Without this identification Hauptmann could not have been sent to the electric chair. Lindbergh had plenty of time to think about it, just as he had time to reflect on his first testimony before the Bronx grand jury in 1932 when he said he could not positively identify "John'' of the cemeteries by his voice.

Two and a half years later he repeated his identification of the body, and changed his testimony on "John's'' voice to identifying him as Bruno Hauptmann!

274

He held rigidly to his convictions; and this may have been the reason he created such a melange of cross-purposes in the most tragic event of his life—the kidnaping of Charles A. Lindbergh, Jr. It may also have been the reason his quiet young wife, Anne Morrow Lindbergh, deferred to his often erroneous judgment, even to the point of erasing from her mind any doubts she may have had at the Hauptmann trial.

The second fact of significance, aside from the blow-by-blow account of the investigation in the press, was the positive evidence, a week after the kidnaping, in one of Edgar Cayce's psychic readings, of a house in New Haven, Connecticut, where he said the kidnaped baby was taken. The reading was not in itself proof that the baby was in the house where he said it was; but the *location* was established beyond question. The fact that it did not emerge as a proved fact until forty years later, when Harold Olson found it, does not detract from the factual content; it *was where Cayce said it would be* in his clairvoyant reading. Failure to find the house was due to the inability of Major Lanphier and the FBI to follow Cayce's directions. The FBI later reported, in an incredibly inaccurate statement, that Cayce's directions had proved of "no value."

In 1972 Harold Olson investigated these directions, using a summary of Cayce's psychic readings, and found the house exactly where Cayce said it would be.

The location of the building in New Haven is not a factor, in itself, in solving the Lindbergh case; but taken with other circumstances, including Cayce's own reading, it begins to shape the various theories that have emerged during and after the kidnaping investigation. Had it been known at the time, it might also have changed the course of the Lindbergh case as a whole, shortening it to about two weeks.

The reason for this involved other parts of Cayce's reading which, if they had been followed up on the basis of the accurate location of the house where Cayce said the baby was held, might have widened the investigation beyond the narrow scope set by the New Jersey police. He had, for example, referred to Betty Gow and Red Johnston, two of the original suspects, as "involved."

Among other circumstances was Cayce's statement that the baby was taken "through Jersey City, and through the tunnel. . .across the city in the morning, carried into Connecticut, in the region of Cordova, and there the body is *yet*—as we find."

While the hard-nosed police of New Jersey might not have been disposed to take action based on a psychic reading or clairvoyance, Lindbergh and his two friends, Lanphier and Breckinridge, did take it seriously and might have followed it up. It will be recalled that Breckinridge had listened to the story of Mary Cerrita, the Harlem mystic; if he and Lindbergh had paid more attention to what she said, assuming she got her message from those involved in the kidnaping and not from spirits, this might also have shortened the entire Lindbergh case. At that time two of the three things she predicted had actually taken place: the entrance of Jafsie Condon into the case, and receiving the next note from the kidnapers in Breckinridge's office in New York both occurred *after* her prediction.

This will be discussed later in connection with a summary of various theories, but it is worth noting that in both cases, failure to follow up, chiefly on the part of Lindbergh himself, who was master-minding the search, sent the searchers off in different—and quite futile—directions.

The third fact of importance was Isidor Fisch. His existence had first been doubted when Hauptmann said he was the man who left the Lindbergh ransom bills with him. Later it was discovered that Fisch did exist—but he was completely disregarded by the police and the prosecution. Yet the knowledge of Fisch's implication in the extortion, if not the actual kidnaping, might have been known at the time through the ransom bills, and might have led to an early solution of the case.

This brings up what might be regarded as circumstantial evidence. When Joe Dunninger and I investigated Mary Cerrita and Peter Birritella, and his spirit church across from Isidor Fisch's apartment, we found a veritable nest of people who in one way or another were associated with the Lindbergh case—Violet Sharpe, Ollie Whateley, Jafsie Condon, the mysterious J. J. Faulkner, and Fisch.

This information was available to the New York and New Jersey investigators, because I wrote several stories on the subject, most of which were carried in New York newspapers. Nevertheless, it was ignored.

The fourth fact, in developing the theories—and there were a plethora in the Lindbergh case—was the unexplained suicide of Violet Sharpe. Inspector Harry Walsh of the New Jersey police maintained, up to the arrest of Hauptmann, that she was deeply involved in the kidnaping. After that he conveniently forgot her, since David Wilentz had decided the case would be treated as a one-man job, and Violet Sharpe would only have complicated the situation!

There may be some skepticism about the psychic readings of Edgar Cayce, but the finding of the house in New Haven many years later proved the point.

One other point, which cannot be described as a fact, and at the time was regarded as a hoax, was the account of meetings with the kidnap gang by John Hughes Curtis. This might have been the key to the solution of the case; but the finding of the body on Mount Rose Heights, and Lindbergh's assumption of the correctness of his identification of the body as his son, effectively closed the door to a follow-up at the time. It was not until after Hauptmann had been executed that Mrs. McLean and later Lloyd Fisher wrote convincing support of Curtis' activities that the story began to be more carefully examined, and then it was too late.

24

A Gang—or a Lone Kidnaper?

David Wilentz did not elect to change the original theory of the Lindbergh kidnaping case from a gang kidnaping to one involving a lone kidnaper. He was forced to do it. The reason was not factual; it was legal.

Under the New Jersey statutes, if a murder is committed during a felony or high misdemeanor, even if the killing was not premeditated, the killer is guilty of felony murder and can be sent to the electric chair. Few believed Hauptmann deliberately murdered the Lindbergh baby (if he was killed), even though Wilentz in his final summation in which he changed theories willy-nilly, portrayed Hauptmann as having beaten the child to death in the nursery with a chisel. Yet Wilentz, in his original statement, did not indicate that a kidnaper, who expected to exchange the baby for ransom, would intentionally murder him.

If Hauptmann had killed the baby accidentally during the kidnaping, it would have been second degree murder and would not be punishable by death. It was only in the commission of a felony murder that capital punishment could be applied. Oddly enough, under the laws of New Jersey kidnaping was not regarded as a high misdemeanor. It was only in the perpetration of arson, burglary, rape, robbery, or sodomy that a felony murder could be committed. It was necessary, therefore, to prove that Hauptmann had entered the Lindbergh house intending to burglarize it—which in this case was stealing the baby—and this required that he be at the scene. Even if the baby died accidentally, he would be subject to execution.

Wilentz used testimony of Millard Whited, a liar by his own statements, and Amandus Hockmuth, a half-blind old man, to place Hauptmann at the scene of the crime, and by contrived evidence tied him to the ladder. Otherwise, even with questionable handwriting testimony and Condon and Lindbergh recognizing the voice of "John" of the cemeteries, he would not have been able to convict Hauptmann of anything, since the extortion was a New York case. The reason he did not pursue the testimony of William Bolmer, the gas station owner who said someone other than Hauptmann had driven a Ford into his gasoline station the morning of the kidnaping, with the ladder strapped to the car, was that this would have shot Whited's and Hochmuth's testimony full of holes.

The reason for shifting from a gang theory to a lone kidnaper was not a question of evidence, either fact or circumstantial evidence. It was a matter of law. It was the only *legal* way of sending Hauptmann to the electric chair.

The investigation of the Lindbergh case can be divided into three periods: from March 1, 1932 to the discovery of the body on Mount Rose Heights on May 12, 1932; the two-and-a-half years that elapsed from finding the body to the arrest of Hauptmann on September 19, 1934; and the pre-trial period of three-and-a-half months.

During the first two periods the entire investigation was based on a gang theory—that is, that more than one person was involved in the kidnaping and extortion. During this time many theories were advanced. The first, lasting for about a week, was based on the supposition that some member of the Lindbergh or Morrow households was involved, either as an informer or a participant. This was held by the police and, with

279

certain reservations, accepted by Lindbergh. He did not believe any of his own servants was involved; but there was Henry Johnson, the seaman employed as a deck-hand on the Thomas Lamont yacht in City Island. It is worth noting at this point that only Red Johnson was arrested.

During the first period the police worked exclusively on the theory that a gang had kidnaped the baby; and someone in the Lindbergh or Morrow households—either Betty Gow, Violet Sharpe, or the Whateleys—informed them that the baby would be at the Lindbergh estate the night he was kidnaped.

When Breckinridge and Schwarzkopf interviewed Mary Cerrita, an opportunity was presented to crack the case. It was at this point that Lindbergh began actively to interfere. Ed Mulrooney, the New York Commissioner of Police, had noted that the letters from the kidnaper (there were two) were mailed in one particular section of Brooklyn. The thought occurred to him that a third note might be dropped into a mailbox in the same area, and he suggested a two-man surveillance to cover all the mailboxes in that section. Every letter dropped in the boxes would be retrieved by a special device that would catch the letter as it was dropped so it could be retrieved and read.

Lindbergh vetoed the suggestion, fearing that shadowing the letter-writer might jeopardize the child. Mulrooney said the man need never know he was under surveillance, but Lindbergh trusted his own judgment more than that of the police. Lindbergh was adamant, threatening to have Mulrooney fired, and the surveillance was not ordered. The following day the third letter—the one predicted by Mary Cerrita—was dropped in one of the letter boxes the police would have been watching!

The police did not abandon their suspicion of Betty Gow and Red Johnson, or Violet Sharpe; but when Jafsie Condon got into the act, Lindbergh turned his attention wholly to Condon and his flow of messages and letters to and from the supposed kidnapers. By this time Lindbergh and Breckinridge were running the investigation, and the police were merely taking orders.

Lindbergh had retained Mickey Rosner, who called himself a government agent but was under indictment for grand larceny in a stock-selling promotion, and Irving Bitz, a former strong-arm man in "Little Augie" Organ's mob, as his contacts with various gangs, including Al Capone's Chicago bootleg ring. But he had authorized Condon to be the go-between with what he now assumed were the real kidnapers.

From March 11, when Condon was named intermediary, until April 3, when the ransom money was paid to "John" of the cemeteries by Condon, Lindbergh and Breckinridge directed the entire operation. The police were told not to interfere. The theory at this time was that "John" represented the group who had the Lindbergh baby.

Meanwhile, John Hughes Curtis and the two men from Norfolk, Admiral Burrage and Deacon Dobson-Peacock, met with Lindbergh at Hopewell and were told to go ahead with their efforts to contact a gang. There were thus two separate efforts being made, one only slightly publicized and one not publicized at all—until April 6, when the Newark *News* broke the story that Lindbergh had apparently paid through Condon, the $50,000 ransom money and failed to recover his son.

The fourth—or perhaps it was the fifth—theory was the abortive effort of Gaston B. Means. He had told Mrs. Evalyn Walsh McLean that he was in contact with the kidnapers, and she had given him $100,000 ransom money. The termination of his effort, which ended in prison, has already been sufficiently covered.

In the meantime, an additional theory had been provided by Edgar Cayce, the Virginia Beach mystic, who directed the search for the abducted child by clairvoyant psychic readings from his Virginia Beach home. This was kept from the police as well as the public; only the FBI, directed by Tom Lanphier and Breckinridge—and, of course, Lindbergh—were privy to this effort.

Thus there were two psychic searches, both producing important evidence, together with three (actually four, if Violet Sharpe is taken into account) more or less conventional searches in progress or abandoned at the time the body of a baby, which Lindbergh had identified as his son, was found on Mount Rose Heights.

Before proceeding to the second period of investigation, from the finding of the baby's body to the arrest of Bruno Hauptmann, it may be well to shake these various theories into perspective.

The three searches for the Lindbergh baby—by Jafsie Condon, John Hughes Curtis, and Gaston Means—were abandoned once the body was found. In all three cases there were clues that—if properly examined—might have provided information as to what happened to the Lindbergh baby. Lindbergh assumed that Condon paid the ransom money to "John" in St. Raymond's Cemetery; the other two were therefore regarded as fakes.

In the case of Curtis, he typed out and signed a statement that his entire effort had been a hoax—that he had not contacted anyone. In a later statement, released by Lloyd Fisher, who was Curtis' attorney at his trial for obstructing justice, he said the New Jersey police had told him that if he would sign a paper he would be released and could go home.

"What kind of a paper?" he asked.

"Just say you never had any contacts with these people.

"But that would not be true! I did. It would ruin me!"

They told him the statement would not be published. It did not occur to Curtis at the time, but later occurred to Fisher, that this was a police trick for developing the only charge they could make against him—that of obstructing justice. They would seek to prove that he did contact the supposed kidnapers. At that time David Wilentz' lone kidnaper theory had not been advanced!

Curtis, as previously noted, was tried, convicted, fined a thousand dollars, and given a year in prison, which was suspended. The accusation against him was not of hoaxing; it was obstructing justice. This meant that he had actually contacted the kidnap gang and had prevented the police from arresting them. In Prosecutor Anthony Hauck's opening address to the jury he said, "We will prove beyond all reasonable doubt that Curtis was dealing with the actual kidnapers."

The same Anthony Hauck, assisting Attorney General Wilentz at the Flemington trial, helped fashion the theory that a lone kidnaper had abducted Lindbergh's son!

Lindbergh completely disregarded Curtis after the body was found; he accepted his statement of the hoax as final. He refused to speak to him, and their only contact was at Curtis' trial. As a result, there was never any police follow-up to Curtis' later statements that he had actually contacted the kidnapers, but denied this when Lindbergh identified the body as his son. Thus Lindbergh again, by his obstinate refusal to change his mind, or to consider anything not previously formulated by him, had closed the door to what might have been a productive source of information.

Oddly enough, Mrs. McLean supported Curtis' story. She had been bilked by Gaston Means, and might have been wary of anyone who claimed to have contacted the Lindbergh kidnapers; yet she later said that although there were many who believed Curtis' story was a hoax, she believed Curtis actually was in contact with the kidnapers.

Since then there are quite a few who have studied Curtis' story and also believe he was telling the truth. In the composite theory in the final chapter of this review,

283

this possibility will be discussed in connection with the theory that more than one gang was involved.

One other possible theory remains to be examined—the accident to Alfred Denzler. Jack Cuddy of the United Press produced the only story on the Denzler incident, which was published in the Hartford *Daily Times* on March 4, 1932. The elements of a police follow-up were there at the time: a record of the accident, which was never found; an investigation of Dr. Pierson, who Denzler said had treated him, which was never made—and which Dr. Pierson said he was unable to recall when Harold Olson visited him in May, 1976.

This lead was never followed by police investigators or anyone else. Olson wanted Dr. Pierson to take a lie-detector test, but nothing was ever done about that.

As the police investigation moved into the second period—from May 12, 1932, when the body was found on Mount Rose Heights, to September 19, 1934, when Hauptmann was arrested—the police concentrated on two phases: searching for "John" of the cemeteries, and tracing the ransom money through the listing of the Lindbergh bills.

They were assisted in this search by a so-called psychological portrait of their quarry, devised by an ambitious young psychologist, Dr. Douglas Schoenfeld. The effort to fit the man finally captured—Bruno Richard Hauptmann—into this portrait was a bit bizarre, and even ludicrous, since it involved several changes in the testimony of Condon to make Hauptmann's character and features coincide with the portrait.

This effort became even more bizarre when Lieutenant Finn, in charge of the interim investigation, began to stick pins in maps of New York City to indicate places where the Lindbergh bills had been passed, until his office began to look more like a military war room than a detective's office. What makes this phase of the investigation significant, largely through omission, is that the man who passed the Lindbergh ransom money might have been identified by the various tradesmen and shopkeepers in which the bills were passed, had it not been necessary to fit the bill-passer into Dr. Schoenfeld's psychological portrait. Anyone who did not have a thin face, a pointed chin and the personality of a megalomaniac—or a Hitler—was quickly ruled out.

Although Isidor Fisch—the fourth fact of those listed above—was not known to the police or anyone connected with the investigation until Hauptmann was arrested, it might have been possible to find him and connect him with Condon's "John" of the cemeteries if the police had been more open-minded in their search. As it was, until the lucky occurrence at the Warner-Quinlan service station on East 127th Street, it began to look as if the investigation of the Lindbergh kidnap case was headed for the ultimate in police obscurity: the unsolved cases drawer.

After the arrest of Hauptmann, it became clear to the New Jersey legal minds—particularly David Wilentz, the Attorney General—that the entire theory of the case must be changed. The various gang theories had to be abandoned, and a lone kidnaper substituted. This was made necessary by the points noted at the beginning of this chapter, having to do with felony murder.

With a reckless disregard for logic, which seemed to be a hallmark of Jersey justice, the facts were quickly shifted around, or abandoned. The voices Condon heard on the telephone—*"Statto citti!"* and a voice asking if Condon "wrote articles for the newspapers" —had to be forgotten. The shadowy figure of the third man in the Woodlawn and St. Raymond Cemeteries— the man who dropped the handkerchief—was totally disregarded. Even the passers of Lindbergh ransom bills, such as the lady in Greenwich, Connecticut, who dropped a twenty-dollar Lindbergh bill on Mrs. Ella

Decornille's pastry shop counter and then picked it up and disappeared, and the mysterious J. J. Faulkner, were expunged from the records.

Every shred of evidence that did not fit with the lone kidnaper theory was scrapped. After this, the police began to fit in various other parts—such as the contrived ladder testimony of Kohler and the expert opinion of Dr. Osborne and the other handwriting authorities—to prove that Hauptmann alone committed the crime.

It was not easy, and a closer examination of the trial record will show that it was not even successful; but the combined influence of "public opinion", a one-sided press and radio, a biased judge and complete disregard of any semblance of coherent evidence by the prosecution, was sufficient to convict Hauptmann.

It may be said, without reservation, that the lone kidnaper theory was not even a theory. It was a rambling, disconnected effort of a conviction-hungry prosecution, a hanging trial judge, inept defense counsellors led by a flaunting publicity-minded chief counsel whose fee was paid by the opposition, and a press corps more gifted in making headlines than in reporting facts.

The result of this ungodly melange was to frame Hauptmann and send him to the electric chair.

This was, of course, an eventuality that cannot be redressed. One thing can be redressed, however; the initial question posed in this review: what happened to the Lindbergh baby? It was never shown where and how the baby died, except by circumstantial evidence or vague stories told by Gaston Means. One thing can be safely assumed: the body found on Mount Rose Heights was *not* that of Lindbergh's son. If this is true—and every circumstance seems to indicate that it *is* true—what was the fate of the child?

25

A Composite Theory

As the apple tree is shaken down, eliminating some of the more or less dead apples, certain significant points in the Lindbergh investigation begin to emerge.

The first of these, in point of time as well as importance, can be framed in a question: why was the New Haven investigation dropped? It has already been explained that Lanphier and FBI agents failed to find the house where Edgar Cayce said the baby was held, but there were enough clues in Cayce's reading to warrant a continued effort. This is partially true in his mention of Megleo and Serceio, who must have been recognized as known Capone henchmen. There was also his remark that Betty Gow and Red Johnson were involved.

Cayce was at his home in Virginia Beach, some 350 miles south of New Haven when he made these statements on March 9, 1932—about a week after the kidnaping—and later on March 25. He could not by psychic means or by physical communication have arranged advance knowledge of the location of the house where he said the baby was held, or of the identity of Paul Megleo, Capone's henchman in New Haven.

Harold Olson's confirmation of the location of the house in 1972 obviously did not indicate whether the Lindbergh child was held in the house when Cayce said it was—on March 9, 1932; but it is reasonable to assume that if the Virginia Beach mystic was able to identify the house, he was probably correct in other parts of his reading. This would include the kidnaping of the baby, the trip across New Jersey, and crossing New York City to the Cordova section of New Haven in Connecticut.

There are certain parts of Cayce's reading that are not clear, but a closer study would reveal whether the Lindbergh baby was originally abducted by Capone's men or perhaps snatched or taken over by the Capone mob as they crossed New Jersey. Cayce mentions a change in transportation, possibly a transfer to another car, one proceeding south and west while the other crossed New Jersey to the tunnel—obviously the Holland Tunnel—and across New York to New Haven.

One reason for not pursuing the New Haven investigation may have been the low esteem in which psychics were held in the 1930's. Alan Hynd, a free-lance journalist, refers to them with skeptical disdain, and Whipple called them soothsayers. The study of parapsychology was relegated to the status of witchcraft.

This was not true when Olson located the house and confirmed Cayce's account forty years later. The scientific community had accepted parapsychology as a valid subject for research, and many experiments in clairvoyance, including some of Cayce's own experiences, had confirmed the existence of extrasensory perception, or ESP.

However, it might have been apparent to Lanphier and the FBI investigators at the time that some of Cayce's story needed further research. The Capone connection was clearly indicated. Yet they abandoned the New Haven angle, and as a result may have abandoned any realistic hope of finding the Lindbergh baby.

This brings up the second point to be considered: the extortion plot. Lindbergh, as noted, had taken full charge of directing the investigation, even to the point of warning the police to stay out of his way. During the period when the New Haven angle was being investigated by Lanphier, Jafsie Condon had injected himself into the picture and was accepted by Lindbergh as his go-between.

This was more than might appear on the surface as an addition to the investigation. When Lanphier and the FBI decided to abandon the New Haven investigation, presumably under Lindbergh's direction, they abandoned a direct search for the Lindbergh baby, and perhaps lost the only chance of finding the baby. Instead, Lindbergh was concentrating on *contacting the extortionists*.

This may have been due to Lindbergh's inexperience as an investigator. He had barred the New Jersey police, except for Schwarzkopf, from having a voice in his decision making. He had assumed that those who demanded extortion money were the kidnapers, and in so doing had foreclosed any effort directed at actually locating his son. He was depending solely on Condon's contacting the extortionists.

It will be recalled that Al Capone was among the first to express his great sympathy for the Lindberghs after the kidnaping. He was at this time enjoying the hospitality of the Cook County jail, awaiting extradition to Fort Leavenworth where Federal Judge James H. Wilkerson, of Chicago, had sentenced him to spend eleven years for income tax evasion. Capone immediately suggested that he be set free to contact his underworld cronies so he could find the Lindbergh child. His reasoning seemed substantial; his underworld henchmen apparently already had the child.

In order to support his offer to help, Capone said he would put up $200,000 to assure his return to jail if he did not deliver the baby. This offer was debated between the Department of Justice and Lindbergh, and finally refused. Lindbergh and Lanphier may not have associated the New Haven investigation with Capone, although there is certainly no reason why they should not have tied the two together in view of the mention of Megleo in Cayce's reading. Paul Megleo must have been known to the FBI as a Capone henchman.

Capone's offer was turned down late in April, 1932, and on May 3—nine days before the body was found on Mount Rose Heights—Capone was transferred to Leavenworth. Under the rules of gang warfare the Lindbergh baby became expendable, but Capone's henchmen in New Haven, who presumably held the baby, had a vested interest in keeping Lindbergh's son alive. It was their insurance against any charge of murder growing out of the discovery of the body on Mount Rose Heights.

Meanwhile Lindbergh had turned his attention exclusively to Condon and his bizarre excursions into the two Bronx cemeteries to meet "John." Aside from the improbable nature of Condon's various stories about his meetings with "John," this marked a definite change in the focus of the investigation, still under Lindbergh's direction. It had become solely an effort to contact the extortionists, rather than to locate the baby.

It may be noted at this point during the entire period of making contact there had not been *one scintilla of evidence that the extortionists ever had the Lindbergh child, or knew its whereabouts!* Lindbergh, and to a considerable extent the New Jersey police, apparently had overlooked the possibility that the extortion plot and the kidnaping of the baby might have been the work of separate gangs!

This possibility was partially confirmed by Murray Bleefeld, a deputy of Ellis Parker, in his interview with Anthony Scaduto during Scaduto's research work on gathering material for *Scapegoat*. It concerned the part played by Isidor Fisch, the man Hauptmann said gave him the Lindbergh ransom money. Bleefeld's account is a bit rambling and disconnected, but there is a ring of truth in much of what he said.

There is a definite similarity between what Bleefeld told Scaduto and the information dug up by Dunninger and myself about the little group that gathered at Peter

290

Biritella's spirit church each Sunday. These included not only Isidor Fisch but also Violet Sharpe, Ollie Whateley, and on occasions Jafsie Condon.

Bleefeld, it will be recalled, referred to an earlier connection between Paul Wendel and Isidor Fisch in a narcotics case, and said Fisch had also been involved in the Lindbergh extortion. There is little doubt that Fisch was in contact with Violet Sharpe. This was confirmed by Gustave Mancke, who operated a restaurant in New Rochelle. He said Violet Sharpe and a man he identified as Whateley came to his restaurant on Sunday nights. As noted earlier, he identified a picture of Isidor Fisch, who sometimes accompanied them.

It would not require much stretch of imagination to link these three to the extortion scheme. Violet Sharpe may have been involved as informer, advising Fisch of the kidnaping of the Lindbergh baby, which she apparently assumed would be returned safely. When the body was found on Mount Rose Heights, she may have committed suicide either in remorse or because she feared further questioning by Inspector Harry Walsh.

Fisch may have master-minded the extortion plot, deciding to cut in with a demand for ransom; or Paul Wendel, as Bleefeld told Scaduto, might have been "John" of the cemeteries, using Fisch as a lookout. In any case, the extortion scheme was carried out, with Condon as a go-between.

This brings to light an explanation of the part played by John Hughes Curtis' Norfolk gang. When Edgar Cayce referred in his readings to the change in transportation as the Lindbergh baby was being taken across New Jersey, he said one car "proceeded south and west." Whether the transfer was effected by a snatch of the child, or whether Curtis' Norfolk gang may have been acting in collusion with Capone's henchmen, will probably never be known. Most of the principles may be presumed to be dead, or at least not answering questions.

The entry of Curtis into the Lindbergh case has been

covered in general, but a few details are necessary to fit him into the composite theory of what is still known about the case.

It will be recalled that Curtis did not inject himself into the Lindbergh case, as Condon did; he was asked by a Norfolk bootlegger to act as contact man with the kidnapers, and much against his better judgment, finally consented.

Curtis, accompanied by Dean Dobson-Peacock and Admiral Burrage, met Lindbergh at Hopewell on March 22, 1932, while Condon's effort to contact the kidnapers represented by "John" was in progress. Lindbergh agreed that Curtis might follow up on the proposal of Sam, the Norfolk bootlegger who had asked Curtis to act as go-between. He did not have much faith in Curtis' efforts, however.

Curtis met Sam in New York and was told that the kidnapers he represented wanted only $25,000 earnest money to be deposited in a bank to the account of Dobson-Peacock, Admiral Burrage, and Curtis, and payable only after Lindbergh had his son back. This offer was conveyed to Lindbergh by Dobson-Peacock and Lindbergh replied, "I prefer to handle it my way."

Lindbergh's way apparently was to secure a preliminary identification of the child. Dean Dobson-Peacock had assured Lindbergh that the ransom would not be paid until Lindbergh held the baby "in his arms" but apparently Lindbergh wanted a preliminary identification in the form of a picture, a description of the baby's condition, and the kidnapers' symbol.

Whether this was another example of Lindbergh's adamant attitude, or whether he fundamentally distrusted Curtis, is difficult to fathom. If he distrusted Curtis, why did he spend days with the Norfolk man, roaming the seas off the New Jersey coast? Why was he friendly until his son was reported dead?

When Curtis later met members of the gang he was told that the baby was at sea, and it would be impossible to obtain the preliminary identification at that time. This apparently confirmed Lindbergh's suspicion that the gang did not have his son, although it did not dampen his confidence that Condon was in contact with the kidnapers.

It was only after Condon paid the $50,000 extortion money and "John" failed to produce the baby that Lindbergh turned to Curtis, and finally joined him in the effort to contact the *Mary B. Moss,* where the Lindbergh child presumably was held.

After discovery of the body of a child, which Lindbergh identified as his son, his attitude toward Curtis, as previously noted, changed. Curtis was ostracized. Accounts differ as to the treatment Curtis received at the Lindbergh home. The New Jersey police later denied having applied pressure, mental or physical, to the man from Norfolk, but Lloyd Fisher, in an article in *Liberty* magazine in 1936, described it as a "terrible ordeal." It was sufficient to cause Curtis, who later came to Philadelphia to testify at the Hauptmann trial, to balk at crossing the state line into New Jersey without assurance of protection. The rubber-hose school of criminal therapeutics, as practiced in New Jersey, had left a lasting impression.

The New Jersey prosecution, as it turned out, did not want Curtis' testimony in which he said he could identify "John" of his kidnap gang with a picture of Hauptmann—testimony which would have shot holes in the State's lone kidnaper theory.

This introduces an additional detail in Curtis' involvement which is of particular importance. Were "John" of the cemeteries, "John" of Curtis' gang, and Hauptmann the same person? "John" of the cemeteries was described as six feet tall, about forty years old, with a long, thin face. "John" of Curtis' account was about five feet nine, more than forty years old, and his face was "filled out". Hauptmann was in mid-thirties, with a thin face, and of medium height. It might have been possible to identify "John" of the cemeteries with

293

Hauptmann by looking at their pictures, but not likely. Curtis' man, however, was so completely unlike Hauptmann that identification would have been impossible. Why had Curtis identified them as the same person?

Probably it was a ploy, as previously suggested. Curtis had good reason to settle his score with New Jersey, and Wilentz must have known what he would say in his testimony.

One point remains to be clarified. If members of the Capone mob did the actual kidnaping, why would they have left a kidnap note asking $50,000 ransom—the amount first mentioned by "John" of the cemeteries? Their interest was not extortion, but pressure on Lindbergh.

The answer may lie in two areas on which there seemed to be considerable confusion and conflicting stories. The New Jersey authorities contended that the original kidnap note, left in the baby's nursery, had not been shown anyone outside the Lindbergh house, but this was not true, even on the record. Morris Rosner had seen it and copied it; Condon had seen it. Later Alan Hynd wrote that "every confidence man, swindler and forger east of the Rockies" had copies of the note, which was probably an exaggeration.

What was important was that the original note could have been planted by the kidnapers and subsequent notes written by other persons. Although the handwriting experts hired by the State insisted all the notes were written by the same hand, this was contradicted by several handwriting experts who were not on the prosecution's payroll.

The second of the two areas referred to above is perhaps the most important in the analysis of John Hughes Curtis' involvement. It is primarily a matter of speculation, and requires an imaginative jump, yet it ties together many of the unresolved questions in the Lindbergh case.

Edgar Cayce, in his reading on March 25—the last he

gave on the Lindbergh case—was asked how many gangsters were involved in the kidnaping. His answer was, "One, as may be termed a gangster. . . .The rest were those rather of the same character, that were not associated with same—until the present circumstances."

He then refers to the change in which the Lindbergh child was apparently transferred to another car which continued across New Jersey to the tunnel, while the first car appeared to head southward.

It would seem quite possible, from a reconstruction of Cayce's remarks, that one group—with only one professional gangster—abducted the baby, turned it over to the Capone group, and then went south, while the baby was taken to New Haven. The group that went south may have been part of a planned diversion, to focus attention on the extortion plot while Capone's representatives, headed by Paul Megleo, were bargaining with Lindbergh. Unfortunately they were unable to reach Lindbergh through Lanphier. Lindbergh, probably not believing Capone could recover his child, rejected the offer made to the Department of Justice, and Capone went to prison.

Much of this analysis is based on Edgar Cayce's readings, which obviously are not very convincing to those who doubt the validity of Cayce's psychic powers. His powers were quite convincing to Harold Olson, however, when he furnished proof of Cayce's accuracy some forty years later. John Hughes Curtis might have furnished the rest of the proof if he had not abandoned the quest in the mistaken belief the Lindbergh baby was dead.

It will be recalled that Condon, in telling the story of his first meeting with "John" to Assistant District Attorney Breslin of the Bronx, had quoted "John" as saying, "The baby is not in Norfolk." This was March 14, 1932, several days before Curtis came actively into the case.

Gaston Means was also aware of Condon's contact with "John" before it was known publicly. He referred to dealings with a school teacher in the Bronx.

The knowledge that each group, and also Means, seemed to have of the other's actions before these actions became publicly known, would seem to indicate that some contact was maintained on both sides. It might also support the theory that the group in the Bronx, which may have been master-minded by Isidor Fisch (or Paul Wendel) was trying to cut into the Lindbergh child stealing by asking for ransom, even though they did not have the baby. The answer to this can only be surmised, since Curtis, through force of circumstances, never followed through on his contacts with the Norfolk gang.

There are many questions in the Lindbergh case that will never be answered because those who could have answered them are now dead. But on the basis of a few known facts, and what might be called reasonable speculation, there can be established a composite theory that is not in conflict with any of the known facts or reasonable conjectures. It can be summarized as follows:

The kidnaping of Lindbergh's son was not for the purpose of extorting ransom from him; it was to bring pressure on Lindbergh, probably in the interest of getting Al Capone out of jail.

The one inescapable fact is the location of the house in east New Haven where the baby presumably was held. This was based on directions from Edgar Cayce, the mystic from Virginia Beach, which were not followed during the investigation by Tom Lanphier and the FBI shortly after the kidnaping, but were confirmed forty years later by Harold Olson in his effort to determine whether or not he was Lindbergh's kidnaped son.

It also seems reasonable to assume that Cayce's reading can be accepted in general content: that is, tracing the kidnaped baby from Hopewell to New Haven, where it was held by members of Capone's mob, headed by Paul Megleo, or Paul (The Waiter) Ricca, as he was later known.

The actual kidnaping may have been accomplished by the Norfolk gang with whom John Hughes Curtis was in contact, the baby being transferred to another car and taken to New Haven.

The Bronx gang with whom Jafsie Condon was in contact was probably trying to deal themselves into the action in an effort to extort ransom from Lindbergh. It was in all probability led by Isidor Fisch (or Paul Wendel) and received information about the kidnaping from Violet Sharpe.

Bruno Hauptmann was executed for the supposed killing of the Lindbergh baby. He might have been involved with Fisch in the extortion scheme, but there is no evidence that he was.

The final point in the summary concerns the identification of the body found on Mount Rose Heights by Lindbergh as his son. Evidence developed at the time, but not widely publicized, indicated the body was *not* that of the Lindbergh baby.

There was never any other evidence produced that indicated the whereabouts of the baby, or whether it was alive or dead.

There has been no attempt in this review to determine the cause of the injury to Olson's head, beyond those references that bear on the Lindbergh connection. The circumstances of the dent in Olson's skull have not been determined by Olson himself, and appear to be significant only in the Denzler theory as previously mentioned.

The theme of this review: What really happened to the Lindbergh baby? probably will not be answered unless the baby's fingerprints, mysteriously missing from New Jersey police archives, suddenly turn up; or some of the copies in the hands of the late Edgar Hoover, or Mrs. McLean, are found.

The purpose of this review has been accomplished; that is, putting together a skein of facts and reasonable speculation that may indicate how the trial went wrong.

There are no facts of importance to be added, although one avenue of analysis remains to be explored: the role played by Charles Lindbergh in the investigation and in the trial of Bruno Richard Hauptmann, which remains a blot in the annals of criminology and a disgrace to the State of New Jersey.

The blame should be shared by many sources: the New Jersey and New York police, who deliberately falsified evidence; the omission of testimony by the New Jersey prosecution; the uninhibited bias of Judge Trenchard. These are all matters that probably belong to the past, and are mentioned only as a guide to the future. Their value lies in what can be gained—as is the case with all history—from a study of what happened: the effect of public hatred and anger that runs amok, a public press interested more in sensational headlines than in justice, and police, prosecution and the court more concerned with protecting their record than protecting the rights of the accused.

This is by no means a news story; it has occurred in countless cases where senseless public anger has dominated judgment. A review of each case, however, may cause a few to reflect on the words of Marc Antony:

> O judgment! Thou art fled to brutish beasts,
> And men have lost their reason . . .

The sad part of the tale, aside from Bruno Hauptmann's execution when he was innocent of the crime of which he had been accused, is the injury inflicted on the son of Charles A. Lindbergh, who—if he is still alive—must walk the earth without knowing his roots, consigned to that fate by a father whose inflexible stubbornness dominated the entire Lindbergh investigation.

Concluding Notes

In 1936 Lindbergh, who had moved his family to England, was asked by Major Truman Smith, military attache at the American Embassy in Berlin, at the suggestion of General Goering, head of the German Luftwaffe, to visit Germany and inspect the German air forces. Lindbergh agreed. With a knowledge of aeronautics far beyond what the Germans had expected, he made an analysis of Germany's air strength, and returned to report that Germany could conquer most of Europe by air "in 48 hours."

This report was passed to General H. H. "Hap" Arnold, chief of the U. S. Army Air Corps; as a result Lindbergh was asked to make a second trip to Germany in 1937. Later he made trips to Russia and Poland. On his return he reported that none of the great powers of Europe, including Great Britain, could stand up to Germany's newly developed air power.

At a dinner at the American Embassy in Berlin, General Goering pinned the Service Cross of the German Eagle, Germany's highest civilian medal, on Lindbergh for his 1927 solo flight across the Atlantic. This became a matter of extreme political concern in the United States, where anti-Nazi groups were forming. Lindbergh was accused of being pro-Nazi.

Shortly after War broke out in Europe he said, "Regardless of which side wins this War, there is no reason to prevent a continuation of the peaceful relationship between America and the countries of Europe.''

This remark, made on the basis of Lindbergh's estimate of German air strength, outraged the Anglophiles in the United States as well as President Roosevelt, and apparently moved Lindbergh to go even further in his dissent.

In April, 1941, the newly created America First group asked Lindbergh to become its chairman. It included such notables as General Leonard Wood, Chairman of Sears, Roebuck, Sen. Burton Wheeler of Montana, and Irving Cobb, all isolationists in good standing. Lindbergh did not join the group, but he was closely aligned with the isolationists. And for six months he gave speeches decrying Roosevelt's effort to get America into the war on the British side.

On December 7, 1941 the Japanese attacked Pearl Harbor and the United States was at war on the side of the Allies.

Two days afterwards, Lindbergh issued a statement: ''We have been stepping closer to war for many months. Now it has come and we must meet it as united Americans, regardless of our attitude in the past toward the policy our government has followed.''

Lindbergh's antiwar speeches had cost him the popularity of both the people and the government of the United States. His attempt to be reinstated in the Air Force was refused. However, although quiet and unobtrusive, his contributions to the war effort were many and varied. He worked with the Mayo Clinic in Rochester, Minnesota, testing high-altitude flights. He helped United Aircraft train pilots for the ''Corsair,'' a Navy fighter. By combat flying he was able to recommend changes in the plane's bomb-load which would double its load factor. While at Nadzab Airfield, near Lae, New Guinea, he tested the newly acquired P-38 ''Lightning,'' a twin-engine fighter built by Lockheed, flying combat missions as a civilian—which would have resulted in his being executed as a spy if the Japanese had brought him down.

After the war Lindbergh bought a home in Darien, Connecticut. He later acquired another home on the Island of Maui, in Hawaii. He was the father of six children—the kidnaped son, John Morrow, Land Morrow, Anne Spencer, Scott, and Reeve.

In the years following World War II Lindbergh achieved the anonymity and privacy he desired. He died on the Island of Maui in 1974.

As indicated earlier, only Lindbergh could answer many of the questions posed in this investigation. What was his role in the Lindbergh case? Since he is dead, most of the answers must be conjectural.

Lindbergh's chief characteristics: his independence of thought, his phenomenal memory, and his absolute reliance on what he believed were facts were demonstrated during the investigation of the kidnaping and the Hauptmann trial somewhat in reverse. He was able to recall the most minute details of the night of the kidnaping, for example, but did not appear able to remember that he had said, under oath, that he could not positively identify "John" of the cemeteries by his voice. At the trial he said, in response to a question asking him to identify the voice he heard in the cemetery, "It was Hauptmann's voice."

Lindbergh's hard-line attitude toward what he believed were facts, and his characteristic stubbornness and self-righteousness, combined with his belief that Hauptmann was guilty, regardless of any imperfections in the prosecution's case, perhaps persuaded him to change his testimony.

This belief in Hauptmann's guilt was also evident in Lindbergh's omission of events that did not fit into his concept of the kidnaping.

The third man in St. Raymond's Cemetery on April 2, 1932—the man who dropped the handkerchief—is an example of this locus. It is true that no question was put to Lindbergh at the trial concerning this; but he knew what had happened. Special Agent Larimer, in his report to FBI Director J. Edgar Hoover, dated March 3, 1933, said:

Colonel Lindbergh's reason for not observing Condon (Jafsie Condon was delivering the $50,000 ransom to "John") more closely was because of the fact that while Lindbergh was waiting in the car alone his attention was attracted to a man who passed along the sidewalk near the car and apparently was interested in the car and in Colonel Lindbergh, who was seated at the wheel. Lindbergh could not discern the features of this man, but took him to be a young man of average size wearing a brown suit and felt hat with the snap brim pulled down in the front. The man walked rapidly and very stooped. The stooped posture might have been natural or assumed. The individual was conspicuous because of the manner in which he held a handkerchief well over his face, as if blowing his nose. This individual passed Colonel Lindbergh while Condon was presumably in the floral shop, and upon Condon's return to Lindbergh at the car, the latter spoke of this individual to Condon, but Condon stated he had not seen the man. In the meantime this strange individual had gone down the street. . .

During Condon's second absence, Lindbergh observed the same stranger dressed in brown suit and hat pass along the sidewalk on the opposite side of the street from Lindbergh, and in walking along this strange man carried the handkerchief in his hand. When he reached a point immediately opposite Lindbergh, he tossed the handkerchief into a vacant lot. This handkerchief has been recovered and is with other exhibits in this case.

This man was never mentioned at the trial.

Lindbergh's motives for changing his testimony, or avoiding any testimony that might have helped Hauptmann, cannot be determined with any assurance beyond mere conjecture. He made no explanation during his life, nor did his good friends, Henry Breckinridge and Thomas Lanphier, offer any explanation.

Later, when he had an opportunity to reflect on the accuracy of some of his testimony, he must have realized what he had done, but it was too late and he was not the man to recant. Above all, he had to protect Anne Lindbergh from the shock of believing that her son might still be alive—a possibility for which he had no direct evidence one way or the other.

It is possible that he spent many long and lonely hours pondering this question—as Bruno Hauptmann spent many hours in the jail cell at Trenton, wondering about American justice.

But, as noted at the beginning of this review, history has a way of correcting itself.